"[Buchanan is] a superb reporter and writer. . . . A fascinating book."

—*Pittsburgh Post-Gazette*

"Lively and tough-talking. . . . Buchanan packs this memoir with punchy accounts. . . . A memorable report on life lived at full throttle, on the edge, with courage."

—*Kirkus Reviews*

"Buchanan crackles, even cackles, with irony. Her life and writing are colorfully woven with twines of grit, street smarts, determination [and] compassion."

—*The Philadelphia Inquirer*

"An informative, highly entertaining book that tells a great deal not only about police and news reporting, but also about Miami. Her style is absolutely delightful."

—*Houston Chronicle*

"Edna is one tough cookie. . . . She tells her own story, plus the story of a lot of her stories. Some are shocking, some are gory, some are poignant, a few are funny."

—*St. Louis Post-Dispatch*

"As colorful and insistent as the Miami sea."

—*New York Post*

"For her, *The Front Page* is not just a play or a movie, but real life."

—*The Houston Post*

Also by Edna Buchanan

THE CORPSE HAD A FAMILIAR FACE

COVERING MIAMI, AMERICA'S HOTTEST BEAT

EDNA BUCHANAN

POCKET BOOKS

New York   London   Toronto   Sydney

Excerpts from the "Sidebar: White Kittens Dancing" and "Missing" chapters were first published in the October issues of *Cats* and *Glamour* magazines respectively.

POCKET BOOKS, a division of Simon & Schuster, Inc.
1230 Avenue of the Americas, New York, NY 10020

ISBN: 0-7434-9364-8

First Pocket Books paperback edition June 2004

10 9 8 7 6 5 4 3 2 1

POCKET and colophon are registered trademarks of
Simon & Schuster, Inc.

Cover design by Tom McKeveny

Manufactured in the United States of America

For information regarding special discounts for bulk purchases,
please contact Simon & Schuster Special Sales at 1-800-456-6798
or business@simonandschuster.com.

For Edna Mae Tunis

Acknowledgments

I wish to thank Gene Miller, Rick Ovelmen, *The Miami Herald* and the staff at Random House for their support, and Michael Congdon, my agent, for his guidance and friendship.

Contents

Introduction

It was my day off, but it was murder. Again.

The phone caught me on the way out. A body in a car in a parking lot. Sure, I said. It was on my way. I'd check it out. It was high noon, during the Christmas rush, in a city parking lot outside a Miami Beach department store near bustling Lincoln Road Mall.

A shiny, lime-green Coupe de Ville sat at a meter, its wheels turned sharply. The red flag signaled VIOLATION.

The driver's time had run out.

The meter maid had written a parking ticket. She leaned over to place it on the windshield and saw the man inside. A parking ticket would not irritate this driver. Nothing would. She called the police.

A knot of patrolmen and detectives ringed the car. I still hoped it was something simple. Maybe a heart attack, or a suicide. A bald, cigar-smoking detective named Emery Zerick stepped away from the car and called my name. I saw the look in his eyes and I knew: My day off was down the toilet.

This cop was no rookie. He had seen it all—and more. It was clear that something was different about this one. "Come on," he invited. We walked up to the Cadillac. I leaned over carefully, without touching it, and peered inside.

The corpse had a familiar face.

To the thatch of silver-gray hair, the ferociously dark and shaggy eyebrows, something had been added: powder burns. They smudged the flesh around the two holes in his left temple. An exit wound on the right side of his face had bloodied his cheek.

"It's your friend and mine, Mr. St. Jean," the detective said. His low, distinctive voice was steady and without emotion. We looked at each other. I took a deep breath and nodded.

My day off was history. So was Harvey St. Jean.

Harvey had it all: money, prestige, and a national reputation as a formidable and flamboyant criminal defense lawyer. He attracted the most colorful and newsworthy people in trouble. I first met Harvey when he represented Jack "Murph the Surf" Murphy, the beachboy jewel thief who stole the priceless Star of India, the world's finest sapphire.

The murdered criminal lawyer and the weathered detective standing beside me went back even further. As young men both wore the badge and the gun.

Harvey began as a Miami Beach cop. He pedaled a bicycle on patrol of the rich residential islands back in the days when Al Capone lived in a big house on Palm Island. Harvey liked the moneyed lifestyle he saw there. He didn't keep his badge long. He studied law at night school and learned how to use it to get people out of jail instead of putting them in there. He had a talent for freeing the accused.

The talent bought him a Jockey Club apartment and his own sauna and whirlpool. His expensive golf clubs lay in the trunk of his Cadillac. It looked as though he had planned to play eighteen holes that afternoon.

Harvey had it all, but somebody with a gun had just taken it away. I scanned the parking lot for a pay phone. I had to tell my editors to start a photographer rolling.

I cover crime for *The Miami Herald,* daily circulation 438,334. In my sixteen years at the *Herald,* I have reported more than five thousand violent deaths. Many of the corpses have had familiar faces: cops and killers, politicians and prostitutes, doctors and lawyers.

Some were my friends.

This book is about them, about life and death in Miami—the place, the people, and the world of a police reporter in a city like no other.

PART
I

*I'm not afraid to die. I just don't
want to be there when it happens.*
Woody Allen

ONE

Miami, It's Murder

The crime that inevitably intrigues me most is murder.
It's so final.

At a fresh murder scene you can smell the blood and
hear the screams; years later, they still echo in my mind.
Unsolved murders are unfinished stories. The scenes of
the crimes may change over the years; highways are built
over them, buildings are torn down, houses are sold. I
drive by and wonder if the new occupants, as they go
about their daily lives, ever sense what happened there.
Do they know, or am I the only one who still remembers?

The face of Miami changes so quickly, but the dead
stay that way. I feel haunted by the restless souls of those
whose killers walk free.

Somebody owes them.

And nobody is trying to collect. Detectives divert their
energies to new cases with hot leads. It is only natural.

But I can't forget.

*   *   *

The first homicide victim I ever wrote about was sixty-seven years old and from New Jersey, a retired dealer in religious books. Somebody beat him to death with a strange object resembling an elephant-sized Q-Tip. The killer dropped the weapon. Police found it, but they could never figure out what it was, much less who used it.

His last night on earth began pleasantly for Edward Becher; he escorted his wife to the theater. The vacationing couple returned afterward to their oceanfront hotel. He left his wife at the front door and drove off alone to park the car in a lot two blocks away.

He failed to return and his wife became concerned. Eventually she went to look for him. In the parking lot, she found the police with a shaken motorist who had discovered her husband unconscious on the pavement. He had already been taken to a hospital, where he died.

The murder weapon was the only clue: an iron pipe, thirty inches long, swaddled at each end with burlap. Everyone who saw it said the same thing: It looks like a giant Q-Tip. Baffled police created duplicates and displayed them to the public hoping for a link to the killer.

The weapon was not, as some citizens suggested, a tool to lubricate machinery or a torch used by fire dancers at a local nightspot.

The circus was in town at the time of the attack; it moved on a day or so later. I always suspected that perhaps the weapon was a tool used in some way by roustabouts or animal tenders. We will never know. Like most whodunits in Dade County, the case remains unsolved. The detectives who investigated it have all since retired or quit. Five police chiefs have come and gone since somebody smashed the skull of the man who dealt in religious books. I doubt that anybody now connected with the department even remembers that homicide.

But I do.

What the heck was that thing? It is still a perplexing and troubling question, nagging along with all the others. I am uncomfortable with unsolved mysteries—and with the fact that whoever did it is still out there.

Somewhere.

The unsolved slaying of Edward Becher was the first of more than three thousand murders I have reported. Every crime, every victim is different. Some remain more vivid in memory than others, but none can really be forgotten. Each time, I want to know it all, everything. If I could just somehow piece it all together, perhaps the things that people do to each other might make some sense.

Years ago, murder was rare and unusual, and almost every killing was front-page news. Then homicide became more and more common and less and less newsworthy. When Miami broke all prior records for violence in the years 1980–81 and its murder rate skyrocketed to number one in the nation, I was often forced to squeeze six, seven, even a dozen slayings into a single story. City-desk editors listed it on their daily budget as the "Murder Round-up." Combining the most outrageous cases in the lead, I would report them in a reverse chronology with the most recent first. Each victim's last story had to be limited to just a paragraph or two.

Despite the constraints of space, I still felt a need to learn all I could about each case. I rushed from one murder scene to another and another, engaged in a daily struggle to cram as much detail as possible into those too-brief paragraphs.

Speeding back to the *Herald* on a deadline one night, with my notes on several homicides, I heard the unmistakable echo of gunfire as I roared beneath a highway overpass near a housing project. Suddenly I felt crazed, uncertain whether to continue on back to the paper, or stop and investigate, perhaps finding another story there would be no room to print. The hesitation was just for an instant. The U-turn left rubber in the road behind me.

Looking back, I see now that for the better part of those two years, I was numb, shell-shocked, and operating strictly on instinct. I remember little of my personal life during that time, only the stories I wrote and the sense of being caught up in something totally out of control. The only reality was what I had to do. That paragraph or two devoted to each homicide was painstakingly put together.

I felt obliged. Often it was the first and last time the victim's name ever appeared in a newspaper. Even at that, I felt a sense of guilt for such a cursory send-off.

The woman left dead by the side of a desolate road in her yellow nightgown wanted to live just as much as you or I do. So did the illegal alien whose charred body was found in a cheap trunk in The Everglades. How dehumanizing to be regarded merely as numbers in the mounting statistics of death.

They deserved better.

Often assistant city editors, short on space and patience, would insist that I select and report only the "major murder" of the day. I knew what they meant, but I fought the premise. How can you choose?

Every murder is major to the victim.

Sure, it's simpler to write about only one case and go home. But some strange sense of obligation would not let me do it. *The Miami Herald* is South Florida's newspaper of record, and I felt compelled to report every murder, every death on its pages—names, dates, facts—to preserve them in our newspaper, in our files, in our consciousness, on record forever, in black and white. On my days off, or when I worked on other stories or projects, some murders went totally unreported. So I would carefully resurrect them, slipping them into the local section in round-ups, wrap-ups, and trend stories about possibly related cases. There was always a way, you could always find an angle. For instance: Victim number 141 in 1980 proved to be the widower of victim number 330 in 1979.

A bright young reporter I talked to recently casually referred to what he called dirt-bag murders: the cases and the victims not worth reporting. There is no dirt-bag murder. The story is always there waiting to be found if you just dig deep enough.

There are many misconceptions about murder in Miami. No one should jump to conclusions. Visitors should fear no harm. A reasonably prudent, law-abiding citizen is in no greater danger here than in his or her own hometown; perhaps less, depending on that hometown.

Innocent victims do get murdered in Miami: a woman on a bus bench, caught in the crossfire between warring Rastafarians; a lovely young career woman who unwittingly moved into a trailer park managed by a paroled sex criminal. They are tragic, but they are rare.

The vast majority of victims contribute to their own demise. They deal drugs, steal, rob, or stray with somebody else's mate until a stop is put to them. They quarrel in traffic or skirmish over parking spaces with other motorists—who happen to be armed and short-tempered. Or they brawl in bars, fight with neighbors, or batter their own spouses, who one day retaliate with deadly force. The average murder victim is not an average citizen. Most Miami murder victims have arrest records; most have drugs, alcohol, or both aboard when somebody sinks their ship.

The crime of murder itself has changed a great deal in Miami. When I was new here, a sex murder usually meant heterosexual rape, a woman assaulted and slain. Now a sex killing more likely involves a homosexual encounter and is characterized by rage and overkill, with the victim stabbed or beaten even after death by a young street hustler, already violent, criminal, and full of rage.

In simpler times, the bulk of cases were robbery-murders and old-fashioned domestic battles. They still take place of course, but by and large murder has become a far more difficult and complex crime to solve. Instead of asking "Whodunit?" Miami police now face the question of who was it? How can you ever hope to identify the killer if you can't identify the corpse?

Many victims come without names. Somebody who flew to Florida to consummate a drug deal most likely did not announce his itinerary to friends and family. If an illegal alien or a resident of Seattle or Montreal gets ripped off and dumped dead in Florida's Everglades, how do you identify him—if you find him. If his fingerprints are still intact, there may be a chance, but if he has no police record to match them to—it is not a simple matter. And the world is full of amateurs trying to break into the drug business.

Good homicide detectives go first to the victim's family, friends, and neighbors to learn who he was, who his associates were, and why somebody wanted him dead. But when a corpse has no name, who do you talk to? Where do you start?

A newspaper story can help. Some detectives are too secretive or too paranoid to talk to a reporter. To avoid releasing the wrong information, they won't release any. Those detectives solve the fewest cases.

I want to write those stories, and I want as many answers and details as possible. What about scars, tattoos, birthmarks, dental work, or jewelry? A distinctive Indian-style bracelet on the wrist of a skeleton was recognized when his former sweetheart, who gave it to him, read my story in the newspaper. Once the victim was identified, so was the suspect, the roommate who had never reported him missing.

Did the remains, often just bones, reveal any old fractures or deformities? A crooked little finger identified one murdered man, a long-healed broken ankle another.

What is most precious seems cheap in Miami. The system makes life cheap. Drugs make it cheaper. So does attitude and perspective: A young city, Miami lacks the history, the roots, and the traditions of other major metropolitan areas. Everybody here is from someplace else.

Miami is nobody's hometown. Ask people here for thirty years where they are from, they don't say Miami. They name the place they left. That is where their loyalty still lies. We are a city of strangers without community spirit or a sense of belonging. When bad things happen, there is no sense of outrage, no attitude of "This is my city. I'm not going to let this happen here."

When the Boston Strangler stalked the women of that city, the horror was national. The attorney general stepped in. Money, manpower, and all the resources of the state were committed to solving the crimes.

The Boston Strangler killed thirteen. He might have operated unnoticed in Miami.

I once wrote a magazine story about more than a dozen unsolved murders and the possibility that they were the work of one man. One young Miami housewife was washing dishes in her kitchen when someone crept up behind her with a knife and cut her throat so savagely that her head was nearly severed. The cases were so terrifying that I felt compelled to rearrange the furniture in my study—so I could work on the story with my back to the wall.

Though well read, the piece inspired no action or indignation. The lone outcry came from the Miami Chamber of Commerce, directed not at the maniac or maniacs who were killing women, but at the magazine editor who printed the story. That was some time ago; awareness is a bit better now—but not a whole lot.

Consider the murder of a man killed at a Miami cafeteria: The employees dragged the corpse out to the curb with the trash and went home. It was the second such incident at the same cafeteria in as many months.

Or the local nightclub where patrons were shot to death on six different occasions: Nobody ever saw a thing. Victims number five and six were carried outside and dumped in the parking lot before police arrived.

The sixth time, police got there fast and rounded up half a dozen fleeing patrons, but to little avail. "They all went blind when the shooting started," a detective said.

At least fifty people claimed they saw nothing because they were visiting the rest room when the killing took place. For all to use the four-foot-by-four-foot rest room at the same time, they would have to stand on each other's shoulders.

Absence of conscience also makes life cheap. Some kids have not yet developed one; some never will. No monster out of a nightmare is more frightening or dangerous than a kid with no conscience. There are fourteen- and fifteen-year-olds on the street who, if given a gun, would kill you as easily as they would sip a soft drink. You look into their eyes and see vacant space: nobody home. There is nothing in there yet, not a glimmer. You wonder if there ever will be.

But the worst of all, the most ruthless killers ever encountered in Miami, arrived among the Mariel refugees. Some men who would have, should have died in Cuban prisons or mental wards will open fire on strangers in crowded bars or cafeterias to simply prove *quién es mas macho*. They consider killing an accomplishment. An arrest enhances their reputation. To charge them with murder is a compliment; they are flattered.

Murder in Miami covers every conceivable scenario. Alfred Hitchcock would have loved the predicament of the killer surprised when a locked iron security door trapped him inside a small South Beach apartment with the corpse of his victim, and the irony of the man murdered while on his way to consult a spiritualist about his future.

Take Terrance Beecham. Both of them.

Their father liked the name so well that he named both his sons Terrance. They were more imaginative. Terrance, twenty-two, and his brother Terrance, nineteen, cut up old newspaper, police say, put a fifty-dollar bill on top, and tried to buy a ten-thousand-dollar bale of marijuana. Somebody got killed in the ensuing gunfight.

Terrance and his brother, Terrance, fled, leaving behind the fake money, the marijuana, and the getaway car, which was registered to Terrance Beecham. The Miami homicide detective on their trail faced double trouble.

Everywhere he went in search of the suspects, people asked, "What's the other one's name?" He would tell them, and they would cry, "No, the *other* one!"

He obtained murder warrants for the brothers, but alert clerks kept insisting there had been a mistake, the same man's name was printed twice. The detective printed and distributed a flier to alert other cops to the fugitives and was quickly flooded with calls from sharp-eyed officers who were eager, not to help with the case, but to point out his "error."

Terrance Beecham—one of them—was arrested, but the witnesses backed off, and the prosecutors never could make a case.

And imagine the chagrin of the disco patrons who all stepped outside to watch a 2:05 A.M. eclipse of the moon over Miami and saw a gas-station murder across the street instead? Or the cop who casually stopped a van to write a routine traffic ticket and was startled when the four men inside tossed five guns out the windows, raised their hands, and surrendered.

Or the Miami man who devised a foolproof plot to murder his wife: He filled the house with propane gas from a fifty-gallon tank, waited until she came home, then struck a match. The explosion did the job, but it also killed the would-be widower. He struck the match just inside the front door, apparently thinking he could escape. Nothing escaped. The walls flew out ten feet in each direction. Police arrived and found a vacant lot.

Hitchcock himself could not have devised a more curious beginning to 1982. In Hialeah, a municipality just

west of Miami, fishermen reported a body in a canal—
the first murder of the new year. Homicide detectives and
patrolmen found it, but to their great relief, it was a
butchered cow. As they stood on the canal bank, slapping
each other on the back and congratulating themselves
that it was not a murder case after all, two excited men
drove up to report a body in a field half a mile away. It
was the real thing.

And what of the plight of Richard Higgins, a man who
spent his life's savings to buy a secluded home on five
acres, so he could operate a plant nursery? Soon after he
finished expensive improvements and renovations, police
arrived asking to dig in his front yard. They unearthed
two bodies: the real owners of the house. Higgins had unwittingly bought the house from the killer, who had
posed as the dead owner.

The little things in life sometimes trigger the urge to
kill: a stereo too loud, a game of checkers. One man killed
his neighbor over the clippings from a Florida cherry
hedge. Temperatures in the nineties sparked a fatal family
fight over a fan. A man shot to death a lifelong friend who
sat in his chair; he had warned him not to sit there. "It
wasn't even any kind of a special chair," a detective said,
"just a plain old ordinary chair."

A man making his way to a vacant seat in a darkened
downtown movie theater stepped on a stranger's toes and
said, "Excuse me." The irate moviegoer killed him anyway.

Gary Robinson died hungry.

He wanted fried chicken, the three-piece box for $2.19.
Drunk, loud, and obnoxious, he pushed ahead of seven

customers on line at a fast-food chicken outlet. The counter girl told him that his behavior was impolite. She calmed him down with sweet talk, and he agreed to step to the end of the line. His turn came just before closing time, just after the fried chicken ran out.

He punched the counter girl so hard her ears rang, and a security guard shot him—three times.

Miami's most dangerous profession is not police work or fire fighting, it is driving a cab. For taxi drivers, many of them poor immigrants, murder is an occupational hazard. All-night gas station attendants and convenience store clerks used to be at high risk, but steps were taken to protect them. Gas pumps now switch to self-serve after dark, with exact change only, and the attendants are locked in bullet-proof booths. Convenience stores were redesigned and drop safes were installed, leaving little cash available.

But the life of a taxi driver is just as risky as it was twenty years ago when I covered my first killing of a cabbie. Bullet-proof glass could be placed between the driver and passengers, but most owners say it is too expensive, and besides, there is no foolproof way to protect yourself totally from somebody riding in the same car.

It is one-on-one, you against them, terror in the night. Cabbies live at the mercy of whoever sits down behind them. They are instructed not to refuse a fare or a destination, which sometimes turns a crosstown trip into a suicide mission—kamikaze cabbie.

I set out one day to find the family of a Haitian-born

cabbie so determined to save the seventy-nine dollars in his pocket that he never gave it up, even after he was shot four times. Hospitalized, his condition was critical, but he was expected to survive.

It was a stunning day as I drove along in the sunshine, music playing on the radio of my silver-blue Cougar. Then I found the poor and pitiful place where the wounded cabbie and a dozen or so of his relatives lived. Serious and polite, they all poured out of the tiny, crowded apartment to talk to me. We stood on the pavement in the shadow of downtown Miami's skyscrapers, shimmering and silvery like a postcard-dream, in the late-afternoon light.

The injured man's brother-in-law also drove a taxi. His eyes were wide and wet. "The people you pick up are the enemy," he said softly. "Always the enemy. It's dangerous. You have to fight to make a living." He held the hand of his eight-year-old daughter.

He had been so afraid that one recent fare intended to rob him that he flashed his high beams in desperation at a passing patrol car. The officer made a U-turn. The driver said he would take his menacing fare to his destination only if the police car would follow. The cop said he was too busy. So the frightened driver asked the passenger to step out and lost the eleven dollars already on the meter.

I asked if his wounded brother-in-law had medical insurance. He did not understand what I meant, which gave me my answer. As we talked, it grew swiftly dark, as it often does with the approach of an afternoon storm. The temperature suddenly dropped ten degrees, and a chilly rain began to fall. The edges of the silver skyline blurred into fairy-tale castles. The day took on an eerie, other-worldly quality. I moved toward my car in the pelting rain, and the cluster of sad-faced Haitians moved with me, disregarding the downpour, wanting to tell me more of whatever it was I needed to know.

I unlocked the door and stopped. How could I slip into my car and continue our conversation, leaving them to stand in the rain? There were too many of them to fit inside. It seemed only right that we be wet and miserable together. We all stood outside the car and talked as the rain continued to fall.

The little girl was the only one who ever smiled, and that was when I admired her and asked her about school.

"People always think cab drivers have money," her father was saying. "Sometimes I drive seventeen or eighteen hours for sixty dollars."

Even unarmed passengers try to rob them. "They curse at you. When the meter reads ten dollars, they offer to settle for six."

Out of fear and despair, he admitted, he often agrees. "It's too dangerous to fight." He spoke quietly so as not to alarm the child who still clung to him.

His fears are not exaggerated. Five cabbies had been shot in the past two months. One careened into the parking lot of a crowded shopping center, shouting in panic for somebody to call the police. Before anybody did, his passenger shot him in the head.

The *Herald* has questioned the cost of taxi trips on my

expense accounts. I cannot blame them. Sometimes the tips exceed the fare. I confess: I grossly overtip cab drivers.

I don't take a lot of cabs. When I deal with taxi drivers it is usually to cover their murders. When I do meet a cabbie who is alive and unhurt, I am always so relieved, so glad he is not dead that I want to give him money, lots of money. Cab drivers don't receive a cop's benefits, combat pay, or high hazard allowance. They don't ever get a Purple Heart.

August is Miami's hottest month, and in August 1980, Miami was hot, breaking all murder records and on the way to becoming number one in violence. There had been a sharp increase in multiple killings. Newly arrived Cuban refugees were figuring prominently in crime statistics. Law-abiding citizens, arming themselves as never before, were mowing down their assailants in droves, taking no prisoners, killing more criminals than the police were.

A grandmother shot down a stocking-masked bandit after several robberies at the convenience store where she worked. The young manager of a fast-food chicken outlet shot it out with robbers—three times. A thirty-seven-year-old woman blasted a would-be rapist with a 20-gauge shotgun kept beside her bed.

A robber dressed as a woman, wearing a long wig, makeup, and false eyelashes, was deliberately run down and dragged half a block by the balding and diminutive middle-aged administrator of a heart-attack prevention program. The incident was witnessed by a weary homicide detective returning from a murder scene. He nearly had a heart attack himself when the robber's wig flew off and landed in the street. The detective thought it was her head and she had been killed. He leaped from his own car and raced alongside, screaming, "Stop! Stop your car! There's a woman underneath!"

"I know, I know," the driver calmly assured him. "I meant to hit her."

The cop rushed to aid the woman and discovered it was a man. "It was the weirdest thing I've ever seen in my life," said the unnerved detective, who has seen a great many weird things.

Crime-weary Miamians began to treat corpses as though they were not there, even those that were difficult to ignore. Like the dead man in punk-rock regalia: Dressed in black and wearing scores of safety pins, medallions, chains, and rock-concert buttons, he lay sprawled in front of an abandoned house for hours one sunny Saturday. There were four earrings in his left ear and several bullet holes in his body. The neighbors went about their business as though he wasn't there.

I wanted to write about a day in the life of a homicide detective, working around the clock, exhausted and barely able to keep up with the body count. I would go where he did, see what he saw. That was how I met Rosa Smith.

Early that morning en route to interview a rape victim, a retarded twenty-seven-year-old man, Miami Homicide Detective Richard Bohan and I were diverted to Jackson Memorial Hospital. An assault victim was in the emergency room.

It was Rosa Smith. "The husband hit her with a steel box and tried to cut off her head—with a weed cutter," a patrolman told us. The woman's skinny son, age twelve, had snatched away the steel box and slammed it over his father's head, knocking him out cold.

An eight-year-old daughter ran for help, pounding so frantically on a neighbor's door that her hand shattered the glass. She was badly cut. A seven-year-old fled in terror, fell, and severely gashed her left knee.

Rosa Smith, a round, soft-looking woman, was seated in a chair awaiting treatment. A blood-drenched bandage was wrapped around her head. The tear-stained little girls sat quietly beside her.

Detective Bohan said he was there to talk about what had happened with her husband.

"Is he dead?" she asked.

"No," the detective said. "He's alive."

"A pity," she said, sighing.

The two little girls stared at the floor.

Rosa had married young. He always beat her. "I thought that if we had three or four kids, he would change," she told us. They had four children, and her husband *did* change. "He got worse," she said. When he left them and went back to New York, she was glad. Free at last, she arranged to take the children and go home to her mother in Costa Rica. Her husband learned of her plans and returned to Miami in a fury.

"He broke a window and came in . . ." She and the children tried to run. "He hit me and I fell down the stairs . . . He started choking me."

She looked pleadingly at the detective. "Please let me take that plane home Monday."

Rosa Smith and her children still had their plane tickets, but no money. Her husband had taken it all, $120. We went to see Edwin Smith, now conscious in an emergency-room cubicle. The detective suggested that Smith return his wife's money. Smith, forty-eight, was surly and refused. The detective relayed the refusal to Rosa. There was nothing more he could do; it would trouble him all day.

Hours later, back at headquarters, we heard that Edwin Smith had made a speedy recovery. Released from the hospital and booked into the jail on assault charges, he immediately posted bond. Rosa, with no telephone, was unaware of his release. It was a busy day, but we speeded miles north to her small duplex apartment. Resting on a couch, a fresh and clean bandage around her head, she smiled at the detective.

"Have you seen your husband?"

The smile faded fast. She jerked to a sitting position. "He's not in jail?"

"He posted bond."

The look on her face was one of panic. "Why? Why did you let him go?"

"It was just a matter of posting one hundred and fifty dollars."

No money, no place to hide, and the flight to Costa Rica was two days away. One of the little girls began to cry. The detective, halfway out the door, turned back into the room. "Pack a few things," he told Rosa Smith. "Stay here. I'll be right back. I'll take you to a safe place."

From headquarters he telephoned Safe Space, a shelter for battered wives. The address is kept secret so violent husbands cannot find it. The person who answered was suspicious, called back to confirm the detective's identity, then left him on hold, interminably. "This," Bohan grumbled, "never happens to Kojak."

He was still on hold when his walkie-talkie began to broadcast a staccato series of signals. A homicide had just occurred, in a crowded restaurant. Bohan, his partner, and I dashed for the door. "That woman is gonna sit in that house and wait until I get back there, and now . . . I won't," the detective agonized.

On the way out, he asked a patrolman to take Rosa and her children to Safe Space. The busy officer said he would try.

The crime scene, a Cuban restaurant, was chaos. The killers, reportedly Colombians, were gone. The victim, a one-legged Venezuelan clergyman, remained grotesquely suspended atop two orange counter stools, still dripping blood from two bullet wounds.

Investigating were Bohan—an Irish cop from Brooklyn— and his partner—an Italian from New Jersey. In the midst of the confusion, with excited witnesses shouting in several different languages, none of them English, the detective's radio interrupted. The patrolman could not find Rosa Smith's house. Closing his eyes to the tumult around him Bohan repeated the address and carefully described the building.

Later, en route to the station with a carload of Cuban and Chilean murder witnesses, Detective Bohan received a message from the patrolman: Rosa Smith and her children had been delivered to Safe Space.

We heaved a collective sigh of relief.

The day that began at 7:00 A.M. stretched to 11:00 P.M., ending with the killers of the Venezuelan and the rapist of the retarded man still at large—but, at least, Rosa Smith and her children were safe. Two days later they took off for Costa Rica. Thank God for small favors, I said to myself.

It was almost a happy ending.

If only it had been the end.

The following May, nearly nine months later, a double murder went undiscovered for days, until neighbors reported the odor. Somebody had broken a window to get in, then attacked a man and a woman inside, hacking them to death with a machete. The man lay in a hallway. The woman made it to the living room. She was nearly cut in half.

It was Rosa Smith. She was thirty-five.

I was devastated. The detectives investigating the murder case were unaware of the family history. To them it was a whodunit, but I knew who did it. Detective Bohan was off. I called him at home, nearly in tears. He too was stunned. We had no idea that Rosa had returned to Miami.

Somehow Edwin knew.

He was found in New York, the children with him. A detective had to explain to them that their mother was dead and their father the killer. He got ninety-nine years.

The saddest, yet most resilient witnesses to violence are children. Perhaps what they see on television prepares them for anything. They seem to take shooting, murder, and death in their stride. It's the small things that disturb them.

A four-year-old blonde with a Dutch-bob haircut was asleep in her own tiny bed in her parents' room, when Uncle David broke in at midnight. He leaped onto her parents' bed, kicked her father in the face, and pumped eight bullets into the couple.

Solemnly, the new orphan told me what she had seen. She knew her parents were dead. She had seen death lots of times on TV. What troubled her, however, was something else that Uncle David did.

"He broke the window," she said, looking shocked, "kicked it right out. He broke it, on purpose," she emphasized, her little face puckered with disapproval. "He'll have to pay for it."

Extracting anything, especially justice, from Uncle David was no easy matter. His niece was nearly six when she testified, like a trouper, at his trial. Adjudicated incompetent, he was sent to a mental hospital. He wasn't so incompetent that he could not escape, frequently. I covered three of his escapes myself. He overpowered guards, forced aides to open doors, leaped from rooftops and scaled fences. Each time he beelined back to Miami, where he had threatened to kill more people.

His escapes so embarrassed hospital officials that they were delighted to oblige the killer's forgiving mother, who requested his transfer to a state mental hospital in Missouri so she could visit him more easily. But there was a slipup in official communications. Shortly after he arrived in Missouri, someone in charge at the new hospital gave him a pass to go visit his mother. He did not return.

She told authorities he had stopped by briefly, then departed, on his way to Miami.

Kids are more matter-of-fact than most of us. A bright and pretty six-year-old who reads newspapers described to me how she ran out to play with her puppies early one Sunday morning and found a murder victim.

"Mommy, there's a dead man out there."

It was 7:30 A.M. The mother groaned and told her to go back to bed. The little girl persisted. "I knew he was dead," she explained to me later. "I thought it was sickening."

She went on to describe in detail to her dozing mother how the man was lying there, eyes half-open and red stuff all over him. Finally the mother climbed slowly out of bed. It must be a wino who went to sleep, she said and padded to her kitchen window.

"My God!" she screamed and dove for the telephone. "He was bloody from head to foot."

Some children witness terrible crimes, others commit them. A great deal of violence is done by people who are still children in the eyes of the law. I mingled with dissident inmates during a Dade County Jail disturbance. One of the prisoners was a slightly built young boy who said he was fifteen. He looked even younger. You don't lock fifteen-year-olds behind barred doors with adult criminals. This must be a mistake, I thought, a bit indignantly. When I asked what crime he was charged with, he shrugged and seemed unsure. He grinned; he had found a champion. Then I asked his name.

Charles Cobb. He did not belong in the jail with the adult criminals. He belonged on death row. He was one of a gang of fifteen- and sixteen-year-olds led by a stick-thin teenager named Nathaniel Pressley. In a twenty-one-day Christmas-season robbery-murder rampage, they had widowed five women and left twenty-one children fatherless. The gang stampeded into small family grocery stores and markets, shouting, leaping atop counters, guns blazing. They were like a bunch of kids playing cowboys and Indians, but their weapons and bullets were real.

At Danny's Market, they killed the owner, shot his wife five times, wounded a customer, then shot the butcher in the back until he fell dead.

He had eleven children.

The owner's widow survived. She sat and described to me how she handed out lollipops to the boys when they were preschoolers, the same boys who had come back, killed her husband, and left her for dead. Their small neighborhood business would never reopen.

The gang left another small supermarket so littered with the dead and wounded—both employees and customers— that it looked like a battlefield when Miami Homicide Sergeant Mike Gonzalez arrived.

The young robbers had so much fun, shouting and shooting, they forgot to take the money. Mike did not sleep for days during the manhunt for Pressley. He and his partner missed him once by ten minutes. Those minutes cost two more lives, victims killed the next day. The detectives finally found the gang leader hiding in a closet at a friend's apartment. The kid was nonchalant; he had escaped punishment for shooting a man in a robbery when he was only fifteen. He had been released just a month before the murder spree began.

Still a child under the law, that is how Nathaniel Pressley was always treated. He expected no less this time. He mouthed off, spouted jive-talk at the detectives and never lost his cool—until a secretary began to type the card necessary to book him into Dade County Jail. "Hey!" he cried, showing his first concern. "You can't put me in jail. I'm only sixteen. I go to Youth Hall!"

Surprise. Prosecutors had already agreed to treat the perpetrators in the cases as adults, no matter what their age.

His jailers considered the boy so dangerous that he was issued a special pink uniform. They wanted to keep him in sight among the other inmates. After he was sentenced twice to die and three times to life terms, prosecutors dropped the other murder charges. It was not worth it, they said. He was too dangerous to take back and forth to court.

I sat next to Pressley on a bench in the jail, under the watchful eyes of guards, and we talked.

"I consider myself an average teenager," he said. His first arrest, at age ten, was for robbery. He could not remember the last time he cried. He slept well, he said, and felt no remorse. He did not feel sorry for his victims. In fact the very question seemed to puzzle him.

His death sentences did not scare him. "I'm not going

to the electric chair," he boasted belligerently, "and that's a fact. I know I will be free someday."

He was right about the electric chair. The U.S. Supreme Court abolished existing death-penalty statutes a few months later. The sentences of Pressley, Cobb, and two other gang members were commuted to life. Whether they will all be free someday remains to be seen.

A year or so after his death penalties were commuted, Pressley sharpened a screwdriver in a prison shop, fashioning it into a weapon. He plunged it into the spine of a young social worker who was trying to rehabilitate convicts by teaching them trades. The victim was left crippled, but Pressley was never tried for the crime. It was another freebie. Again, authorities decided it was simply too dangerous to escort the gang leader back and forth to court.

And Charles Cobb, the "child" I met at Dade County Jail, also sentenced to die twice, was transferred from the prison to a hospital for an eye operation. The surgery was so successful that while recuperating the patient managed to climb out a window and disappear. Three years later he was recaptured in Los Angeles.

When arrested, he was carrying a gun.

Murder gives you a glimpse into lifestyles that would otherwise remain private. If nothing else, the insight demonstrates again and again that strange things are happening in suburbia—I mean plain old *Twilight Zone* weirdness.

What are they doing out there? And *why*?

The double murder of a Coast Guard lieutenant and his wife, bludgeoned to death in their handsome, well-landscaped home, has never been solved. But a bigger mystery to me is why the couple had eighty-one neglected, dirty, and unkempt poodles caged in the garage of their expensively furnished home.

Eighty-one.

What about the highly respected art teacher? Police found him dead in his small apartment with more than one hundred multicolored finches. The tiny bodies of six more birds were found in the freezer, carefully wrapped in aluminum foil. Homicide detectives who arrived to investigate the murder were dive-bombed by some of the small, short-beaked songbirds, who then soared over their heads to freedom. The body and the birds were a complete surprise to the landlord.

A murder in the family provides a slice-of-life look at that family and those surviving. A man named John Wooden, shot at a weekend party, died at Jackson Memorial Hospital. An arrest was made. That was the contents of a terse police press release.

I wanted to know more about the party, what it was all about. Sergeant Mike Gonzalez said he thought it was a birthday party. It was—a surprise party for the dead man. During the festivities, a stranger shot the guest of honor through the heart. Mike told me the victim was part of a large and affectionate family and that their grief had created quite a stir at the hospital.

A daughter answered my call. Trying routinely to learn

more about her dad, I asked how many children he had. She hesitated, seemed to be ticking off names. Finally she said, uncertainly, "Thirty-one, or thirty-two."

"No, no," I said, "how many *children?*"

"Thirty-one, or thirty-two," she said, and began conferring with other relatives present, debating the number.

Obviously crazed by grief, she did not know what she was saying. I expressed my condolences, thanked her, and redialed a few minutes later. A son answered. This time, I asked how many brothers and sisters he had. "Thirty," he said firmly.

It was true. John Bell Wooden, a construction superintendent, had fathered seventeen sons and fourteen daughters, ranging in age from three to thirty-one.

They had arranged the surprise party in honor of his fifty-third birthday. A brother took him out to dinner so the family could decorate his apartment. They brought refreshments and a gigantic cake. One hundred people shouted "Surprise!" when he opened the door at 9:30 P.M.

At about a quarter to three one of Wooden's daughters refused to pose for a Polaroid picture with a party crasher, age nineteen. He felt insulted and showed her a gun. She told her dad. He was a nice guy. He took the young gunman aside to speak to him in a fatherly fashion. The guests heard five shots.

A son wrestled the gun away. He and a brother bundled their injured father into a car for a wild ride to the hospital. At one point he stopped breathing. Frantically, they pounded on his chest, and he again began to gasp.

They carried him into the emergency room, where he died.

The rest of the birthday celebrants attacked the shooter. They fractured his skull and were still battering him when police arrived. Officers and paramedics rescued the teenager from the infuriated crowd and saved his life.

The partygoers all ran for their cars, headed for the hospital. As they got the bad news, the gunman was wheeled by, unconscious. They all charged him.

Bewildered officials reported a riot at the emergency room. It was no riot, it was just the immediate family.

Sergeant Mike Gonzalez, his partner, Detective Louise Vasquez, several patrolmen, and hospital security tried to hold back the crowd, including a Wooden son who had won a college football scholarship.

"My father was a good man," the husky football star told me. "Everybody loved him."

Murder exposes the uncommon in people's lives; sometimes one detail will reflect the motive or the warped dreams of a killer.

Christopher Wilder's favorite novel was *The Collector* by John Fowles. It fueled his dark fantasies. The book's central character, an inhibited young man, tired of collecting butterflies, stalks and kidnaps a lovely young woman. He holds her captive in a secret room at his home. There he photographs and torments her and when she dies, he buries her body on the grounds. The chilling book concludes with his plans to capture another specimen for his collection.

Wilder liked to photograph beautiful women and race expensive sports cars. A wealthy, Australian-born contractor, he was also a serial sex-killer, or about to become one, when I first telephoned him. It was shortly before he embarked upon an eight-thousand-mile, coast-to-coast odyssey of rape, torture, and murder.

All I knew was that two Miami women were missing. Each was a stunning part-time model. Neither had any reason to disappear. Rosario Gonzalez, age twenty, was deeply in love and planning a June wedding with her college sweetheart. Beth Kenyon, age twenty-three, a former University of Miami cheerleader and Orange Bowl princess, had close family ties and a teaching career.

Suddenly they were gone.

Rosario Gonzalez vanished amid the roar of engines at the Miami Grand Prix, on February 26, 1984. She was one of ten identically dressed models—in red shorts and white T-shirts—hired to distribute aspirin samples. Wilder, age thirty-nine, blue-eyed and bearded, had competed in the race, driving his black Porsche.

Beth disappeared a week later, on March 5. Her parents learned she was last seen with Wilder.

Coincidence? Bad luck? Two police departments were investigating: Rosario had vanished in Miami, so city detectives were looking for her. Metro-Dade, the county police, took a missing-persons report on Beth. I first suggested to Miami investigators that there might be a connection, but they doubted that the cases were linked.

Beth's wealthy parents retraced their daughter's steps to where she was last seen, in a service station talking to Christopher Wilder. No one has ever been found who saw her again. When police showed little initial interest in the disappearance, the frantic couple hired private investigators.

One of their detectives spoke to Wilder by phone on Saturday the tenth. The following day, he checked Wilder's home and usual haunts but was unable to find him. On Monday, Beth's father and brother and their private eye met with Wilder at his office. He lied to them. He said he had not seen Beth for weeks.

But he gave himself away when he said he understood that they had found Beth's car parked at Miami International Airport. They had, but no one had ever told Wilder.

Beth's brother wanted to force information out of him at gunpoint, but the private detective restrained him. He said it was a matter for the authorities to handle and turned all the information over to Metro-Dade police. "I think Wilder's your man," he told them.

They would have to start from square one, they said, to see if they reached the same conclusion. The police did not want to jeopardize Mr. Wilder's rights. They began by interviewing a number of pretty cheerleaders Beth had coached at the high school where she taught.

I called Wilder's home to ask him about the disappearances. The cops on the cases never went to see him, never spoke to him. Wilder lived north of Miami, in Palm Beach, across two county lines, and that complicated matters. Detectives would need special permission to leave their own jurisdictions and go there.

They did not have sufficient reason to do so, they said. "We had no proof he was a maniac," a Metro detective said later. Wilder was on probation for a Palm Beach rape. He was also free on $350,000 bond for a rape in Australia.

Wilder's machine answered my call. "This is Chris," the recording said affably, inviting me to leave a message. I did, asking him to call me. He did not.

The first news story referring to Wilder appeared in *The Miami Herald* the next day, on March 16. I did not use his name. The story said "a thin thread may link" the two missing women to a Boynton Beach man who drove in the Grand Prix. A detective investigating the disappearance of Beth Kenyon was quoted. He still considered "everybody a suspect."

Her parents had only one: Christopher Wilder. They knew the man. Once they had dined on crêpes with him at a fancy restaurant. He had even proposed to their daughter. He told Beth he would take her back to Australia and make her a princess. She hardly knew him; she did not take him seriously.

The day after the story appeared, Christopher Wilder was gone.

The families of the two missing girls had feared he might leave town, or the country, before they found their daughters. Both had offered to pay private detectives to watch Wilder night and day. But police told them not to worry; Wilder was not going anywhere. The distraught parents were convinced that he was under constant police surveillance, that his every move was monitored.

But it was not. Anyone watching would have seen Wilder deliver his three English setters to a boarding kennel and load a suitcase into his car. They would have seen him drive to his office to say goodbye to his business partner. But no one did. No one investigating the cases even realized he was gone until a week later. A hysterical college girl brought it to their attention. She escaped from a kidnapper in Georgia after a harrowing ordeal. A man had abducted her from a North Florida shopping center. Bound and gagged and zipped up in a sleeping bag, she was raped and tortured. The attacker had poured Super Glue in her eyes, but she could still identify him. It was Christopher B. Wilder.

Then the brutalized body of a twenty-one-year-old aspiring model, reported missing days earlier, was discovered facedown in Florida's Green Swamp. She was the daughter of a policeman.

As Christopher Wilder traveled across the nation, beautiful girls continued to vanish. A seventeen-year-old contestant disappeared after a beauty pageant in Las Vegas. A nursing student was reported missing by her husband in Beaumont, Texas. A young woman never returned from a shopping mall in Grand Junction, Colorado.

Bodies began to appear, in deserts, in woods, and along country roadsides. The FBI—always a day late—followed his trail of credit-card receipts, never knowing where Wilder would surface next.

During that monthlong travelogue of terror, I wrote the stories, week after week. The FBI joined the case and an agent confided to me that he would go home at night and cry, out of rage and frustration, knowing that somewhere out there, somebody else's daughter was next.

His cross-country rampage catapulted Wilder to the top of the FBI's Most Wanted list.

The FBI advised Miss America officials to warn the organizers of their fifty-one preliminary pageants to be on the alert. The publicity was national and intense, yet the most-wanted murderer in the nation still had no problem attracting lovely women. He had learned something since the 1981 Miami dating service videotape on which he said softly that he wanted to meet more members of the opposite sex. He had found the perfect ploy, the irresistible lure. It worked better than big bucks, which he had, better than flashy cars, which he drove.

It was a camera—and a promise of cover-girl fame.

Beautiful girls, especially star-struck teenagers, are fond of posing for pictures. It thrills them to be told that they should be top models. Every girl nourishes a secret dream: her face on magazine covers and billboards, put there by somebody who will make her a star. Those dreams became nightmares at the hands of a twisted and sadistic killer. Eleven women were caught up in the terror; eight are dead or missing. One survived being left for dead, another escaped, and Wilder gave the last one safe passage home. A Torrance, California, girl, her name was Tina Marie, age seventeen.

It was his final gesture.

I think he let her live, not because he suddenly developed a conscience, but because she was not a ten. Unlike the others, Tina Marie was no model, no beauty queen. She was a somewhat-pudgy teenager who had problems with school, with her parents, and with her boyfriend. She was not perfect. It saved her life. Christopher Wilder felt no need to destroy her.

And he knew the chase was nearly ended. At a Boston airport, he gave her a fistful of cash and put her on a plane bound for California. Tired of running, he told her he "felt they were going to catch up with him real soon."

He was right.

He drove north, toward the Canadian border. At Colebrook, New Hampshire, a resort town of twenty-five hundred, just nine miles south of the border, he stopped at a Main Street filling station. In Los Angeles, twenty-five hundred miles away, Tina Marie's plane was about to touch down. An attendant pumped gas into his car as Wilder struck up a conversation with an old gentleman. He asked directions to the border and appeared curious about the documents he would need to cross.

As he asked questions, two passing state highway patrolmen saw him and stopped. As one walked toward him, Wilder suddenly ran for his car and the gun stashed in the glove compartment. The passenger's door was locked. He scrambled around to the driver's side and dove for the weapon, but the 240-pound trooper was upon him. They grappled for control of the gun. Two shots rang out.

Wilder was killed, a hole blown through his heart, the trooper wounded. It was April, Friday the thirteenth.

Word of Wilder's death brought mixed emotions.

Jubilant South Florida police offered the two New Hampshire state policemen a free trip to Miami Beach for ending Wilder's rampage. The parents of the two missing Miami women broke down and sobbed. How would they find their daughters now?

They never have.

Whatever happened to Rosario Gonzalez and Beth Kenyon took place at a time when Wilder hoped to go on living his double life undetected. He hid them well. Once he had become the nation's most-wanted fugitive, it no longer mattered. He just dumped dead women by the side of the road.

For the two families, the nightmare will not end until their daughters are found. I even sent the FBI photocopied pages from my copy of *The Collector.* I hoped they would study the original building plans of Wilder's lakefront home, seeking any unaccounted-for space. He was a contractor; he had remodeled the house.

The FBI did not reply.

But police did arrest somebody in this tragic case—the heartbroken parents of Rosario Gonzalez. Unable to restrain themselves any longer, they went to Wilder's home on Mother's Day, seeking some trace of their daughter, missing then for two and a half months. Officers collared them. The charge: trespassing. Prosecutors later dropped the case.

On the day in June that Rosario Gonzalez was to

marry her college sweetheart, he kept the appointment. The young man prayed alone in an empty church.

The parents of Beth Kenyon have searched as far as Mexico and South America for their daughter, grasping at straws, hopeful that Wilder's white-slavery fantasies might mean that she is alive, smuggled into Mexico and sold into prostitution.

At least the other families each got back a body.

If only Christopher Wilder had been kept alive long enough to talk. His friends and business associates, shocked and disbelieving, could offer little information about his secret life.

It is difficult to keep in mind that the people who commit monstrous acts may look normal, even personable. It is always a surprise to me. Swallowing my own sense of outrage and indignation, I go off to the jail, or to his or her home, or some neutral turf, to talk to a killer. No matter how despicable, the killer always proves to be human, somebody you can identify with in some way.

That is the problem with judges and juries and parole commissions: All they see is a human being. The victim is history, old news, a name on a piece of paper, not like the flesh-and-blood human being standing before them, alive and breathing and even shedding a tear or two at the propitious moment.

A man who had spent half his life in prison and his buddy, an ex–Philadelphia cop, both junkies, wanted the few dollars in the cash register at the convenience store where Annie Ruth Oliver worked. They hit the store at

midday. Annie Ruth Oliver was nibbling her lunch between customers. She had been robbed seven times in the
past, and she knew the procedure. She passively handed
over the money without argument. But one of the strung-
out robbers was shaky, the one with the sawed-off shotgun.

He didn't mean to squeeze the trigger, he said later. He
was as surprised as anyone when the blast cut her in two.
She was dead behind the blood-soaked counter when I
got there.

The moment you dread most at a murder scene is the
arrival of next of kin; in this case it was Annie Ruth
Oliver's two teenage sons. The oldest, his face tear-
streaked, told me, "She just worked, came home, and
went back to work. She never even went anywhere."

I never forgave the men who killed her. Captured and
convicted, they were sent to prison. The ex-cop was a terrific talker with a high I.Q., a smart man, but not smart
enough to stay off drugs. He attended college in prison
and hosted his own radio show. Hailed as a glorious example of successful rehabilitation, he organized a group
to counsel troubled convicts, so they would be able to return to the community with an education and a better
attitude—and less chance of going back to jail.

Then he split. One day he just failed to come back
from his college classes. A year later, he was arrested in
San Francisco. As soon as he was back behind bars, his
professors and social workers were clamoring that he deserved a break on the escape charge. The "Cinderella"
syndrome made him do it, they said: The fact that he had

to go back to prison each night, or turn into a pumpkin, was too stressful for the man.

Maybe I am unkind, but what about the "sudden orphan" syndrome? Were any social workers or college professors clamoring to assist the children of Annie Ruth Oliver? She chose to work and support her family. He chose drugs and crime.

Maybe I have just seen too many victims.

I would not have given him a break. But nobody asked me, and he got one.

Sometimes the only justice is street justice. Some slayings seem, if not poetic, to be logical conclusions that were inevitable and only a matter of time. Take Jessie Lee Stuckey, an unpleasant fellow whose brief and violent life ended at age twenty-seven in a littered field near a rock pit. He died of unnatural causes.

His killers kidnapped Stuckey at gunpoint in front of witnesses. But they all knew the abducted man and his lifestyle and did not think it unusual, so nobody called the cops.

His sweetheart, with whom Stuckey had been living for a year, also saw him kidnapped. They had been quarreling lately, she said. And she "was kind of glad to see him leave," no matter what the circumstances. In addition, she said, she had no phone, so it would have been inconvenient to report the crime.

So police never knew that Stuckey was in trouble until a woman looking for firewood discovered his scarred, tattooed, and bullet-torn body. She did call the police, probably because she didn't know him.

His face was a familiar one to the cops. They had shot him once themselves, while trying to arrest him on assault charges. A nickel-and-dime dope dealer and thief, Stuckey had a history of resisting arrest and shooting into people's houses, and he had killed a man in a fistfight three months earlier. There was no lack of motives for his murder. When solemn-faced detectives arrived to break the bad news to his nearest and dearest, they all said, oh yeah, he was kidnapped by guys with guns.

They had been meaning to call.

Finally, consider the case of Karate Al: That's what they called him, and they stayed out of his way on downtown Miami's steamy sidewalks. He was tough. Known as the Bully of Northeast Fifth Street, he claimed to be a martial-arts expert. He posed and postured in karate stances—and if that didn't work he used broken bottles and two-by-fours.

A violent bully, he had the crowd at Abe's Rooming House cowed—until it was discovered one morning that Karate Al had picked his last fight. Somebody had pounded in his head with a pipe or hammerlike weapon as he dozed in a peaceful wine-induced slumber.

He was asleep and never knew what hit him.

Oddly enough, none of the other tenants at Abe's—where the manager was nursing a split lip and a tenant still hobbled on crutches, both after encounters with Al—could tell police how he happened to be killed there.

It was a mystery.

The tenants all discussed Al freely. They told me he could render people unconscious just by pressing their necks with his fingers and that he did not hesitate to demonstrate the talent. They said he had busted the manager's mouth the night before for no reason at all. A week earlier, he had kicked a boy in the stomach so many times they thought he would kill him. They said he had a knife in his back pocket and a big mouth. They said that whoever did it must have known that sneaking up on him as he slept was the only way to get rid of Al. All said they didn't have the faintest idea who could have done it.

"You die like you live," said one of the tenants, as morgue attendants carried Al's muscular body out of the rooming house.

They all nodded wisely. And nobody cried.

It is characteristic of New Jersey that not even the horrible here attains really heroic proportions.
Edmund Wilson

TWO

Paterson, New Jersey

Some people avoid Florida in July because of its scorching heat. But July was when I first saw Miami, and I knew at once it was for me. That first deep breath of steamy summer air, heat waves shimmying off the sizzling pavement, palm fronds feathered against a sharp and brilliant blue sky—it was like coming home at last.

When the temperature atop the bank building at 407 Lincoln Road registers eighty-plus at midnight, I am most comfortable. The summer sun and the salty sea breeze feel good on my skin. I even love the giddy near-dizziness that almost overwhelms you as you slide into a car that has been baking in the midday midsummer sun.

The same ovenlike heat will, in a matter of minutes, kill pets and small children left in a closed car. What it will do to a dead body in the trunk for twenty-four hours is unspeakable.

I visited Miami from Paterson, New Jersey, on a two-week vacation, and fell in love—with the city. It was July 1961. The summer romance has lasted. If anything, it is more intense. Everything is exaggerated in Miami, the clouds, the colors too bright to be real, the heat, and the violence. Ugly is far uglier in Miami, but beautiful is breathtaking, it hooks you for life.

I did not intend to become the city's chronicler of life, death, and human conflict. Somehow it happened. Anyone who knew me in my life before Miami would find it difficult to believe.

My mom was twelve when she lost her mother to pneumonia. She was seventeen when I was born. She named me for her mother, who was a descendant of early colonists, French Huguenots who came to the new world by way of Holland two years before the Indians sold Manhattan. One of them, Samuel Provost, was the first Protestant Episcopal bishop of New York. He officiated at the inauguration of George Washington and was highly respected. I believe that another, called Ready Money Provost, was this nation's first loan shark. He charged the soldiers at Valley Forge high interest rates during the Revolutionary War.

Commander David Provost was the first colonist to refuse to surrender a fugitive slave and successfully beat back an attempt to take her by force. That was at Fort Good Hope in 1646. Distinguished activists and patriots, the Provosts fought the English in the Revolution and each other in the Civil War. According to my grandmother's carefully kept family tree, a number of them married their cousins, which may explain why the family is no longer so distinguished.

My grandmother did not marry a cousin, but she did shock everyone by rejecting her wealthy fiancé to marry a poor schoolteacher, the son of a German sailmaker. My mother, an only child, shocked everyone by eloping with my father, the son of a Polish factory worker. She was just a teenager. She claims he threatened to leap from a bridge if she refused.

She rejected her own relatives as snobs compared to "real people," like her tiny, barefoot mother-in-law who was born in the Ukraine. My grandmother spoke little English and always wore a babushka. Her first husband died in a Pennsylvania coal-mine disaster. A pregnant widow with small children, she married her dead husband's best friend, a huge and bad-tempered man. It must have seemed like the right thing to do at the time. I have an old photograph of my grandfather astride a horse, wearing the uniform of some foreign army. He looks like a Cossack; he behaved like one. Drinking unleashed rages so towering that his children, as young adults, would leap from second-story windows to escape his wrath.

He would toss down a few boilermakers and it was monster-movie time. Like many such drinkers he seemed to relish holiday performances. One memorable Christmas when I was small, he upended the kitchen table, laden at the time with the holiday feast my grandmother had been preparing for weeks.

As a youngster I heard whispers, I don't know how

true, that a barroom brawl was the reason the family had hurriedly departed Pennsylvania to resettle in New Jersey. In one version he killed the man, in another he broke both the man's legs. In most versions, the man was his brother.

We lived in a yellow two-story house on Main Street in Little Falls, New Jersey, a town best known for a laundry. Highway billboards that depicted three little kittens washing their mittens touted the Little Falls Laundry up and down the turnpike.

My mother read to me when I was a tot. Cuddled together on a couch, we shared warmth and adventure. Stories became my passion in life. When she was too busy to read them, I looked elsewhere. The quest was constant. My grandmother, two doors away, was always delighted to see me. She always had Jell-O, with sliced bananas, in the refrigerator, but she could not read English.

So, clutching a story book, I would roam the neighborhood in search of someone who could, even beseeching the mailman to stay and "read a book-a to me?"

My mother resorted to tying me to the apple tree in our backyard so I would not wander away. Some neighbors complained that it was cruel, but I was content, seated in the shade amid falling blossoms with a Sears and Roebuck catalog. It was a terrific book, with lots of pictures to make up stories about.

Our house was full of real books, and the newspapers my father bought for the sports section and the race results. To a new reader hooked on stories, a newspaper is a gold mine.

I was addicted by age six, burning with a fervor to share these exotic stories with others. Up the street I would hurry, to my grandmother's house, newspaper folded under my arm. I no longer had to be read to; now I could read to others. I sat on one of her wooden chairs, put on my hated glasses—they were ugly—and read her the news while she puttered barefoot about her kitchen.

Her sheltered life revolved around family, food, and her backyard garden, where she grew vegetables, herbs, and glorious giant flowers. Sometimes she chuckled; more often, she was shocked. At the more outlandish stories, my grandmother shook her head, muttered in her native tongue, and moaned. I learned later that she was convinced I made them up. It was the first, but not the last time I would be accused of such a thing.

The New York *Daily News* was my favorite. It had lots of pictures and easy-to-read headlines. The tabloid size was just right for me to handle. The *News* also published fiction, a short story every day. The Sunday magazine and features were a bonus. The best of all was A JUSTICE STORY, a double-page spread on a juicy crime case, most often a murder. I devoured it. Other kids cried for nickels for candy, I yelped for nickels to buy newspapers.

Avidly I followed the adventures of Willie Sutton, the Babe Ruth of Bank Robbers; George Metesky, the Mad Bomber; and all the larger-than-life desperadoes whose stories splashed across the front pages.

And by age seven, I had finished the Ellery Queen books and *Forever Amber* and had amassed under my bed a huge collection of the *Reader's Digest* and *The Saturday Evening Post*.

That was the year it all changed.

We left the yellow house on Main Street and moved to Singac, a blue-collar community a few miles away. A doctor had warned that factory work was too hard on my father's heart, so my parents invested everything in their own small business, a neighborhood tavern. We lived in the basement. Those living arrangements were to be temporary, my father said,

I clearly remember the familiar sounds of beer barrels being tapped and the jukebox playing the "Beer Barrel Polka" and "I'm Looking Over a Four-Leaf Clover," over and over again.

My mother built thick boiled-ham sandwiches for the working men who came by in the evenings, carrying empty buckets to fill with draft beer. My father's new career as boss, with ready access to the cash register, unlimited liquid refreshments, and the female customers, gave him the opportunity to indulge in his favorite pastimes: gambling, drinking, and carousing.

One Sunday my father and some of his friends burst in, all sweaty, disheveled, and out of breath. He and Jimmy the Rabbit, One-Armed Eddie, and a man named Stinky were running from the cops, who had raided their big crap game in the woods. Another morning I woke up and found him passed out in the middle of the floor wearing only his underwear. His clothes were scattered all over the room, along with money, dollar bills everywhere.

I did not mingle much with kids my own age because I had to look after my little sister who was three years younger. I had even more responsibilities after my mother took us and left my father. A judge ordered him to pay child support.

He never did. He simply left town, took off, never to be seen or heard from again by any of us.

The youngest in my class, I was the tallest girl, self-conscious, and gawky—a mess. I wore hand-me-downs that co-workers at a sewing machine factory gave to my mother. Very shy, I thought everybody laughed at me. Sometimes they did.

School was an ordeal. We moved a lot, and I was lousy at math. Worse at phys ed: If somebody tossed a ball, I did not catch it or swing at it with a bat, I ducked. I could never learn to climb a rope like a monkey, roller skate, or even stay successfully upright on a two-wheel bike.

An unkind arithmetic teacher announced in class that I would not be anything—not even a good housewife—because I would be unable to count my change at the supermarket or figure out the correct measurements in a recipe. Everybody laughed.

But it has all turned out okay; I don't get change at the supermarket, I write checks. Recipes rate low on my list of priorities, and I do not want to be a housewife, good or bad. But as a child, I dreaded Sunday night because Monday morning meant school. I have never dreaded anything as much since.

Covering murder, rapes, and riots is a breeze by comparison.

Stories were my sole escape. They were wonderful. I read them, I wrote them, I daydreamed them.

The bright spot in my life taught seventh-grade English. Her name was Edna Mae Tunis, and in front of an entire class, she once said something I never forgot: "Promise you will dedicate a book to me someday."

She thought I could write; she made me believe I could. By term's end I had my first rejection slip, a printed form from *The Saturday Evening Post*. Mrs. Tunis said it was okay, that I would get a lot more. But keep at it, she said, you can do it. Or words to that effect.

I think of her each time I sell a story. She saw none of them. I was in the eighth grade when she died. She was in her forties. They said it was kidney failure.

I got my first job that summer when I was twelve. I plucked off loose threads and wrestled almost-finished coats right-side out at the South Paterson coat factory where my mother worked. They were big and bulky, fuzzy winter coats. It was summer; there was no air conditioning. The itchy fuzz stuck to your damp skin and drifted up your nostrils. Some of it, I am convinced, is buried still, deep in my sinuses.

My mom worked two full-time factory jobs and was a waitress on weekends. Whenever she was too exhausted to go to her midnight shift at the candle factory, I took her place. As long as the night's production quota was reached, it did not matter who did the work. Time flew;

you ran to keep pace with the machines. It was fun, except for the hot wax that splashed onto your clothes, your shoes, your hands, and arms. When it cooled and you plucked it off, your skin came with it.

Sometimes I substituted for her as waitress on the all-night shift at the Market Street Spa, near the Greyhound bus station in downtown Paterson. A huge newspaper and magazine stand in the front, it had a horseshoe-shaped coffee-and-sandwich counter at the back. We told them I was eighteen, though I was not quite sixteen. The tide of business ebbed and flowed through the city night: cab drivers, occasional travelers, a mix of local insomniacs, and the drinkers, swept out of the bars at 3:00 A.M. closing time.

Two well-dressed black men, wearing top coats and nicely blocked fedoras, took seats at about three o'clock one morning. As I fixed the sandwiches they ordered, a light-haired man in a leather jacket climbed unsteadily onto a stool on the opposite side of the counter. Slurring his words, he demanded immediate service. I said I'd be with him in just a minute.

He mumbled drunkenly, then spoke up. I hoped I had heard wrong, but he said it again, loudly: "Wait on me first, honey, ahead of those niggers."

He continued the slurs and the larger of the two black men became agitated. His companion tried to calm him, urging him to ignore the insults.

Instead, the big man reached over the sandwich board in a flash, snatched up the big bread knife I had just used and charged around the counter, brandishing it. The drunk saw him coming and took off running. He ran fast for somebody so drunk. They raced past the racks of newspapers and magazines, out the front door onto Market Street, and into the night. The black man's companion pounded after them, shouting, trying to stop his friend.

I never saw any of them—or the big bread knife—again.

Leaving work at 7:00 A.M. did not promote good school attendance. Paterson Central was a big high school, and I got lost in the crowd. My mom was too busy and too tired to be available. She was often too exhausted to make sense. I had no other adult to confide in. I never remember seeing a school counselor.

We lived on the top floor of an old wooden tenement that creaked and moaned and seemed to sway in heavy winds. The bathroom was out in a hallway. It was freezing in the winter. The ill-fitting door stopped about two inches off the floor. One night as I took a bath, I saw movement on the other side of that door: feet—little rat feet. Rats were scampering around in the hallway. Paralyzed, I kept perfectly still, afraid to budge, as the water I sat in got colder and colder.

Eventually, I called for help. If someone came, it would frighten them away. But nobody came. Finally it was freeze to death or face them. They ran, of course. So did I.

At sixteen, I was old enough for working papers, my own Social Security card, and my own job, behind the sock counter at F. W. Woolworth. A pervert was following me. He was probably exposing himself, but I never noticed. Teenage vanity kept glasses off my face. The pervert would later tell police that it all began when he followed me home after a dance at the Polish Home in Passaic. We were now living in a small house in South Paterson.

He became known as the Prowler. Neighbors noticed him first. He would lug a milk box down the alley, place it under one of our windows, climb up on it, and peep inside. The man next door chased the Prowler, but he got away. Other neighbors and the police also chased him, but the man scaled fences and fled through backyards in the dark. Soon everyone had seen him, except me. By the time somebody shouted "The Prowler!" and I fumbled for my glasses, he was gone.

My mom dozed on the couch one night, right under a window facing the alley. It was nearly eleven o'clock, time for her to go to work. I called her, and she slowly opened her eyes, focusing on the face of the Prowler, as he leered down from his milk box. She screamed. He ran.

I was folding socks at F. W. Woolworth a few weeks later, just before closing time, when a bloodcurdling scream froze shoppers in their tracks. It was my kid sister. She had stepped into the store to say that she and a boyfriend were waiting outside to drive me home. As she approached my counter, she saw the Prowler standing at the far end. He was staring at me and fondling a pair of sweat socks.

I saw the back of his head as he ran.

Not long after, the man next door and the police collared him after a chase. My mom had caught the best look at his face, and she could identify him, she said, without a doubt. Downtown at a police line-up, she positively identified a tall detective as the Prowler. When detectives pointed out the real Prowler, all of five feet four inches tall, she cried: "No. No. He's too short. You've got the wrong man!" Luckily, he had already confessed.

Standing on his milk box he did look taller, particularly to someone lying on a couch. When I listen to eyewitness descriptions and positive identifications now, I sometimes think of the Prowler. So many variables exist. A gun is a good example. It always makes the person holding it look taller.

The Prowler did not have a gun, but he did have a record of sex offenses. He pleaded guilty, got some jail time, and I don't think I ever saw him again—but I wouldn't swear to it.

I left Woolworth's for an after-school job in the baby clothes department at W. T. Grant and left that for a photo studio, to sell families a "photo of your child every year for three years." I also worked for a mail-order house and in a dry-cleaning shop.

College was obviously out of the question and never discussed. It was simply understood that I would work full time after high school. The job was at Western Electric. My mom was already working there. For the first time she did not need two jobs to make ends meet. We assembled switchboards, wielding wiring guns and soldering irons.

I bought my first car, a wonderful little Nash Metropolitan convertible, and drove everywhere, top down, hair blowing in the breeze, feeling free and exultant. But something terrible happened only ten days after I bought the car.

"You will be famous," said my fortune cookie on that hot August night. I laughed and zoomed away from the Chinese restaurant, headed home alone, never dreaming my car and I would make the pages of the morning paper.

The roof down, humming along with the radio, I became aware of something sinister, a dark car following me. At the next red light, it pulled alongside. Two young men called and shouted. I ignored them and floored it on the green. So did they. I drove faster. So did they. In my efforts to escape, I wound up on a dark and deserted downtown Paterson street. A figure loomed in the darkness ahead.

A man, his back to me, was lurching down the dividing line in the middle of the street. Glancing over my shoulder at my pursuers, I zigged around him. He chose that moment to zag. I hit him. He fell back, arms outstretched, a hefty, grizzled man, spread-eagled on the hood of my car. I slammed on the brakes. His nose was mashed against the windshield like that of a wistful child, but his face was upside-down. His eyes, big and blue, stared, unblinking, into mine. They were bloodshot.

I froze in horror. It was the eye contact. My foot slipped off the brake and the man slid slowly off the hood and into the street. As I sat clutching the wheel, the car rolled over him. The two men in the car behind me were no longer sinister. One was reaching in to pull the emergency brake while my car was still moving.

They lifted the front of my Metropolitan off the man

who was wedged beneath, facedown in the street. Two detectives in an unmarked unit appeared almost at once. A patrolman arrived in seconds, siren screaming. He leaped from his squad car, sprinted to the prone man, lifted his head—then dropped it abruptly back onto the pavement. "Oh," he said, as he slowly straightened up, wiping his hands on his trousers, "it's only Archie."

Bewildered, I fished for a dime in my purse and stumbled to a phone booth to call my mother. A detective reached past me and hung up the phone with a hammy fist. "No need to upset your folks," he said. "Now, how fast were you going when you saw the man lying in the street?"

"He was walking," I whimpered. "I hit him."

To my surprise, they neither took me to jail, nor gave me a traffic ticket. The detective who drove me home tried to be comforting. My insurance company would pay to repair my car, he said. I saw no damage, all I could see was that man lying in the street. The medics had splinted his leg. It must have been broken. When they lifted him into the ambulance he looked unconscious. I was panicky and puzzled. The police seemed to be treating the victim in a rather cavalier fashion.

The detective explained it to my mother: The man I ran over was Archie Beal, Paterson's most-arrested drunk, jailed hundreds of times since 1938. So far that year—and it was only August—he had been run down in the street seven times. His most recent misfortune involved the intercity bus, which ran over him as he lay in the gutter, breaking his leg. The morning of our encounter, he had appeared before a judge who released him in exchange for the promise that he would never drink again. He walked over to Mill Street, earned a few dollars washing cars, and bought a jug of wine to quench his thirst on that hot summer night.

Outraged residents called police soon after to complain that Archie had shed his clothes and was strolling naked in the street. Reluctant to jail him again so soon after his release, they simply ordered him to get dressed and move on—which he did, moments later, into the path of my car. At least he was wearing clothes at the time. I spent a sleepless night worrying about his injuries.

I was stunned next morning to see that the hood of my car was concave, the grille mangled, and that his head had shattered the windshield.

I took a bus to the hospital, carrying magazines, candy, and cigarettes. His bed was empty.

"Why are you looking for *him*?" a middle-aged nurse asked.

"I hit him with my car last night," I said tearfully.

She screamed with laughter and asked about damage to my car. "It must have been like hitting a bull moose!"

He had sobered up and been released.

I hoped to keep the accident secret from my co-workers, who often teased me because I was young and shy. But when I picked up the morning paper, there was a photo of Archie sprawled in the street in front of my shiny and unmistakable little Nash Metro. The headline said I hit him three times: with the fender, with the windshield, and then with the entire car when I ran over him.

The story was meant to be clever. It mentioned his record, the intercity bus, and my name.

I recalled a splash of light. I had assumed it was the police, shooting pictures to use against me. But a newspaper . . . ?

How on earth, I wondered, do reporters ever get these things?

Wiring switchboards became a tedious job—so did waking up in the cold dark of winter to punch a time clock by 7:00 A.M. Restless, I transferred to office work at the same plant. The pay was no better but the hours were. Even the nine-to-five job was dreary. So was life. Winters were long, the days short and gray. Something was missing.

I soon found it. My friend Joanne, a sylphlike clothes horse with a warm and eager passion for fashion, enrolled in a night course in millinery design at a local high school. She never liked going anywhere alone. I thumbed idly through the catalog of classes; I had no interest in hats. Creative writing leaped off the page. Writing had been my life's ambition. Somehow I had lost track of it.

The teacher was a struggling writer, a lean young man with a limp. A war veteran, I assumed. When he asked who had been published, it seemed like almost half of the large class responded. Intimidated, I was afraid of embarrassing myself. But I remembered Mrs. Tunis—she said I could do it.

He told us all to write something and mail it to him in Greenwich Village before we met again. I stayed up all night pounding out a story of suspense, about a young woman in jeopardy. My mom complained that the typing kept her awake. I couldn't help it, I didn't want to stop, this was exciting. I mailed it.

In class our instructor said that something special had happened, something every teacher hopes for. He described a story one of us had written, comparing it to early Tennessee Williams. As he went on, I slowly began to realize that it was my story he was discussing. Embarrassed, yet pleased, I slouched self-consciously in my seat. He gave me a list of writers to read and books to buy. His classes left me stimulated, my mind racing, more eager than I had ever been about anything.

He quit teaching to write and his career flourished. As a reporter in Miami, I once covered a mindless murder that police suspect may have been set off by the violence in a screenplay he wrote. I often wished I could tell him how much he helped me, but I never expected the chance. Then a California novelist visited the *Herald,* to pick my brain for his new book. We drank wine, talked, and discovered that he and the screenwriter, my old teacher, share the same agent. He got me a telephone number, in Connecticut.

I dialed it on Christmas Eve, more than twenty years after the fateful writing class that set my life in a new direction. The call from a stranger surprised him. He remembered the class. He even recalled one of his students, a young black man who drove an old sports car and wrote poetry.

He did not remember me at all.

He was apologetic. I didn't want him to be. I felt no disappointment. I don't know what I expected. It was not a reaction or a reunion; I simply needed to say, "Here I am, alive and well in Miami. And thanks to things you shared in a classroom a long time ago, I not only make a living but have much more than just a job."

Heck, maybe Mrs. Tunis would have forgotten me, too, but I will always remember her. And that is what counts.

Western Electric shut down for two weeks in July, and my mom and I took our first vacation. My sister had eloped young and had a family, so it was just us. We rented a seaside cottage at Point Pleasant to spend a week at the Jersey shore. It rained every day. We never saw the sun, not once, or even glimpsed a patch of blue sky. When it rains in New Jersey, the skies stay gloomy gray and drizzly all day, day after day.

We vowed that on our next vacation we would find a beach with some sun and blue sky. Where else but the nation's best-known beach?

"The Playground of the World."

This Miami spirit is a great thing. It is infectious.
Dr. James Jackson, 1896

THREE

Miami Dreams and Legends

Miami Beach: I saw it first from the backseat of a taxicab. Traveling due east from the airport to the sea, you ascend a slight rise in a silver stretch of expressway and suddenly, there it is across the water, spread out in front of you, all pink, radiant, and bathed in sunlight. The glittering bay sprawls at its feet, its rooftops and Art Deco towers are surrounded by vast sky, and drifting clouds glow golden at sunset and rosy at dawn. It is the image of a fairy-tale kingdom full of dreams and legends.

In reality, it is a wild and wacky town where outlandish events occur, but from that spot, it seems enchanted.

I caught my breath. I still do each time I see that view. Sometimes I need to see it, when things are wrong or scary. I drive by there often. It is something that has not changed and will not change.

Our hotel was small and pastel, in what is now the heart of the city's Art Deco district. We stayed in an oceanfront room. I went back to New Jersey only to un-load everything I could not pack. No regrets. What to miss? Ice on the windshield, freezing feet, and sore throats? What to say goodbye to, except wicked winters and brief, dingy days that seemed all the same. All I have ever missed about New Jersey is the summer harvest of juicy beefsteak tomatoes—and the pizza. It does not taste the same in Miami, probably because most of the pizza chefs were born in Havana or Port-au-Prince.

Young journalists today study, train, and prepare for the profession. I stumbled and fell into it. Western Electric in Miami turned me down. Hiring anyone from the New Jersey plant was forbidden, the personnel officer explained tersely. Why, then, would anyone stay in New Jersey?

It was easier to find a creative writing class than a job. In downtown Miami, "the Magic City," they taught every-thing from massage to auto mechanics. My classmates were mostly old folks. They all had stories, most of them sad. Many were Jewish immigrants who escaped the Nazis, who lost families, who survived with little else but memories.

One of them, a tiny, shriveled man, lived with his wife near the small South Beach apartment my mother and I shared. He plodded daily to the Miami Beach Public Li-brary on Collins Avenue, across the street from a strip joint called the Place Pigalle. There, in air-conditioned quiet, he labored in longhand on his book. Twice a week, I drove him to class in my pint-sized convertible. He wolfed down sandwiches in my car and, spewing crumbs, tried to talk me into typing and correcting his manuscript. It needed more than corrections. In broken and barely decipherable English, he wrote wistfully of golden-haired Katya, the goddesslike lost love of his Russian youth. I felt he was being disloyal, somehow, to the round, cherubic wife who dutifully fixed his sandwiches. It was a relief when I could no longer help him. I was too busy.

I got a job.

It emerged unexpectedly out of the writing class, through another student. His Tennessee drawl was more a nasal whine and his palms were always damp, but he was oh-so-so polite that the teacher and the sweet old ladies just loved him—and I can't complain. He suggested that I apply for the open job of society page reporter at the small Miami Beach newspaper where he worked as an editor.

The suggestion was startling. I had never thought of working for a newspaper; it just never crossed my mind. This, I thought, could be a perfect way to support myself while writing the great American novel. I had no clue that a newspaper will swallow up your life until little is left for a novel, great or otherwise.

At the Miami Beach *Daily Sun,* a tiny tabloid with a circulation of ten thousand, "Serving the Gold Coast of Miami Beach," somebody handed me a press release about a church social and said to write a story. I did. They hired me. It was that simple.

"Now you're a journalist," announced my classmate. He shook my hand with his damp one. I had a nagging suspicion that somehow, there had to be more to it than this.

There was no hint of what lay ahead: that life in Miami would bring joy and amazement, interspersed by moments of sheer terror, absolute panic, and an army of dead people—five thousand corpses.

My boss was Maude Massengale, the society editor. She knew everybody and everything and had been there forever—since before I was born. She was beyond retirement age, but beneath her sagging breast beat the heart of a love-struck teenager.

Maude lived, loved, and breathed sex and romance. To her, everybody was "Darlin.'" Her standard greeting was "How's your love life?" She waited for an answer. Maude was vintage southern belle. When her two grown daughters were hungry youngsters, she told me, they complained constantly that there was nothing in the refrigerator but orchid corsages.

Suitable escorts for all the parties and society balls Maude had to attend were in short supply and great demand. Her favorite was Timothy Smith: tall, dark-haired, and elegant in his tux. She was crazy about him. After an evening at the country club with Timothy, her tired blue eyes shone starry above a road map of wrinkles. Maude had heart. Her abiding faith in romance was an inspiration. When Timothy Smith later married a rich widow, she was inconsolable. It broke her heart. She was never the same.

Maude taught me how to cover society bashes, do the makeup and layout of pages, and write headlines. Sometimes, when she was mooning over Timothy, she even let me write her column. This did not seem unusual at the

Miami Beach *Daily Sun*. I had never been to the dog track, but I picked the greyhounds for the sports department. There was no one else to do it. And occasionally, when the need arose, the sports editor and I wrote the Letters to the Editor, signing fictitious names, of course. We wrote them volatile, hoping to rile real readers enough to send in their own and relieve us of the job.

Those were the dying days of old-time newspapers, the days of linotype machines, hot type, and metal engravings. The *Sun* paid less than minimum wage, and there was no such thing as overtime pay.

It never occurred to me to complain.

I covered Hadassah meetings, the PTA, luncheons, and teas, worked with the pressmen, helped lock up the pages, and learned how to read upside-down and backward, a skill that would come in handy later in my career. As soon as I could afford it, I bought a simple black dress to wear to balls and the opera. Not to worry that it is not terribly trend-setting or chic, Maude explained. The people who wear expensive designer originals to these events are not pleased if upstaged by a reporter. She was right. And it was not as if I was going to actually listen to the opera. I was working. My job was to mill about outside, watch the Baroness Adele von Poushental and her friends make their entrance, and record for future generations what they were wearing.

Maude had no illusions about her role in the lives of these people. They invited her everywhere and clamored to be her pals—so long as she could drop their names into her well-read society column. It was better read than even Maude suspected. Big time jewel thieves later confessed to me that her column was their bible on the habits, habitats, and recent glittery acquisitions of the rich and social.

I insisted to Maude once that many of these socialites surely sought her out for herself alone—not just because she wrote a column. She smiled and shook her head. I was wrong, she said.

A day or two later, one of the grande dames of local society dropped by to invite Maude personally to a small, but swank, dinner party. "Now Maudie," she said, fluttering around my boss's desk, "we want you to come strictly as a friend. Leave your ol' notebook at home. We just want you there because we *love* you. You *know* how much we love you."

Maude consulted her appointment book. An unfortunate prior engagement forced her to decline. The would-be hostess marched dejectedly to the door, turned, and pouted, "Well can you *at least* send a photographer?"

Occasionally, back in the composing room, a handful of type would somehow spill to the floor and scatter. Some cigar-chomping pressman who lacked the proper respect for society news would scoop it up in a grimy hand and stuff it back into the page—anywhere it fit.

You have not seen fury until you have seen the mother of the bride whose wedding story was garbled with lines from a recipe for roast loin of pork. I learned a lot about human nature—and raw emotion—working for the society pages.

I learned something else. The editor with the Tennessee whine liked me—too much. He kept prancing into our little office with pleas, impassioned notes, and poetry. I enjoyed pointing out his misspellings. Once I locked the door when I saw him coming. He pounded on it, waking Maude, who was napping after a rough night at the country club and a vitamin B_{12} shot from her doctor. She checked her mirror, applied fresh purple lipstick, and insisted I invite him in. Maude loved romance; she loved to experience it, talk about it, instigate it.

His name was James Buchanan. He was my Pearl Harbor.

I always had lousy taste in men. It seems traditional among the women of my family.

I wanted to write books. He said he did too. Our goals were the same. Maybe, I thought, he is not so bad after all. He was not my type, but that was good. Perhaps this was meant to be. The sex-smart and worldly Italian women I had worked with back in Paterson, New Jersey, had warned: Be sure the man loves you more than you love him.

I am insecure. Maybe that is because the first man in my life blew town for good when I was seven. Jim Buchanan was always there. No matter how many times I said no, he bounced back, pitifully humble, hat in hand, gazing adoringly. Back in Paterson I was always impatient for boyfriends to call; sometimes they didn't. I never had to wait for Jim Buchanan's call. I had to take the phone off the hook to make him stop.

We ate Chinese dinners, we dated.

The management changed at the *Sun*, and Jim Buchanan got fired, along with some ambitious others who had dabbled in office politics. A few more staffers quit in protest. I was one of them. I had been there eight months.

We got married and honeymooned at Sanibel Island, an unspoiled paradise of sea shells and beach off Florida's west coast. I remember the sand fleas most of all. They were terrible.

Jim went to work for a newspaper in neighboring Broward County. I was going to write a book. We were going to play house. It was a disaster. I fled after only a few months—back to Miami. Not without anguish; I never planned to be a divorcée. I never planned a lot of things.

I decided to try for a real reporting job at *The Miami Herald,* the biggest and the best newspaper in the South. The woman in the personnel department was quite blunt when I asked to fill out an application.

"Unless you have a degree in journalism or five years experience at a daily newspaper," she said coldly, "don't bother."

I would remember her words.

The *Daily Sun* was under new management again, and I needed a job. A pale, chubby editor named Ted Crail wanted to know if I had studied journalism. My heart sank. I had not.

"Good," he said happily, "you won't have to unlearn anything."

I thought they would hire me, but days dragged by with no word. When I inquired, the news was bad. Rolfe Neill, the publisher, had rejected me based on marital status. "A divorcée," he was quoted, is "unstable and unreliable."

To pay the rent, I free-lanced to stodgy trade journals. My mom was busy with a new job and a new life, so it was just Niña, my white cat, and me. We survived feast and famine in our tiny Miami Beach canalfront efficiency. I ate canned hash and Skippy peanut butter and Niña dined on cat food from a sack. When the mail brought a check, we splurged on steak and cat food from a can. We could hear the music, the bouncing beds, and the busy feet of an ever-changing number of chorus boys and girls who worked in the nightclub revue at the Fontainebleau Hotel and shared an apartment upstairs. They would even plunge exuberantly into the canal for a swim—from their second-floor balcony. They were vibrant, exciting, and friendly, but we didn't mingle. I can't even swim, much less dive, and my work was as dull as dirt.

The trade journals paid by the inch, so I wrote in as excruciatingly rambling, lengthy, and wordy a fashion as possible. If one short word would do, I used three long ones, four if possible. Editors trimmed and tightened the copy and then paid only for the inches published, but I managed to slip a lot of useless verbiage by them. It was a matter of survival.

I even adopted a male persona to sell an article to a national magazine: *Action for Men*. They used only male bylines, so to *Action*'s editors I was Mr. Buchanan. I profiled the tough-guy mayor of a pie-shaped municipality on the fringe of the gator-infested Everglades. A rough-and-ready Clint Eastwood–type, the mayor had used bare fists and bravado to clean up Florida's "last frontier town."

Some time after the story was published, the town was cleaned up again, this time by authorities who carted the mayor off to jail. It was my first encounter with the good-guy–bad-guy syndrome, a familiar pattern among police, politicos, and judges. Today's hero is often the man caught with his hand in the cookie jar tomorrow.

Finally Rolfe Neill, the *Sun*'s publisher who had rejected me, got his big break. The New York *Daily News* offered him a job. The instant he was out the door, the *Sun*'s editors hired me.

This time I was not writing society page puffery or covering the PTA luncheon beat. I was hired to report hard news, hit the streets, see life in the raw, ferret out the real story, and bear the torch of truth into the darkness of ignorance. Could I do any of that? Was I capable of it? I had no idea. It scared the heck out of me. But I needed the paycheck because I had to move.

Niña had gotten pregnant and the landlord was furious. A handsome silver tomcat had come to call one night while I was still intoxicated by Richard Burton's movie version of *Hamlet*. The long-haired stranger and Niña crooned softly to each other through the screen door. Moonlight sparkled on the water behind them. Somehow I thought it wildly romantic, let her out, and they eloped. I must have been out of my mind. Two days later the neighbors told me they were holed up under the building. I lured her out with a saucer of cat chow. He followed, wailing plaintively. She called back, from over my shoulder.

At least somebody in our household was in love.

We never saw him again, but the damage was done. The landlord did not want a cat to begin with, now there were three.

My favorite sound in the world is a kitten's purr, a soothing signal that something is right in a world full of bad dogs, bad people, troublemakers, and complainers. The kittens were entrancing, but impossible to hide in a one-room apartment. Lord knows I tried. When the landlord showed up to collect the rent, the kittens fastened their furry bodies to his polyester pants with needle-sharp claws. Cats instinctively know an ailurophobe when they see one. It was time to move.

The rent was higher at the new place, and I was desperate to make good at the *Sun.* I had no idea how to use a camera, much less shoot news pictures, which was a requirement of the job. Ted Crail, my editor, pasted a brief set of instructions to the side of an old Yashica. Luckily, my first target was a patient man—a minor city official— and not some felon-on-the-run. Together we read aloud the instructions, and after several false starts, I successfully snapped his photo and it was published in the newspaper.

Next came my first hero: a skinny college kid who dragged an unconscious three-hundred-pound woman from her submerged auto after it had plunged into Biscayne Bay. There is something about a hero—people love to read about them, and it is a joy to write about them. They feed our secret fantasies. Every man, woman, and child yearns in dreams to possess the right stuff when it counts, but few are ever tested.

Heroic cops and fire fighters make good copy, but they are trained and paid to be heroes. And when they are heroic, they often use it as leverage to protest pay scales and win promotions or more benefits. The finest, truest heroes of all are the uninvolved passers-by: the teenagers with acne, the overweight truck drivers, the weary housewives, and the middle-aged myopics who rise to the occasion, suddenly transformed into real-life superpeople.

They are the stars of the few happy-ending stories in a business where I am too often the bad-news messenger.

Ted Crail told me not to worry, or hurry, that people love having their picture taken, that they will be patient and endure what they must, especially if it is for the newspaper. He was right.

The fire chief in Surfside, a tiny oceanfront municipality just north of Miami Beach, doused his hand with lighter fluid, set it on fire, and lit his cigarette with his blazing thumb all so I could snap the picture. This was not a stunt, he explained gravely. It was a simple demonstration of the principles of fire. To be certain I had captured it on film for our readers, he did it again.

Miami Beach Mayor Chuck Hall, a silver-haired patrician, was larger than life, like everything else in South Florida. Rich and quotable, he was always accessible. His new forty-five-foot yacht was just a few days old and still uninsured when a storm cloud sailed across Biscayne Bay, stopped right over his boat, and burst.

In Miami, the heavens crack open with a deluge that nearly drowns you. Black clouds roll in from the west, the sky grows so dark that street lights kick on at midday, and thunder crashes like it is the end of the world. Cats run for cover, small children scream, and lightning streaks the sky. Twenty minutes later, it is all over. The sun shines. The sea is calm. It's a beautiful day.

Often it rains hard on one side of the street and not at all on the other. It will drown the front yard, but the back stays dry. It rained in only one place that day, and it flooded and sank the mayor's new boat. I took my camera to the marina—too late. The mayor had hired half a dozen workers. They had pumped for hours and resurfaced the boat. I was disappointed. "Gee, Mayor," I said, "we wanted to get a picture of it when it was still underwater."

"No problem," he said. He spoke to the workmen—who shook their heads and squirted hoses, refilling the boat with water. They sank it again, so I could take the picture. I was new in the business—and worried.

"Mayor," I said, "is this ethical?"

"Of course it's ethical," he said. "We're only recreating the scene."

This was before the days of riots and refugees, and the mayor's good humor remained constant, despite crisis after crisis, including the jewel robbers who waited in his penthouse to congratulate him at gunpoint after an election-night victory. Somebody shot the windows out of his Silver Cloud Rolls-Royce on another occasion, and I photographed His Honor with a well-tailored arm extended through the shattered glass. *The Miami News* had been there before me, he said. They shot the same pose.

"Let's see," I worried aloud, "what can we do that's different?" The eyes of the silver fox met mine—two minds as one. Without a word spoken, he sighed and loosened his expensive silk tie. Next day we front-paged the mayor, his handsome face framed by the jagged edges as he obligingly stuck his head through the broken window.

Another surprisingly good sport, to my infinite relief, was Lefty Rosenthal. A convicted basketball fixer and nationally known gambler, Lefty had taken the Fifth Amendment thirty-eight times before a Senate subcommittee. Barred from Florida racetracks and a bit miffed about all the publicity, he had recently cursed a *Miami News* photographer who tried to shoot his picture at the Orange Bowl. Another man then attacked the cameraman with a chair seat. The unfortunate incident made headlines.

Now Lefty was due to appear in Miami Beach city court on some minor infraction. An editor sent me to cover it. "Don't forget to take his picture," he called after me.

I trotted along at a safe distance behind Lefty after court. As I wondered where I would get another camera should he break this one, he turned to ask what I wanted.

I told him.

"You must be kidding," he said.

I am only a girl reporter trying to make a living, I said unhappily. He posed and even flashed a smile for the camera.

My greatest fear was of not getting the story, of failing somehow, or making a mistake. It still is, every day. Panic has a permanent place in my psyche, probably fed by neurotic fears of being fired and sent back to New Jersey, doomed to a factory full of fuzzy coats forever. It propels me forward on the job, looking for more, more, more.

Another prime motivator, of course, is unquenchable curiosity. Miami was always a magnet for people on the run, even before it became the new Ellis Island. It is a city of constant surprises. You never know who, or what, is waiting behind the next door.

Once it was Sam Houston Johnson, and we briefly shared the same bed.

Lyndon B. Johnson was president. A guest, grandly welcomed as his younger brother at a posh oceanfront hotel, was causing growing concern among the staff. The man was closeted in his suite with a platinum blonde, their bills were skyrocketing, and they seemed to be having a far better time than first families should. The staff began to doubt his identity, but dared not accost him. The hotel's press agent asked for help.

Our newspaper morgue had nothing. The president did indeed have a younger brother Sam according to the public library. Strangely enough, Sam seemed conspicuously absent from official family portraits.

I pounded on the door of his unnumbered eighth-floor suite. The blonde welcomed me, offering a beer. It was 10:00 A.M. She ushered me to "Mister Sam's" bedside. He lay atop the spread, in casual clothes and hand-tooled, black leather cowboy boots. He was guzzling clear liquid from a water glass. There *was* a family resemblance.

The woman righted his glass when it slopped over and slid ashtrays beneath his burning cigarettes. Why isn't the

Secret Service protecting him, I asked, if he really is the president's brother? He sat straight up in bed.

"They're everywhere," he said, "too damn many Secret Service men," then collapsed back on his pillow.

He had not seen the president since the inauguration, he told me, but added that Lady Bird had called him first after LBJ's gall-bladder operation.

He and the blonde were delighted to have photos taken. Then he insisted that I pose with him. She helped him to a bedside chair and took my camera. I sat beside him. She found us in the lens. I said "cheese." He lunged, grabbed me around the neck, and planted a mushy kiss on my cheek. Then he tumbled back onto the bed, rolled over, and went to sleep in one violent motion.

I tiptoed toward the door. The blonde stopped me. It would be positively disrespectful, she drawled, to leave without a proper goodbye. Mister Sam would be downright insulted.

Mister Sam did not look insulted. He appeared to be unconscious. Nonetheless, I approached the bed and thanked him politely for his valuable time. The eyelids flickered and I extended my hand. He took it tightly in his.

"Honey, you're delicious," he cried. "You look like Jackie Kennedy!" He jerked me closer with both hands and, caught off balance, I sprawled forward, landing on top of him.

My bulky box camera, hung from a leather strap around my neck, was caught between us. I struggled awkwardly to get up, but he was surprisingly strong. During the tussle I caught a glimpse of the blonde calmly pouring herself a drink.

I wrenched myself away and staggered to my feet as Mister Sam rolled over, eyes closed. I asked if he had been drinking. "He is perfectly all right," the blonde snapped.

From the newsroom I telephoned the Miami office of the Secret Service. "Tell me about Sam Houston Johnson."

The agent's response was expressionless, by rote. "Any information on the president's family has to come from Washington."

"Why aren't you protecting him?" I cried. "If he falls into the wrong hands . . . "

"You know where he is?" The agent's voice had changed, it sounded urgent. When I told him, he hung up quickly, without saying goodbye.

Less than fifteen minutes later, I got an outraged call from Mister Sam's suite. His companion demanded to know why I had called the Secret Service. He took the line and whined, "Now why'd you go and do that, honey?"

He and the woman now wanted my roll of film. I refused. They called my editor. Sam mumbled something unintelligible before they were cut off by a crash, as though the telephone, or Mister Sam, had fallen to the floor.

The woman called again a short time later, her manner pompous. The nation's top Secret Service agent was there, she announced, and wished to speak with me. She tried to put him on, but he refused to come to the phone.

The hotel staff told me later that Secret Service and

FBI agents had arrived en masse. They quickly rolled Mister Sam out, strapped in a wheelchair and wrapped in a blanket. A private plane, registered to Johnson Enterprises, was waiting at the airport. The Secret Service left the blonde and the bill behind. She picked up the tab and left town after one last angry phone call to me.

My editors now believed that Mister Sam was authentic and were baffled about how to handle the story. After several closed-door conferences, they instructed me to write a perfectly straight interview with the president's brother. The story ran the next day, with photos, one with his companion and one of him alone.

In it, we quoted Sam as saying that he was in Miami Beach for a rest after living in Mexico for three years and being divorced twice. His plans were to travel on to San Juan next. The most colorful aspects of our hotel-room encounter were missing.

I got one more call, weeks later; the blond woman's husband, a disillusioned Democrat, had hired a private detective to track down his wife and Mister Sam.

They wanted to know if I had any other pictures.

Part of my beat was a string of four small waterfront towns and villages just north of Miami Beach, some no longer than eight oceanfront blocks, each with its own government, police and fire departments, and uniquely virulent strain of small-town politics.

Most were peopled predominantly by senior citizens, tough old-school street fighters from the New York metropolitan area. They did not spend their retirement days drowsing in the sun. After working hard all their lives, they now had the time, the energy, and enough fire left to raise hell. And they did. Each of the towns teemed with these gray gadflies, activists, and rabble-rousers. Many became my sources. They taught me the truth about politics.

There is no place like a small town for mudslinging, bitterly fought elections, and blatant skullduggery. Digging into these controversies titillated my aging tipsters— me too, ditto my editors. Together we exposed cover-ups, election frauds, sinister plots, and all sorts of misfeasance, malfeasance, and nonfeasance—some of this in towns where the registered voters numbered hundreds, not thousands. Penny-ante stuff in the scheme of world affairs, sure, but it was big time to them and did boost our pitifully poor circulation.

A reporter could mine gold in those tiny towns. On one day a firebomb exploded on a North Bay Village councilman's lawn, the mayor died suddenly, of natural causes, and another councilman was mourning three relatives lost in a fiery cruise-ship disaster at sea.

On that same day I interviewed my first cop. Too old and too short for the job, Miami Beach Officer Bennie Hyman fought a five-year legal battle to win the badge. God knows why he wanted it. Something about a very short and extremely aggressive middle-aged cop provoked people. They shot at Bennie, slugged him numerous times, ripped off his shirt, and knocked out a tooth. He was attacked on the street, in a patrol car, in the squad room at headquarters, and in the police elevator.

One woman, who later said, "I always wanted to throw something at a cop," hit him in the face with a roast beef sandwich. She paid a fifty-dollar fine and went away happy. "It was worth it," she said.

As for Bennie, he was criticized for shooting the earlobe off an elderly woman as she sat in a lawn chair on the front porch of a South Beach hotel. He was aiming at fleeing felons, he said, but his eyesight was not so good anymore.

The late 1960s were golden and glamorous days for Miami Beach: Miss Universe, *The Jackie Gleason Show*— "direct from the sun and fun capital of the world"—major revues in the big hotels, top stars during the season. Frank Sinatra was actually nice to me and Joan Crawford sadly confided that she was lonely. Miami Beach had everything. The city was full of colorful local characters, celebrities passing through and crazy politicos.

Fueled by youth and enthusiasm, I worked six-day weeks and long hours. We were always short-staffed. For one eight-month stretch, I was the *Sun*'s sole reporter, scribbling copious notes about everything, anything, all the time. It was insurance. We never knew exactly how much space we would have to fill. One night, at 1:00 A.M., my editor, Ted Crail, a gentle but driven man, stood over my desk wearing the face of a man with a desperate need. He wanted what they all want. More copy. More news. More stories. He still had blank space to fill. I had been working since 7:00 A.M. I hadn't had any dinner. I had to be back at 7:00 A.M.

"I can't, I can't," I wailed. Exhausted, I slumped over

my battered old Remington typewriter and began to cry.
He did not go away.

"One more story," he urged, "one more story." His
pudgy fists clenched tight, his knees flexed, he was cheer-
ing me on as if I were a punch-drunk fighter on the ropes.

"One more story, one more story."

Wearily I sat up, leafed numbly through my notebook,
and found—one more story.

One night I needed more information to finish a story
and went out looking for Detective Emery Zerick, who
was off duty. That was the night I met Detective Sergeant
Emmett Miller. He was blue-eyed, with sinfully big biceps
and a Kirk Douglas dimple. Our romance taught me to
never mix business with pleasure.

I always learn everything the hard way.

The first place I went to look for Zerick was just a
block away from the *Sun:* The Southwind Bar, a favorite
all-night hangout for Beach police officers. The chief had
assured its popularity by declaring it off limits. If you
wanted a policeman, the Southwind was the place to find
one. Emery Zerick was shooting pool with Emmett
Miller. Somehow Emery disappeared, and I found myself
giving Miller my home telephone number. I give it to lots
of policemen, for tips when news happens; it is strictly
business. This was not. Neither of us had stories in mind.

As I said, the bar was off limits. Emmett Miller should
have been.

He had three children by prior marriages and was
about to be divorced by his second wife. Sober, he was

super. Drinking, he was not. He feared at first that romancing a reporter would make him suspect, that he would be accused of being "the leak in the department." But he did it anyway.

Sergeant Emmett Miller and I got engaged. Then unengaged. Again and again. Single seemed simpler: When surly, a single man could be sent home. I should have stuck to that theory.

Our work limited our time together. We managed to meet on Lincoln Mall one day for lunch. Our sandwiches arrived just as his walkie-talkie announced a three-seventeen, the signal for a traffic accident with injuries. We ignored it; his officers could handle it without him. Then the dispatcher changed the signal, to a three-eighteen, a hit-and-run. Lunch was obviously not going to be leisurely. Then the dispatcher spoke again. The victim was a forty-five: a corpse. There was no lunch at all. We left our sandwiches on the table.

Sirens wailed in the distance. "They're playing our song," he said.

Emmett speeded there in his patrol car, lights flashing, his siren joining the cacophony. Running traffic lights in his wake, I got there right behind him.

The man on the pavement was seventy-nine years old. He had stepped out of a bakery carrying a sack of doughnuts, was hit by a van, and hurled more than seventy feet. The driver left him lying in the street, doughnuts scattered over half a block.

Lunch in this job is an exercise in indigestion.

The *Sun* had a new city editor, Bob Swift, formerly of

The Miami Herald. Thin and mustachioed, he had a lively blonde-bombshell of a wife named Elvalee. They liked to party. I had stayed out of trouble during frequent management and ownership changes by working hard and avoiding the bosses, but the entire *Sun* staff was invited to the new editor's big house party. Lots of important people would be there, lots of *Miami Herald* editors. The invitation seemed to be a command performance. Everyone was going.

My date was Emmett. I wore a glamorous black dress, sinfully short, with fluffy feathery stuff floating around the neckline.

I would later refer to it as my Doomsday Dress.

Emmett had visited the Southwind before picking me up. I knew better than to dance with him, but our cute-as-a-button switchboard operator did not. She was always making ga-ga eyes at him. She had a new nose job and looked cute. You could tell she *felt* cute. "Dance with me, dance with me," she trilled, throwing open her arms, all bubbly and adorable, with flowers in her hair. Emmett beamed. I stood aside, hoping my new boss did not see me arrive with him.

She was very tiny, just about five feet tall and a hundred pounds. He was six foot and two hundred pounds. They danced nicely together for all of forty-five seconds. Then they swirled, and he bent her back, way back, into a dip. I did not want to watch. I heard the crash, saw the dance floor clear, and heard the switchboard operator screaming, "My nose! My nose!"

Things went downhill from there.

Hugo Wessels was sipping a drink as we talked. A topflight United Press International photographer, he is a notoriously feisty fellow. Once, when shooting the wrestling matches at Miami Beach Auditorium, the wrestlers, for some reason, attacked him. Fans joined in, and harried police radioed for reinforcements. The melee did not end until Hugo was carried out, still struggling, over the heads of half a dozen cops.

Hugo is no hulk; he is deceptively thin, but wiry. Heidi, his fiancée, was with him at the party. She was talking to friends. He asked if I had seen the new addition to the Swift home, an upstairs bedroom built out over the treetops. I had not.

We climbed the stairs to admire it, stepped out onto the Romeo-and-Juliet balcony, chatted for a few moments, then returned to the party. Emmett saw us descending, me in front, Hugo trailing behind. He greeted us at the foot of the stairs. I smiled at him. He slapped my face. I was stunned. Hugo stepped in front of me and said, "Where I come from, we don't treat women like that."

Emmett hurled his drink at Hugo. Booze splashed up onto the wood-beamed ceiling. The glass smashed on the tile floor. Emmett drew back to throw a punch. Before he could let it go, Hugo hit him on the jaw so hard that he spun completely around. As he did, his jacket flew open, exposing the .38-caliber revolver in its shoulder holster.

Hugo had never met Emmett. He did not know he was a cop. All he saw was that the man had a gun. He decided to hit him again before he could pull the gun.

Made sense to me.

He made the split-second decision while Emmett was still spinning. As the bigger man's face came around, Hugo punched it hard. Emmett crashed to the floor among the shards of shattered glass and fractured his ankle.

Suddenly, I was sympathetic. Family tradition perhaps. Some people cannot, must not ever drink at all. Emmett said he realized he was one of them, all the way to the hospital.

And I was touched: When they cut his clothes off in the emergency room, he was wearing the leopard-print briefs I had given him for Valentine's Day.

Surgeons screwed his ankle back together with metal pins. The bone around his eye was also fractured. It proved what I had long suspected: that a man who is big and burly is no match for one who is thin and wiry.

Emmett was now a lieutenant, due to take the test for captain of police. I hated to see something so stupid set back his career, particularly since he had reformed, or so he said. Somehow we had to keep the chief from learning what happened. But all the eyeball witnesses were media types, in the business of spreading the news. It would surely wind up in print, in somebody's column.

Gene Miller, the *Herald*'s two-time Pulitzer Prize winner, had been at the party. I called him and explained the situation. He promised to see what he could do, and he did. The police department investigated the battering of one of their lieutenants, but they never found out what really happened—though every reporter in town knew. It was a unique reversal of our usual roles: The press usually clamors to learn what the police try to keep quiet.

Emmett explained that a gang of hoodlums, total strangers, had attacked him from behind in a parking lot.

To me he swore he would never drink again. There I was, helping to save his career, when I should have been running for my life.

Bob Swift, my new boss, blamed the thrown drink for the mildew he discovered months later spreading across his wood-beamed ceiling.

I did not wear the Doomsday Dress again until New Year's Eve nearly a year later. Emmett was again my date. The year blasted off to an ill-omened start. After a party, we went out for coffee. Two noisy teenagers were drunk and rumbustious at another table. One hurled a heavy, round menu like a frisbee, sending it spinning across the room. It missed me by a foot. But it offended Emmett, who had forgotten his vows and had been vigorously toasting the new year.

He stalked to their table, grabbed each by the shirt-front, lifted them out of their seats, slammed them back down, and ordered them to behave. Suddenly sober, they agreed. Other patrons, the waitresses and management, applauded.

It was all Emmett needed.

When the boys left, Emmett hurried to depart also. The reason did not occur to me until we reached the parking lot. He cornered them at their car and was about to take another shot at the kids, when a stranger intervened. He was thin and wiry.

Quietly, he said that what Emmett did *inside* was okay; this was not. Made sense to me. He said to leave the boys alone. Emmett reacted poorly to the advice, and the stranger decked him.

On this trip to the hospital I began to rethink the relationship.

He swore to his colleagues that a gang of unidentified hoodlums attacked him from behind in a parking lot. He swore to me that he would never drink again.

His reputation for being attacked from behind in parking lots did not stall his career. He was sent off to the Southern Police Institute, in Louisville, Kentucky, a hint that he was being groomed for greater things. He swore he never touched a drop of Kentucky bourbon while there.

I flew to his graduation, and we drove back together, talking marriage.

I was dubious.

He found us a breezy corner apartment, on the Beach across from the golf course. He knew, he said, that he could never again have even a single drink and promised he never would.

It was a quiet wedding, with no time for a honeymoon. We spent the night on Key Biscayne. There were no sand fleas.

The marriage was a good one for almost twenty-four hours.

We moved into the apartment the next day. Emmett and I and my friend Bill Gjebre, a reporter for *The Miami News,* lugged boxes of books. It was a hot day in June. A neighbor welcomed us, all smiles, and invited us in for a cold drink.

We trooped gratefully into her air-conditioned living room. "Would you like iced tea?" she said, "or our own private-label imported Scotch?" I said tea, so did Bill.

"I'll try the Scotch," said Emmett.

I nearly fell off the chair. I had been had.

Our hostess asked if we wanted a refill. Emmett accepted. She brought out the bottle and stood it on the coffee table. I wondered how the heck I was going to get myself out of this mess. And how that woman would ever get Emmett out of her apartment. The marriage officially ended the following March, but for me, it ended in my new neighbor's living room.

I know a few judges now. If I ever even begin to talk marriage again, they will have me committed until the urge subsides. They promised.

During that brief period of wedlock, I shared the trials and troubles and the stark terror that haunts the hearts of women married to police officers. How could I ever forget the Police Benevolent Association's Fourth of July picnic? That was when I learned what playful police use for noisemakers when the firecrackers are all gone. The other wives and I crouched under the picnic tables, hoping they were solid enough to absorb the shock of stray bullets.

As the marriage skidded toward its demise, so did the *Sun.* Its current owner, the fifth since I was hired, was a wealthy politician. He bought it while promoting himself for statewide office, won the election, and was ready to unload us again. It looked like we were in deep trouble this time.

The rumored buyer operated a little throwaway called *The Miami Beach Reporter*. The front page was always reserved for his column and a cheesecake picture of a bathing beauty. Inside, he printed puff pieces about the people who bought his ads and attacks on those who did not. He bragged all over town that he was about to buy out the competition, fire the staff, and have all the local advertising to himself.

It was time to bail out and I needed a job. I remembered what I had been told at the *Herald,* then picked the name of executive editor George Beebe off its masthead.

Dear Mr. Beebe,

Five years ago I called The Herald to ask how to apply for a job as a reporter. I was told not to bother unless I had a degree in journalism or five years experience at a daily newspaper.

As of August 14, 1970, I have five years experience at The Miami Beach Daily Sun.

How about it?

Edna Buchanan

His secretary called the next day and invited me to a daylong battery of interviews and tests.

"Do you ever have any irresistible impulses that you find difficult to control?" asked the company shrink.

Christ, I thought, what has he heard? The man's voice

had a peculiar edge to it. I had to come up with some-thing.

"Yes," I said, averting my eyes, "about twice a week. I just can't help myself."

He leaned forward, intense. "Tell me about it."

Sighing, I confessed, "I drive to a Dairy Queen for a Hawaiian Isle sundae, the one with pineapple and co-conut."

It was the best I could do on short notice. It was even true.

I heard nothing from the *Herald* for weeks. I was des-perate. The decision had been left to Steve Rogers, the city editor.

Dear Mr. Rogers,
    Obits?

                                    Edna Buchanan

The day after receiving my one-word letter he called to ask when I could start. My heart pounded as I told him when I would be there and said goodbye. "Wait, haven't you forgotten something?" he said.

I had no idea.

"Salary," he said, "you haven't asked me the salary."

FOUR

Nobody Loves a Police Reporter

I was in over my head.

Steve Rogers showed me my mailbox and said to check it frequently for assignments. Nodding attentively, I tried hard to look alert. This was it, *The Miami Herald,* the big time. He asked if I had any questions. Struck dumb, the attentive look frozen on my face, I shook my head and fled his office to check my empty mailbox.

I still check it compulsively a dozen times a day. God knows what other important instructions Rogers gave me that first day. Overwhelmed, I remembered nothing else.

From the beginning, it was a comfort just to see the *Miami Herald* building looming huge and permanent against the skyline. It made me feel secure. It still does. You can see it from the expressway, the causeways, from downtown, and from the bay. Just look up. The *Herald* building sprawls over an entire block of prime water-front. Employee parking lots are slowly swallowing the surrounding neighborhood. Sometimes the world's biggest barge is moored at the back door, delivering newsprint.

The yawning fifth-floor newsroom is the size of a concert hall, with a spectacular view. To the east, beyond the glass cages of the executives, lies Biscayne Bay, its surface dotted by the bright sails of weekend regattas, the spans to Miami Beach, and the resort skyline with the sea beyond. The panorama is so clear and beautiful that any imperfection is quickly noted. Twice over the years one sharp-eyed editor has spotted from his office desk, and hastily reported to the proper authorities, dead bodies adrift in the bay. The vista to the west is an overview of stunning skyscrapers, Overtown slums, spectacular sunsets, and the lights of the Orange Bowl, above which the Goodyear blimp hovers during big games. Brown pelicans and Chalk's seaplanes swoop gracefully past the newsroom's picture windows to land at Watson Island just southeast of the building. The blue-and-white seaplanes arc in a sharp turn so close to our windows that even veteran newsroom habitués sometimes catch their breath. A stranger visiting my desk gasped and would have hit the floor had he not realized that all around him it was business as usual.

Somewhere in the heart of that mammoth structure, buzzed by birds and planes and strafed by the politicians that it gores, a newspaper is actually printed. I cannot tell you precisely where. Most new employees take orientation tours; I dashed out to my first assignment instead—a feature about a Cuban refugee whose Russian parents had fled the Bolsheviks to settle in Havana in 1918. Now the son had fled Cuba with his wife and children and, thanks to an award from the Small Business Administration, had set up shop for himself as the only American flag manufacturer in the southern United States.

I settled in to work, quickly reporting a Miami Beach houseboat ban, dangerously antiquated North Bay Village fire-fighting equipment, a Hialeah garbage strike, Golda Meir's appeal for Israel bonds, the inadvertent insecticide poisonings of Miami Beach police dogs, the clout of senior power, and the arrival of a new aardvark at the zoo. Some other reporters soon objected to my stories. Too damn many, they said. They, all of them men incidentally, accused me of diarrhea of the typewriter. They suggested it would be to the benefit of us all if I held it down to one a day.

I couldn't; asking me to cut back on stories was like asking me to cut back on breathing. The manic work habits, forged in daily desperation at the *Sun*, had become a way of life. The more stories I wrote, the happier and more productive I felt. If I could write four, five, or more stories in one day, it only made me want to write more, more, *more*. It was addictive. When one of those reticent reporters later became an editor, he totally about-faced. Suddenly, productivity delighted him. He wanted as many stories as I could churn out—and more.

Despite my diligence, some editors failed to take me seriously during those first months at the *Herald*. I thought I knew why: *Something* was missing.

I threatened to buy one at an adult toy store and display it in a flowerpot on my desk.

It never quite came to that, but you can understand my frustration the day the roof blew off a restaurant near Lincoln Mall. I had been at the *Herald* for three months and was at Miami Beach police headquarters that day, researching a story on jewel thieves. Fumes from a slow gas leak next door to the restaurant built up near the ceiling, then detonated. The roof soared skyward, raining down debris and rubble. The explosion blew a passing cop right off his motorcycle, demolished the restaurant, a print shop, and a fruit shipper, and damaged eighteen other stories. I called the city desk first, then raced to the scene, just seventeen blocks from headquarters.

Firemen were carrying out dazed victims in their arms. Police, fearing the worst, were calling the medical examiner's office for body bags—most of which, happily, would not be needed. Casualties were not as heavy as it first appeared, because after the roof went up, most people were quick enough to stampede out the front door before the roof came down.

I watched the rescues, itching for a camera, and wondered why the *Herald* photographers were so slow to arrive. It was a straight shot across the causeway, yet they missed all the heroics. I later learned that, after my breathless call, the man in the slot, the editor in charge, leaned back in his chair and said, "Edna Buchanan claims some restaurant just blew up on the Beach." Casually, he asked someone to add it to their list of tips to check out. Had he thought to glance out the picture window on his left, he could have see the towering mushroomlike cloud of black smoke. When they finally did confirm the news, a mob of male reporters was sent to back me up.

Soon after, I was the first *Herald* reporter to arrive at the scene of a Chalk's seaplane hijacking—a misguided fellow demanded to be taken to Africa on a seaplane that could hold just enough fuel to get to Bimini. Editors hastily sent another reporter who followed me about, interrupting my news gathering to interview me about what I had seen so *he* could write the story.

I swore to myself that somehow I would not let that happen again.

Therefore, I was delighted late one Saturday night when the man in the slot sent me off to cover a fatal shooting outside a Liberty City bar. The cops were horrified to see me elbow my way through a raucous and jeering crowd. "What are you doing here!" they cried. We were the only white faces there. This is real progress, a breakthrough, I thought happily.

Next day I learned that the editor, new on the job, was severely criticized for sending me there. It was not new policy. It was a mistake.

Few women were sent out on police stories in 1971.

I covered a few that year, when I was the only reporter available or got a fast-breaking tip from an old source—like my mother. After she came upon a wounded Miami Beach police officer crouched behind a patrol car exchanging bullets with a Black Panther, she called, suggesting I look into it.

Eventually I made a real breakthrough. I knew it when a reporter sauntered into the newsroom, mentioned that he had just passed a Volkswagen in flames on the express-way, and suggested that someone check to see if there were casualties. The same editor who doubted me when the restaurant exploded was infuriated that the reporter simply drove on by. During the tongue-lashing that fol-lowed, I heard him bellow that had Edna Buchanan seen the flaming Volkswagen, "she would be talking to Ger-many on that phone right now, interviewing the assembly-line worker who put it together."

During my second year at the *Herald* I covered crimi-nal court, another beat where a reporter can mine gold. You meet the cops, the crooks, the judges, the bondsmen, and the lawyers: the good guys, the bad guys, and the ma-jority who are a mix of both. You see more honest-to-God drama, intrigue and acting in a criminal courtroom than you will ever find on any stage. Award-winning per-formances every day: so many stories, so little time.

I often found the guilty parties eager to talk—for a va-riety of reasons. Some try to build alibis or protest too much out of nervousness. Others believe they are misun-derstood; if you show a real interest in the call girls, the cat burglars, or the serial killers, they invariably will want to tell you all about it.

Kim Brown was the first practicing Satan worshiper I had ever met. Young and exotic, a dark-eyed former model, she had been the welcome houseguest of a Miami Beach retiree. She badly abused his hospitality by stab-bing him fifty-six times and stealing his car.

The sign of Satan was tattooed on her left hand. Kim

prayed daily in front of a hexagram she had drawn in her jail cell. This unnerved her fellow inmates, most of whom discover Jesus in jail, if only temporarily. Chiefly interested in an interview about her religious beliefs and practices, I talked to her lawyer. He kept wisecracking that he was having a "devil of a time" building her defense. I promised not to discuss the homicide charges pending against her.

They locked us together in a hold cell for a one-hour interview. Kim told me that she had been worshiping the devil for five years and that she was a lesbian with an intense dislike for men. Instructed not to discuss the murder, she insisted on doing so, in loving detail. She enjoyed stabbing the old man and even laughed while doing it, she said. That explained the overkill. As she described it, she became agitated and more intense. She talked faster, moved closer, her eyes glittered. It occurred to me that the hour must be up by now and it was time to go.

I discreetly tried to catch a guard's attention without offending Kim, who squeezed my knee in a surprisingly strong grip as she discussed the sexual stimulation stabbing achieved. I realized that the shift had changed. The guards on duty now had no idea I was in there, locked in a cell with a devil-worshiping, sexually crazed, homicidal lesbian maniac.

Luckily, a jailer strolled by and asked, "What are you doing here?"—a question I am usually not so pleased to hear—and I was sprung.

Kim plea-bargained, pleading guilty to a reduced charge of manslaughter in exchange for a seven-year sentence. The public was furious. The prosecutor resigned under fire and roundly criticized his boss in public, creating quite a furor. Kim was pleased. Satan did it, she said. Despite the relatively light sentence and her almost-instant parole eligibility, she escaped soon after.

I learned a lot on that beat and worked incredibly hard. One benefit of covering courts is having weekends off. On one of them, I attended an Orlando conference of women journalists. Feminist Gloria Steinem and *New York Times* reporter Judy Klemesrud talked turkey to us, explaining that we had to be sure we were receiving equal pay. *Herald* reporters have no union and are paid on merit and experience. That, the speakers warned, is how the white-male–dominated press gets away with underpaying women.

I had never even suspected I was being treated unfairly. I had already had a few raises, but now I was curious. How do you find out what the men are making? Simple they said—young men in particular tend to be generally candid. Agree to tell him your salary and he will tell you his. It worked. I chose a reporter hired at the *Herald* a year before I was. If I could get him to divulge his salary and then adjust for his year's seniority, I would know. To my surprise, he readily agreed and named the figure. It struck me speechless. It was one hundred dollars a week *less* than I was being paid. "Now," he said, "how much do you make?"

I froze. How could I tell this man my salary was higher than his? "How much?" he said.

"Never mind," I said, and hurried away. He is still at

the *Herald* and vaguely pleasant, but I am sure he has never forgiven me. I don't blame him.

By the end of my year on the court beat, I had seen how stories can make a difference. They often produce results. Stories can get people out of jail or put people into jail.

Stories can even change the law.

When I learned that a wealthy Miami Beach socialite, convicted of two murders and sentenced to two life terms, had been quietly paroled to another state after only five years, I wrote a three-part series on the parole system. It examined the question of how long "life" is—in prison, in Florida.

Life for many was surprisingly short. Lawyers told clients it meant six to ten years. Many terms were shorter; technically, parole was possible the day of sentencing. Thousands of people in Dade County went free not long after being sentenced to spend the rest of their natural lives in prison. Many committed new and nasty crimes.

In its next session, the legislature decreed that those convicted of first-degree murder must serve a mandatory minimum of twenty-five years before parole. Not everyone agrees with the law. Some would modify it because of prison overcrowding and public sympathy for certain convicted killers, but the penalty still stands.

I returned to general-assignment reporting for my third year. Based on what I had seen in court, I could see that something was lacking. Miami's crime rate was not about to lighten up, but we still "covered the cops" with any general-assignment reporter who happened to be free when the shooting started. It seemed to be a catch-as-catch-can method.

I had caught a number of good stories in court that we had overlooked at the time of the crime. So I casually suggested to Steve Rogers that a reporter pay daily visits to the major police departments, read the reports, rap with the troops, and then drop by the morgue and the jail to check the overnight arrivals.

"Sounds good. Why don't you do it?" Rogers said, without skipping a beat. Never the sort of editor who needed memos and meetings before making a decision, he walked away jauntily.

I stood frozen in panic. It was only a suggestion. I did not intend to volunteer, but somehow, I had.

That is how I came to cover the police beat.

It is what I have been doing ever since. It is why I have been threatened repeatedly with arrest, had rocks thrown at me, and had my purse stolen. It is why I regularly get ominous letters, subpoenas, and obscene phone calls—some of them from my editors.

Nobody loves a police reporter. It can be lonely.

It's lucky I like being alone. If I must mutter about my day, I can tell it to a cat, who won't flick a whisker no matter how weird it is. She could probably tell some pretty crazy stories herself. As for my dog, he'll listen, but he doesn't give a damn.

Covering the police beat does little to enhance one's social life. Sure I meet new people every day, but my first words to them are usually, "Did you hear the shots?"

Hardly the sort of opening line that leads to a long-term relationship.

I had been on the beat for about a year, when a date took me to see *Jesus Christ Superstar* at Miami Beach Auditorium. The night was still young as we emerged from the show, but I heard sirens. The wail of a siren is a familiar sound in Miami Beach, but there were lots of them. I paused and listened. Some were approaching across the causeways, which means that the Beach, which has a terrific fire department, called other jurisdictions for help.

What it means is major disaster.

A deranged man had walked into the popular Concord Cafeteria—always crowded with senior citizens—and dumped a pail of gasoline. Then he struck a match. The place exploded in flames, the lights went out, and people were trapped. Couples who had never been apart in fifty years lost each other in the dark and the panic. About thirty people were hurt. Several died later. Cafeteria employees, police, and firemen made heroic rescues.

I called the *Herald* to be sure photographers were on the way, rushed to the Concord, dashed into the still-smoldering building to talk to the fire and police chiefs, got as much detail as I could, and called it in from a pay phone across the street. It was right on our deadline. Keeping the phone open so nobody else could tie it up—especially other reporters—I had my date round up witnesses, people who had escaped, and those who had helped. He herded them over so I could interview them and pass their quotes directly over the phone to the city desk.

We had a thorough front-page story the next morning,

but the performance at the auditorium was erased from my memory. Also missing was my date. The evening was obviously not what he had in mind.

Ditto the heart surgeon I saw briefly. It was hopeless from the start. It was always either his pager or mine. On our last night together, it happened simultaneously. Our pagers began to beep in unison as we sat in the bar at his club waiting for a table for dinner. We looked deep into each other's eyes and knew—this was pointless. All we had left was the question of who would get to use the telephone first. Next time he called me, it was to announce his plans to marry a nurse.

Unlike the other men in my life, the arsonist who torched the Concord remained constant. From a wealthy family, he was quickly cured after commitment to a mental hospital. Soon, he was released. Not long after that, I began receiving calls from concerned employees at another restaurant. He was in their establishment, they complained, throwing lighted matches at waitresses.

My worst fear was missing or being beaten on a police-beat story. That is why I reacted with concern one Saturday when a *Herald* editor paged me with an assignment. He wanted a feature story on a big shopping-center sale. Covering crowds and color is fun. I love features, but the police beat is my job, and I hadn't even been to Miami police headquarters yet. What if we missed something important?

He insisted I forget it and go straight to the shopping center. Once, I believed that a good reporter follows orders like a marine, but that changed when I was at the *Sun*.

A plane crashed in Miami, on Thirty-sixth Street. I called from a pay phone to tell my editor I was on the way to the crash site. No, he said, it's not a Miami Beach story. The *Sun* was a local newspaper, but no paper is that local—the crash was at the other end of the causeway. I said the only thing I could at the time: "Hello? Hello? I can't hear you . . ." I held the phone at arm's length. "Something's wrong with this phone."

Picking through rubble at the scene, I met the *Sun*'s other reporter. Hearing of the plane crash, she had leaped to her feet to go cover the disaster. "No, wait!" the editor cried, as she ran out the door. "It's not a Miami Beach story."

Our coverage and pictures were award-winning, and our editor accepted praise for sending us.

Now I faced the dilemma of the shopping-center-sale assignment. I did the only thing I could: "Hello! Hello!" I cried, holding the phone at arm's length . . .

I was lucky. At headquarters I found a story we might have missed: A well-known police supervisor had been surprised in a stolen car during the night. Off-duty and disguised in blackface and a wig, he was armed and lurking near a room at Miami Jai Alai, the room where $333,695 wagered the night before was being kept. He had no explanation.

The pressures of covering a beat and meeting constant deadlines cause you to do things you would never do otherwise. Certain dismaying experiences lose significance in the face of more pressing considerations. Two young men tried to rob me one night as I left a crime scene. I shook them off and escaped safely back to the *Herald*. It did not even occur to me until later to notify the police. I was on deadline.

"Don't even think about it," I growl at strangers eyeing my purse or about to break into my car. That is not me talking. That is a feverish somebody who works for the *Herald,* is on deadline, and has no time to be distracted by incidents unrelated to the story.

Once, on deadline, I was leaning over a second-floor balcony into a street on fire below, for a better view of the still-burning wreckage of a plane. It had crashed with a full fuel tank when its cargo of Christmas trees shifted. The railing buckled. Pencil and notebook in my hands, I fell forward asking "What street is . . ." A homicide detective named Arthur Felton grabbed me and dragged me back as we both teetered on the brink for one dizzying moment. ". . . that over there?" I continued, still engrossed in mapping out a proper diagram to pinpoint the plane's fatal path for my editors. Trembling, the shaken detective shouted that I must be crazy. He never let me forget it.

In real life I am basically shy and can't do a lot of things, but on the job, the story is all that matters—the deadline is coming at you, unstoppable, like an avalanche down a mountain. You brave the wrath of crooks and cops and bad crowds and mean dogs without even seeing them. There is no time. Do what you have to and worry about it later. And fortunately, you do not worry even then, because later arrives with the hot breath of a new deadline on its heels.

That is why I went speeding off into the dark without

directions my first year on the police beat, the night the Eastern Air Lines L-1011 crashed in The Everglades. It was the big one that everybody fears, the disaster we all know will come someday.

The New York–Miami flight went down in the middle of the week, between Christmas and the New Year. Called at home close to midnight, I was told survivors were being airlifted to Palmetto Hospital in Northwest Dade. We were perilously close to final deadline. I had never been there and did not even know where the damn hospital was, but I was going there, headed in the general direction at ninety miles an hour. I hoped to spot a police car, for directions. None was in sight. The highway was long and lonely. The only sign of life was a motorcycle gang, ten or twelve bikers congregated at the side of the road in their leather jackets and boots. I hit the brakes, veered off the pavement, screeched to a stop and rolled down the window. "How do I get to Palmetto Hospital?" I screamed. They looked startled. Maybe the panic in my voice brought out the best in them.

"Follow us!" they cried, running for their machines. We rumbled off, three bikers leading the way, the others in a pack behind me.

The hospital was ringed by the flashing blue lights of Florida Highway Patrol cars. The bikers waved, turned, and thundered into the darkness. Helicopters throbbed overhead. Some of the crash victims the choppers were bringing in were badly hurt; many died later. The Palmetto staff was remarkable, as though they had rehearsed their response.

They had. Three days earlier the hospital had staged a disaster drill. The entire staff, even those now racing in from home, knew exactly what to do.

The first passenger I talked to was a young woman in a wheelchair. Her injuries were not serious, but she was hysterical. She had been holding her baby in her arms during the flight. On impact, the infant flew out of her grasp. She couldn't find him in the darkness. A stewardess arrived on the next helicopter, carrying the baby. She had heard his cries in the pitch blackness of the swamp and picked him up. He was unhurt. Mother and child were reunited there in the emergency room.

We needed to find out fast if there was major loss of life. Deep in The Everglades, the crash site was remote and inaccessible, and naturally, the rescue crews were only airlifting live victims. Eastern Air Lines public relations people, well aware of our imminent deadline, were hopeful, saying that since so many survivors were being brought in, it was possible that no one had been killed.

I found a perfect witness, a private detective, an ex–New York City cop, bound for Miami on a case. Unlike the average traveler, here was a man who knew a dead body when he saw, or felt, one.

Lying flat on an examining table, he said he wanted to run from the plane because he feared it would explode. Unable to stand because of a back injury, he crawled away. To do so, he told me, he crawled over bodies, "lots of bodies." How many are lots, I asked. He said twenty to thirty. That was our first word from a credible eyewitness that a great many people were dead. The truth was that about one hundred survived and about one hundred did not.

We were trying even then to piece things together. What happened? Was it pilot error? Did a bomb explode? Was the plane struck by lightning?

A black, middle-aged longshoreman had a clue. He had been on his way to visit a married daughter in Miami. He was still in shock, badly hurt, but feeling no pain. He saw the lights of the city and Miami International Airport, he told me, as the plane approached for a landing. But then the pilot apparently swung the big jet back out over The Everglades. Moments before the impact, he said to the man next to him, "Where did the city go? It's all dark down there."

He was right on the mark. That is exactly what happened. The pilot, distracted by a malfunctioning light, had chosen to abort the landing and circle over The Everglades. As we talked, the passenger began to come out of shock and feel the pain of his injuries. He groaned loudly. The electronic media had arrived by then. TV and radio reporters were milling about. At the sound, they stampeded across the emergency room in their usual herd, microphones extended, to send the poor man's groans coast-to-coast. Lights, cameras, and wires trailing, they nearly knocked over two nurses who were running with plasma to save somebody's life.

Newspaper reporters can be kinder. We can talk with victims of tragedy without blinding them with bright lights and hitting them in the mouth with a microphone. Reporting news live, as it happens, must be exciting, but while I envy the immediacy of radio and TV, I don't regret staying with print journalism. Only once did I come close to leaving it. Officials at a network affiliate wanted to talk to me about a job. When the news director stepped into the office where I was waiting, he found me on hands and knees. I was not praying to be hired, I was seeking my lost contact lens. In spite of it, they offered $137 a week more than the *Herald* was paying me. Tempted, I told my editors on Friday that I probably would give two weeks' notice on Monday. But, at the last minute, I couldn't do it, and I'm not sorry.

In those early years, when I was competing almost exclusively with men, it would not be quite true to say that I never used sex to beat them. I was the first reporter—and probably the first willing woman—to step into sex killer Albert Brust's torture chamber.

Albert Brust was a mild-mannered Dade County housing inspector. He lived quietly in the suburbs until a summer storm struck one morning, and the housewife next door ran out to snatch her clean wash off the clothesline. Brust was stretched out in his backyard, on a lounge chair. Thunder crashed, lightning streaked the sky, and rain began to fall. He did not move. It occurred to this busy young housewife that her neighbor had not moved in two days.

She called the police.

Brust had downed a chocolate drink laced with cyanide. His death, which first appeared to be a simple suicide, quickly became bizarre. The walls of his house were padded and soundproofed. His freezer was stocked with carefully wrapped meatballs, each containing enough cyanide to kill three people. There was a torture chamber with psychedelic lighting, and under a layer of freshly poured cement, something terrible in the bathtub.

Albert Brust had kidnapped a runaway teenage couple. He killed and decapitated the boy, put the corpse in his bathtub, and covered it with cement. He raped and tortured the girl for days, then took her to Fort Lauderdale and set her free. She went straight to police. They did not believe a word of her outlandish story and sent her home to Indiana.

She was fifteen.

An otherwise immaculate housekeeper and efficient handyman, Brust was undone by a detail: The cement failed to seal. The body began to decompose, and the terrible odor permeated the entire house. The only answer would be to free the body with a jackhammer. The corpse would then have to be disposed of somewhere else.

A messy job.

"I have miscalculated," Brust confided to his diary. "I know I could save the situation by a lot of disagreeable work, but the whole business is not worth the trouble."

He left the disagreeable work for police. Sweaty homicide detectives took turns with the jackhammer. The press and a crowd gathered behind the yellow crime-scene rope outside. It was a sizzling Saturday in July 1973. The storm had blown over, and ice-cream and soft-drink vendors worked the crowd. Stunned neighbors described Brust to reporters as a loner who was kind to stray cats.

They often saw him feeding them meatballs.

The presence of reporters had excited the neighborhood children to a fever pitch. They demanded to know what channel I worked for, a common question. I explained that I work for a newspaper. "But what channel? What channel?" they cried, puzzled. I explained again. This time a tyke about age seven comprehended.

"*The Miami Herald!* Boo! Hiss! Boo!" he bawled, turning his grimy thumbs down. What grudge could this child, barely old enough to read, have against our great newspaper? I hunkered down to his level, eyeball to eyeball, to gently ask the problem. "It's too heavy," he howled. "On Sunday it's too heavy!"

He wanted to be a newsboy, but the paper was too fat and bulky for somebody his size to handle. I could live with that.

The press that was assembled outside Brust's two-bedroom house included reporters from newspapers, wire services, radio and TV—all of them men, except me. It took hours for detectives to free the body. Meanwhile we waited out in the hot sun—and my deadline was approaching, fast.

A husky homicide lieutenant finally agreed to escort the press inside—one at a time—to tour the house and the torture chamber for our stories. That could take the rest of the day. I was pushing deadline. I still had to drive all the way back to the *Herald* and write my story.

"Ladies first!" I shouted.

It was instinctive, in desperation. It worked.

I filed the first story on this classic case of madness and

murder. I asked myself if what I did was aggressive, which is considered good in this business, or sexist, which is not. There is a fine line. I think that is as close as I have come to crossing it.

Albert Brust's story was front-page in the morning *Herald.* My byline was also on the lead story on the local page, and I had written the cover story in *Tropic,* the *Herald*'s Sunday magazine. It was a good day. I realized, perhaps for the first time, that maybe I *could* do this after all. But of course in this business there is never time for the glow of accomplishment.

All that matters is the story—the one for tomorrow's paper.

Hollywood came to the *Herald* to shoot the movie *Mean Season,* and the wardrobe woman, Linda Benedict, visited the newsroom to observe how to authentically attire Kurt Russell and the other actors portraying newspaper people. We did not impress her.

"Reporters don't care how they look, do they?" she sniffed, gazing around the newsroom.

I plead extenuating circumstances, at least in my case.

For the first few years, conscious of representing the *Herald,* I primly wore dresses and high heels to work. Wearing them, I slogged through The Everglades and scrunched across the scorching sands of Miami Beach, hunting down witnesses to shark or barracuda attacks and heroic rescues by lifeguards.

Then the Drug Enforcement Administration building collapsed. It was 1974 and the DEA had begun confiscating drug dealers' wheels. They stored the seized autos on the roof of their downtown Miami headquarters. They apparently parked one confiscated car too many on the roof, and it caved in one day, taking the entire building down with it. Seven federal employees died, sixteen were injured.

Some were still trapped under tons of debris and automobiles, and a major rescue effort was under way. I was up front with the fire chief, who was directing the operation, when a TV reporter set up a howl from far behind the yellow rope. "What is Edna Buchanan doing up there? Why is *she* allowed in there when we aren't?"

I hate that. Naturally they couldn't allow the TV crews, with all their cumbersome equipment, to get in the way of the rescue workers, so I was captured and marched back behind the police line.

At one point, just as I leaned across to ask a question, a nearby cop jerked the coarse knee-high rope up to let some city official pass beneath. The line caught the synthetic material of my dress in a Velcro-like grip, dragging my skirt up around my waist. It was very embarrassing.

Minutes later, a group of DEA agents returned to their office with more confiscated cars, found the building in ruins and became highly perturbed. Their reactions attracted eager cameramen. That perturbed the agents even more. Their cover as undercover narcs would be blown if their pictures appeared. There was quite a scuffle, with threats, shouting, and lunging at cameras. I seized the opportunity to slip under the yellow rope for a few final words from the rescuers before my deadline. That provoked some cops, who said I was under arrest and threw me in a police car. Luckily somebody opened the door on the other side, and I got away.

After that, however, I began to wear slacks to the office and stashed thigh-high, reinforced, black-and-orange, authentic fire-department boots in the trunk of my car.

So much for fashion.

For his role as a police reporter in *Mean Season,* Kurt Russell wore cheap, drip-dry suits and 100-percent-cotton shirts. Linda Benedict spun them in a hot dryer until they were wrinkled enough to look authentic.

How can you dress for success when you never know your next assignment? It could be a funeral, a riot, or a three-alarm fire.

Or you could be sent off to ride an airboat out to the site of a plane crash in The Everglades. I wore a dress and high heels as I clung to the back of the airboat, much to the amusement of Dr. Joseph H. Davis, the Dade County medical examiner. Also a passenger, he was more sensibly dressed. A plane carrying a cargo of foam-rubber falsies had crashed. The doomed aircraft broke open and spilled them all over The Everglades. There were falsies in the trees, in the swamp, in the bushes—falsies everywhere. I don't know the long-term ecological effect, if any, on the environment.

This is just not the sort of job where you can dress up or plan ahead. It never works out. When a predawn house fire killed five children and their dog, I worked for seventeen hours. When somebody shot Florida Highway Patrolman Bradley Glasscock, it was twenty hours.

I first met the husky young trooper at a major traffic snarl created by a carload of Rastafarians. A Jamaican sect, they wear their hair in dreadlocks and claim marijuana as part of their religion. In a perfect example of how marijuana may damage the thought process, particularly the ability to think ahead, a passenger in the backseat shot the driver in the head during a quarrel, at sixty-five miles an hour in the fast lane.

The car careened across the highway, caused several wrecks, then crashed. The passengers who could still run, jumped out and did so. Patrolman Glasscock, an earnest and good-natured cop, was trying to piece it all together. He handled the accidents and called in those detective whizzes from the city, Sergeant Mike Gonzalez and Detective Louise Vasquez, to investigate the homicide. I abandoned my car on the shoulder of the road and hiked through the backed-up lanes of traffic to work the story.

Not long after that, I found myself pounding the pavement in the middle of the night on the same highway, on another story. Highway Patrolman Bradley Glasscock was dead, murdered by a driver who did not drop his dime into an expressway toll. I got a call at 4:00 A.M. and went to cover the manhunt.

A police K-9 dog, a German shepherd, was set loose to track the gunman. He leaped a seawall and splashed into the bay, much to the dismay and embarrassment of his handler. Moments later, the shouts were electrifying. The big dog scrambled back out of the water—the murder weapon clenched between his teeth. Dogs can't smell under water; how did he do that?

I don't know, but I was there, and he did it.

A year later, I took my mom out to dinner and was paged as our meal arrived. A highway patrolman and a tow-truck driver had just been shot to death on the expressway. I left my mom in her doorway, clutching a hastily wrapped turkey dinner. At the office, I pushed aside a package to work on the story. Later, after I turned in the story on the latest murder of a trooper, I idly picked up the package and tore it open. The contents seemed right out of *The Twilight Zone:* a plaque—a journalism award for the story of the trooper's murder a year earlier.

Sometimes reporters are drawn personally into cases. A hit-and-run driver struck a young girl on a bicycle, backed up, yanked her and the bike out from under his car, and threw them to the side of the road, where she died.

She was twelve years old.

The police worked the heck out of that case and solved it—two days before the statute of limitations would have let the driver go free forever. They brought him in in handcuffs. TV cameras were outside; I was waiting in the police station lobby. I stepped aboard the elevator with him and the two detectives. They were not crazy about my joining them, but they were gentlemen. During the brief ride to the second-floor homicide office, I had the chance to ask only one question: "Do you remember the accident?"

"Yes," the suspect said. "I do, very well." I quoted him in my story.

He confessed to the detectives that day. Later, he hired a sharp defense attorney and pleaded not guilty, repudiating his confession, which was ruled inadmissible. I got subpoenaed to a pretrial hearing.

We get lots of subpoenas. *Herald* lawyers usually have them quashed. It is not good policy for reporters to testify. But this time was different; this guy might actually walk. All I would swear to was the accuracy of what I wrote.

I testified that I was wearing press identification, carrying a reporter's notebook, and had identified myself to him as a reporter. He did *not* think I was a cop. So, although his formal confession to police was ruled out—his comment to me was not.

Rather than have a jury hear it, the defendant and his attorney decided to plead guilty.

I had been called as a witness before. During my final year at the *Sun*, the police radio on my desk signaled a robbery in progress at a South Beach liquor store twelve blocks away. I pulled up out front as the owner, a tough old guy who had been robbed five or six times, came running out the door. He waved frantically, then darted past me and down the street toward the first approaching police car. I waved back and ran inside to see what happened. A rack of whiskey bottles lay smashed on the floor. A man was crouched in a far corner. He was trembling and panicky. I asked if he was all right and fished out my notebook.

He was a terrible interview.

He kept rolling his eyes and saying, "I don't know,

man. I don't know nothing." I thought the poor fellow was in shock.

"Did you see the robber? What did he look like? Which way did he go?"

The owner and three policemen had their noses pressed against the plate-glass window. They were beckoning me to come out. They usually whisk away witnesses before I can interview them, and I still did not have even a single usable quote from this guy. Trying to ignore them, I kept asking questions.

He was a lousy interview.

I glanced up again and the police looked angry this time, waving their arms and demanding I come out. I gave up trying to get any quotes and walked out on the sidewalk. The police ran past, rushed inside, tackled the guy and handcuffed him.

He was the robber.

I was subpoenaed to his trial—by the defense. They wanted me to testify in his behalf, that he was a perfect gentleman in my presence. I did testify. It did not do him much good. The judge was Ellen Morphonios, referred to by the prisoners in the jail as the Time Machine because she gives them so much time behind bars.

I testified that he was a perfect gentleman, but a lousy interview.

She gave him twenty years.

To be a police reporter is to be an unwelcome intruder. It can be lonesome and arduous. People blame you for the bad news. It's human nature: Somebody gets in trouble, you report it, and he turns on you like it's your fault, not his, that he is in this mess. The truth can get you in a lot of trouble. The Greeks used to kill the messenger who brought the bad news.

It would delight some people to revive the custom.

Writing a story is an uncertain business. You never know if you are really finished. There is always something else to check, another detail you might glean that could change everything. A newspaper story can ruin a life or come back to haunt it twenty years later. It is there in black and white, on file, like a police record—forever. You never outlive it.

Police reporters deal with lives, reputations, and careers. So you keep on—ask one more question, knock on one more door, make one last phone call, and then another.

It could be the one that counts.

The smallest of the felines is a masterpiece.
Leonardo da Vinci

SIDEBAR
White Kittens Dancing

Never again, I swore after Niña died. Losing a pet is too hurtful. There is pain enough in the world without inviting it. Within days, of course, I longed for a white kitten just like Niña. I even dreamed of white kittens, watching when I drove, half-expecting to see one dance out from under a parked car. But none did.

People I knew kept trying to bombard me with kittens—black ones, fuzzy ones, gray-striped balls of fur. Even Sergeant Mike Gonzalez acquired a kitten somewhere and tried to foist it upon me. I was shocked at his insensitivity.

The right white kitten will come along again someday, I thought, dancing out of the shadows, as kittens will. Then Elayne Wolfenson, my friend from the missing-persons bureau, called. A kitten, she said, black and white. No, I said firmly. A policewoman and her husband, also a cop, had spotted it skittering in bewildered panic in the middle of busy South Dixie Highway. They jumped out of their car, stopped traffic, and successfully made the rescue. They had three German shepherds, their vacation was coming up, and they had heard I was bereft. It's amazing how word gets around. I even got a kind note of sympathy from another animal-loving softy, Judge Ellen "Time Machine" Morphonios, also known as the Hanging Judge.

At police headquarters next day, I was adamant as Elayne and the policewoman pushed a Polaroid picture at me. It was a portrait of the ugliest kitten I had ever seen, obviously the product of an unfed stray with poor prenatal care. The head was huge, too big for the scrawny body, the front legs were crooked, and a strange, jagged white mustache stopped short halfway across her black face, giving it a lopsided, unfinished look. I knew instantly, I had to say yes. Had she been beautiful, she would have been easy to refuse, but nobody else in the world would ever want this waif.

Dixie Darling came home with me. The timing was poor. In addition to long hours at the *Herald,* I was spending all my free time in jail interviewing a sex killer. When I did arrive home late at night, I could hear the lonely cries of Dixie Darling before I even got out of the car. I was guilt-ridden. The poor little creature had been happier dodging traffic on South Dixie Highway. In her desolation, with time on her paws, she upended every flowerpot, shredded every paper, and began to dissect the drapes.

She needed a partner to keep her occupied—two cats

are better than one. But I had no time to go out and find
her a suitable companion. As they searched me at the jail
one day, I remarked to the sergeant in charge that my situation at home was desperate, I had to find a kitten.

"See me before you leave," he said. I did, and we went
to the kitchen. He stepped out a door and came back carrying a gray-and-white kitten. Frightened and wailing, it
was the runt of a litter delivered by the jail mascot, a gray-
striped cat named Trustee.

I sighed and gave up all my wistful thoughts of a dancing white kitten. This one cried like a baby all the way
home.

I presented Baby Dear to Dixie Darling, who stopped
howling for company and viciously attacked the new-
comer. She regretted it quickly. Like a great many of the
creatures who emerge from that jail, Baby Dear proved to
be incorrigible, unrehabilitatible, a vicious sociopath at
heart. She has always behaved more like wild animal than
pet. One veterinarian, clawed a time too many, offered to
put her to sleep, permanently, absolutely free. It would be
his pleasure. "Pets should be a joy," he explained gently,
gripping his bloodied hand, "and she is not."

I was shocked. It might have been unnerving to open a
harmless-looking pet carrier, tagged with the name Baby
Dear, and have the occupant lunge snarling for your
throat, but capital punishment is a bit stiff for a bad dis-
position. We found another doctor.

At ten, Baby Dear has mellowed some, but when provoked, her attack is lightning fast. She slashes once, then
follows up with a double-barreled second strike, more vi-

cious than the first, sort of the old one-two—a habit picked up behind bars no doubt.

Her first doctor may have been right. When she foamed at the mouth, I rushed her to the animal hospital fearing the worst. The doctor merely plucked out a sand-spur stuck between her upper lip and her teeth and presented his bill. Another time it took a dozen sutures to close a ragged wound in her side. It looked like a skirmish with a wild animal, the vet said. How this slinky street fighter from the jail crossed the path of a wild animal in downtown Miami Beach, I don't want to know.

Worse was the incident in the dining room at the Boulevard Retirement Hotel.

Baby Dear was gone all night. A busboy from the Boulevard, next door, rang my doorbell at 11:00 A.M. He looked like bad news, his face grim. "Is the gray cat yours?"

"Where is she?"

"Follow me."

We trotted out to the street and made a left, into the hotel and its cavernous empty dining room. In a far corner, under a table set for two, crouched Baby Dear, her back to the wall, eyes glazed in the gloom of the deserted hall.

The night before, when the room was full of retirees enjoying their evening meal, something came crashing, squalling down out of the ceiling. It landed on a table occupied by an elderly couple. The woman screamed. The man clutched his heart. Brisket and potato pancakes scattered in all directions. Baby Dear scrambled off the table, fur and utensils flying, and dove for cover in a far corner.

They hoped she would go away. But next morning she was still there, apparently injured and disoriented. When they tried to give her milk and water, she snarled at their efforts.

I dashed home, called the vet to say an emergency case was on the way, then took a carrier back to the dining room. Fearing that her back was broken, I lifted her into it gently.

The vet X-rayed her entire body, announced that she was unhurt, and handed me his bill. Apparently she had been chasing a rat up in the false ceiling of the dining room when she tumbled through a weakened panel. Stunned and uncertain as to where she was, she simply waited until I came for her.

Now of course, since I had my quota of two cats— carefully spelled out in my lease—a lovely *white* cat did appear, meowing at my back door. My neighbor Mrs. Goldstein and I fed her. She was so friendly that I decided that the next time I saw her I would take her to be neutered, then try to find her a good home. Weeks later, when she reappeared, she was hurt—scraped, battered, and holding up a pitifully injured paw.

The vet who treated her paw commented that this cat had had kittens. Starving babies out there somewhere? No, he quickly reassured me. "I don't think it's too recent." Since I was already at my quota, I took the white cat to my mother's house to recuperate in her guest room. I inquired if my neighbors had seen any kittens. They had not, so I forgot it. A day or so later, at dawn, I thought I heard faint cries, like baby birds. When I stepped outside to listen, the cries stopped. I thought I heard them again when I was in the shower, but I couldn't be sure. Next morning, there they were again, as though baby birds had fallen from a nest. I walked about twenty feet to a thick hedge separating the property from the old hotel next door.

The high-pitched cries came once more. I crouched down to look and saw a tiny thumb-sized white kitten run. And then another and another and another and another, all scrambling, terrified, starved. They were all snow white and all hungry and thirsty, because I had stolen their mother. I ran back inside for warm milk, then ran so fast coming out the door that I spilled it onto my welcome mat and had to go heat up some more. Though wild and frightened, the kittens could not resist the aroma. They did not know how to drink from a saucer and two clambered into it and splashed about. I touched the milk to their little pink tongues and noses. They were far too young to be without their mother. I scooped them all into a carrier, called the office to say I had a family emergency, and rushed them to the vet, the same man who said the mother had not recently borne kittens. She would reject them now, he said with solemn certainty. They would have to be painstakingly fed formula with an eyedropper. In fact, he warned, if the mother got her paws on them now it was curtains. She would kill them.

He gave me their formula and his bill. I took the kittens to my mother's house and cautiously opened the carrier, ready to pounce to the rescue if their mother really tried to hurt them. She trotted straight to the carrier, mewing softly, jumped inside, and began nursing her kittens, washing them enthusiastically.

If only all my daydreams and secret desires were answered so abundantly. I had wished for a white kitten. Now I had more white kittens than I ever dreamed of—and I was six cats over my legal quota.

The five white kittens tormented Baby Dear, Dixie Darling, and me. As I sat working in my study, they climbed right up my clothes to the typewriter, tapped the keys, and attacked the carriage.

I found homes for three, but Fancy Flossie and Misty Blue Eyes stayed.

It is hard to admit you live with four cats. People's expressions change. They exchange knowing looks.

It is even more difficult to admit you have five.

Lost and abandoned, a tiny, gray tiger kitten meowed plaintively at passers-by strolling along the South Beach seawall. They all ignored it, though I could hear it from the other side of the park. Instinctively, I crouched and called to the kitten from more than one hundred yards away. It came running in mad relief, scrambling straight into my arms. I walked for an hour, trying to talk strangers into giving it a home. I was so hopelessly over my quota already that I could not possibly take it with me—but nobody else would, and it was small.

A day or two later, my blood ran cold as I stroked the purring kitten's tummy. There was a lump. It was larger the next day. I called the vet. It's either a hernia or a fast-growing tumor, I told him. At his office he felt the lump and nodded wisely. "It's either a hernia or a fast-growing tumor," he said. Surgery was the only way to find out.

It was a hernia. It was repaired the same day that actor Burt Reynolds underwent his double hernia operation. Burt's latest film, *Sharkey's Machine*, was showing in Miami at the time. That is how the kitten came to be named Sharkey. When Sharkey's hernia was repaired, he was also neutered.

I doubt they did the same for Burt.

PART
II

The policeman is the little boy who grew up
to be what he said he was going to be.
Raymond Burr

FIVE

Cops

No better human being exists than a good cop and no worse creature than a bad one.

The truth is, the good cop and the bad cop are often the same cop, at different moments, on different days, with different people.

Cops have saved my life and tried to arrest me. I have reported the deaths of half a hundred of them, including six suicides, and written about scores more—shot, battered, or in bad trouble. I have cried at their funerals and shared confidences with their widows, ex-wives, mothers, and children.

I briefly shared bed, board, and bank account with one.

People tend to forget it, but cops are human.

As a child, I was taught to look up to cops. They were strong, invincible, the people to turn to when there was trouble. I think that is why I am always so moved when a cop cries—and they do.

They also break the law.

Cops are all too human, but they are not like you and me. Their job sets them apart and divides their world into *us* and *them*. Their mistrust of outsiders, particularly the press, is instinctive. They draw their wagons into a tight circle. Most cops socialize together; they intermarry; they buy houses in the same neighborhoods, on the same streets. The closeness makes them feel comfortable. Some small communities outside of Miami, particularly across the county line in south Broward, seem to be enclaves populated almost solely by police officers.

In the good old days, when life was simpler, the neighbors felt safer when a cop lived next door. Then things changed. The cop became the guy who was left out of backyard barbecues because somebody might light up a joint. If they did it in his presence, should he ignore it? Join the crowd and break the law? Bust his next-door neighbor or his brother-in-law? Or let the barriers down and look away?

Young cops almost all start out eagerly, with pure hearts and common goals, helping people, performing public service, and changing society. They fight the bad guys, but they see even good guys turn against them. They are engaged in constant conflict, almost always the adversary. The public resents authority, but the public wants to be protected. No wonder cops feel alienated.

No wonder they complain constantly about morale.

Miami cops are subjected to everything that is ugly or evil: drug smuggling, money laundering, mass murder, the Mafia, deposed dictators, foreign fugitives, illegal aliens, serial killers, street people, spies, terrorists, international intrigue, bombings, grave robbing, exotic diseases, bizarre sects, bizarre sex, animal sacrifice, voodoo, gunrunning, vast wealth, utter poverty, crazy politics, racial tensions, refugees, and riots.

After the riots in 1980, when the pressure was on to hire more police officers, particularly minorities, recruiters parked a trailer down on Calle Ocho, Southwest Eighth Street. They stopped young men on the street, saying, "You want to be a policeman?"

Some of the young Latins they recruited are outstanding, but among that group are most of the cops suspected in million-dollar cocaine ripoffs, murder, robbery, racketeering, and corruption—one of the most devastating police scandals in modern America.

It is tough to recruit good police officers. Once there was a vast pool of former military men, but the draft is long dead, and supervisors cope with me-generation rookies who refuse to cut their hair, want weekends off, and argue, instead of obey, when a sergeant issues an order.

Police officers have to be honest and honorable people, with good intentions. Giving badges and guns to people who are not is asking for trouble, which of course is exactly what we have.

We have young cops driving fire engine red Ferraris and Porsches and an occasional Lotus. Two young Miami cops, who drove to their deaths, crashed with cocaine in their blood.

Temptation on the street is stronger than it ever has

been: big money and drugs. Just ten years ago street cops never saw kilos of cocaine and people carrying hundreds of thousands of dollars. They do now.

A big case, years ago, was a boatload of marijuana; a big worry was somebody offering a twenty-dollar bribe to escape a traffic ticket. Today, cops find closets, suitcases, trunks, satchels, and briefcases stuffed with drug money.

They are only human.

During the height of Miami's crime problems, when the city was number one in murder, some people compared the situation to the frontier days in Dodge City. That is not accurate. We have more people shot in a bad week in modern Miami than were ever shot down in the entire history of old Dodge City. But people want to cling to the image of the wild West and the rough, tough lawmen of the movies. The man who wore the badge knocked the bad guys on their rear ends if he had to, to keep law and order. Most of today's bad guys are far more violent. Yet the lawman of today must behave like a gentleman.

If a cop was spit on, he used to be able to do something about it. If some foul mouth cussed out his neighbors or was disorderly in the street, a policeman used to be able to take action and put him in jail.

Now we have community relations. Cops must constantly back off, back off.

Which is why everybody cheered Metro Officer Joseph Pesek. In Greater Miami, where dozens of officers have recently been accused of police brutality, this paunchy, middle-aged cop fought back. Bruised, battered, run over, and oft-abused, Pesek, fifty-six, decided he was "mad as hell and not going to take it anymore." He sued a man for civilian brutality and won. A jury awarded him twenty-five hundred dollars for a single punch to his forehead by a drunk driver.

It was not the first time civilians had brutalized Pesek. An angry motorist, told he could not park illegally, deliberately ran him down as he directed traffic. A crazed drug suspect once chewed savagely on his fingers.

"Why should a cop have to take this crap?" Pesek demanded. It's not easy being a cop in Miami. "People curse and swear at us. As far as they're concerned, we're the lowest things in the world. But when they need help, they sure forget what lousy so-and-sos we are."

Amen.

Mike Gonzalez is the best cop I know. Policing is a young person's profession, yet Mike has been solving murders longer than most of his colleagues have been alive. A Miami cop for thirty-six years, he has been a homicide detective for more than thirty-two.

Tall and lanky, he affects the somber dress of a funeral director or a priest, with small, gold-rimmed reading glasses and dark suits. Such attire seems only appropriate when dealing with survivors, grieving relatives, and remorseful suspects on the brink of confession. His unassuming garb nearly got Mike killed once at a murder scene, in the middle of the night. He spotted a possible witness standing across the street and trotted toward him. A woman motorist, distracted by the flashing lights and police lines, said she never saw the man in the dark suit.

Mike bounced off the hood and was hurled dozens of feet. He was fifty-seven then. The cops all panicked, except Mike. Many younger officers would have remained flat on the pavement while computing their disability benefits. Not Mike. He climbed to his feet and continued the homicide investigation. Over his objections, concerned colleagues hauled him off to a hospital. An hour later, he checked out and returned to work, limping and battered, his good suit torn.

The conservative image of homicide cops, epitomized by Mike, seemed to change a few years back. Some of the county's young detectives became the flashiest men about town. Their hair was styled, their fingernails manicured. Their suits were three-piece, custom-made, and their ties were silk. Heavy gold gleamed richly from their necks, wrists, and fingers. At murder scenes they tried hard not to get their hands dirty or splash mud on their Gucci shoes.

They also solved fewer cases and became increasingly secretive with the press. They had good reason. They were able to dress so fashionably because most were moonlighting for a cocaine kingpin. When it erupted, the scandal was of major proportions. Much of the homicide bureau was transferred, fired, or arrested.

I always knew I could never trust a man whose manicure was better than mine.

A woman in my occupation has to convince the cops to forget she is a woman. You want them to think of you as a confidante, a professional who will always be fair, or if nothing else, a piece of the furniture, someone they are so used to seeing that they forget you are there. And you do not mix business and pleasure. I think I finally have it down pat. The basic rule to follow on the job is that if something you are doing is really fun or makes you feel good, it *must* be unethical. But that does not prevent me from noticing little things like smoldery eyes, neat laugh lines, a good body, truthfulness, and sincerity.

They are nice to see in any man, even if he is a cop.

The first time I ever saw Miami Homicide Sergeants Mike Gonzalez and Ed McDermott was on a sun-dappled Saturday morning in Coconut Grove. A gunfight in a liquor store had left somebody dead. The year was 1971, and the assignment was one of my first police stories for the *Herald*. Determined to succeed, and unable to find out what was going on, I clambered over the yellow rope surrounding the crime scene. Angry shouts froze me in my tracks. Two men, both tall and black-haired, in dark suits, rushed toward me, asking loudly how would I like to go to jail. They talked tough and were menacing; I had no doubt that they meant it. Mike Gonzalez and Ed McDermott scared the heck out of me.

It was the start of a beautiful friendship.

Most cops who are surly with the press behave that way because they are unsure of themselves—their jobs, their intelligence, their manhood—or because they are concealing something illegal or embarrassing. Sergeants Gonzalez and McDermott were not at all uncertain, nor did they have anything to conceal. They were merely startled. Few women went out on crime stories in the early 1970s.

Mike Gonzalez now insists that it was not he, but Mc-Dermott, who threatened me with arrest. Mike's memory is excellent—he can even describe the pink dress I wore that day and how I "hiked it up to step daintily" over the crime-scene rope in my high heels—but I seem to recall being threatened by both.

Once they recovered from their initial surprise, they were cooperative. It is wonderful to meet cops who know what they are talking about and are not afraid to do so.

The liquor store owner was badly wounded but had won a gun duel with a robber. Flying bullets had shattered whiskey bottles, the counter, and the hold-up man's skull.

His unused getaway car still sat outside, a SUPPORT YOUR LOCAL POLICE tag on the front. The dead robber was an ex-convict—and a security guard. In his pocket, he carried "a badge three times as big as mine," Gonzalez complained. The gold badge, similar to that of a sergeant, identified the robber as "Special Police." The detectives pointed it out as a prime example of poor hiring practices by security firms. That issue was later covered in depth by the *Herald*, and subsequently, new legislation required background checks and licensing for all guards.

Mike Gonzalez is a lieutenant now, the nation's dean of homicide cops. In Miami the average age for cops is even younger than in most cities. The attrition rate is high, due to the riots, stress-related burnout, and the cocaine-corruption scandals. Yet Mike, unlike many cops from his generation, has never clung to the old ways of the past. He constantly forges ahead with new enthusiasm, new ideas. The only elements about him that never change are his sound practical judgment and sensitivity. I learn a lot from him and the detectives he has trained.

I certainly learned from Ed McDermott, a quiet Irishman and a strong, old-fashioned sort of cop. Divorced, he lived alone and kept to himself. He was very private and sort of sad, a man you could call friend but never really know.

He took me where no other man did before—to the morgue.

I was with him one day when a homicide call was dispatched: a woman shot at her home. En route, his radio again crackled to life. A man had just screeched his car to a stop outside Jackson Memorial Hospital and staggered into the emergency room, his throat cut.

The man was still alive, and we were closer to the hospital. The woman could wait—she wouldn't be going anywhere.

The man was not hard to find. We just followed his trail. It was everywhere, splashed all over his car, his white trousers, and in a growing pool under the hospital table where he lay gasping, unable to speak.

McDermott studied the man's identification, his only reaction a raised eyebrow. The address on the driver's license was familiar: It had been our destination before we were diverted to the hospital, the same house where the dead woman waited.

She was sprawled across the back-door sill, wearing just a bra and slacks. She had almost escaped. A bullet had caught her between the shoulder blades at the very last instant.

Splintered fragments of a shattered crystal bowl littered the living room carpet. A bloody trail led out the front door.

We sat at the table in the dead woman's comfortable kitchen, looking for an ID and some clue to what had happened to her and her husband. We emptied her purse: lipstick, a comb, and her wallet, with a receipt from a dress shop where she had left a deposit on some clothes she would never wear.

It seemed so intrusive. Strangers in her home, rifling through her personal belongings—but that's death.

A corpse has no privacy.

Until you are dead, you are usually a total stranger to homicide detectives. Then, with a single-mindedness matched only by that of a jealous lover, they must know all about you—everything—even details your sweetheart or your spouse does not know. Secrets you would not tell your best friend. Particulars you didn't understand about yourself. Nothing is sacred.

They want to know what you ate, what you wore, what you read. Your drinking habits and your sex habits. They will read your diary and your mail and scrutinize the contents of your safety-deposit box and your stomach. They are there, examining all that you held private, including every nook and cranny of your corpse, once they begin to disassemble it at the morgue.

That knowledge has imbued me with certain neurotic tendencies. Periodically I feel a compulsion, an urge to empty my overstuffed purse, my glove compartment, and my dresser drawers to sort the jumbled contents. It is not because I am basically neat—I am not—but I am reminded from time to time that if I am hit by a bus or gunned down by some irate reader, the cops will routinely inventory the contents of my handbag. I don't want them to find the aging granola bar at the bottom, along with the crumpled packet of Tender Vittles and the green cough drops that are stuck together.

McDermott called the hospital from the dead woman's kitchen and was told that the husband would survive. The wife went to the morgue, and we followed. It was my first visit. She lay on her back, her face frozen in a look of disbelief, as though this unfortunate turn of events was totally unexpected.

We stood on either side of her and stared down. She stared back. McDermott looked sad, but then he always looked sad, even when he smiled. He was not smiling now. I had no idea what we were looking for. He lifted her right arm and scrutinized it carefully. We were looking for defense wounds, he said, cuts, tears or bruises, broken fingernails, old injuries, signs of drug abuse, anything significant. "You check that one," he said briskly, without looking up.

I had never touched a newly dead person before. Her arm was unexpectedly soft and still warm. It bore no injuries, no needle marks. She had recently manicured her fingernails and polished them with a glossy petal-pink lacquer.

We were not alone. Other bodies rested on the

stainless-steel tables in the autopsy room, referred to by those who labor there as the Pit. The faces of a few looked weary and resigned, but most wore the distinct expressions of someone rudely interrupted. The graying hair of a woman in a nightgown and housecoat was carefully set, big rollers at the top, small curlers at the sides. She obviously had plans and wanted to look her best.

A young man of nineteen looked clearly astonished at his broken front teeth and smashed face. A doctor at the other end of the table inserted a needle and withdrew a clear fluid—urine. It would reveal what the young man had in his system before crashing his car into a giant ficus tree. No secrets of that sort when you're a corpse.

A chubby and beautiful curly-haired infant boy seemed to be napping. His chart was marked SIDS—sudden infant death syndrome—crib death. Hearts had to be broken. How unfair to end that little life's journey so soon. Death is mean.

It left me indignant. A reporter's consciousness is often raised by the plight of the downtrodden, the little guy shoved around, the victim of injustice. Death too soon is an injustice. You cannot be more downtrodden or pushed around than that. I wanted to know all their stories, what went wrong, why they were there.

Unfortunately, McDermott only wanted to know about his case and dragged me out of the morgue.

We learned later, from the husband, why the woman was shot in the back and how his throat was cut. The motive was a new see-through blouse. Too revealing, he said, and demanded that she change it before leaving the house.

When she refused, he ripped it off her. Furious, she snatched the big crystal bowl off the coffee table and flung it at his head. It caught him by surprise, smashed against his Adam's apple and slashed his throat. Blood streaming, he ran for the gun they kept in the house to protect them. She tried to beat it out the back door. He nailed her before she did.

A simple case, thousands of murders ago in Miami. But I won't forget it or Ed McDermott.

If you think a cop's life is tough, try it if you are a woman. The pressures are more powerful, both professionally and personally. Police officers, both male and female, who excel in their work often do so at the expense of their personal lives. Yet Louise Vasquez is the best at both—a real live superwoman who successfully leads a double life.

A plain-speaking, pistol-packing mother of eight and grandmother to thirteen, she has solved more murder mysteries than Sherlock Holmes and caught enough rapists to fill a prison. In her spare time she can build, panel, and paint walls and mother a house full of babies and a yard full of pets—I once counted a horse, a pony, a raccoon, a mother cat, a litter of kittens, and Freckles, a springer spaniel that loved to sing when someone played the piano. Louise also helped forge new criminal law in Florida, she is captain of a softball team that won the police olympics, and she does it all with the direct, down-home, no-nonsense approach that has become her trademark.

Blue-eyed and Irish, she married a man named Vasquez. His name is Eddie and he is not a cop—he sells sporting goods. A soft-spoken man, he is proud of his wife's accomplishments and queasy at the sight of blood. He worries.

"The bad part," Eddie tells me, "is when I'm home and she's on the job—on a stakeout."

She shot it out with an armed robber once. Another time she posed as a woman seeking an illegal abortion. At the crucial moment, just before surgery was to commence, fellow detectives were to burst in and make the bust. But the men who were her backups got lost in traffic.

When she realized no one was coming to the rescue, Louise Vasquez, alone and unarmed, made the arrests herself.

Louise was not sure she liked me when we met. In fact I'm sure she didn't. She was Mike Gonzalez's partner. Homicide detectives also investigated sex crimes then, and the department was accused of juggling rape statistics and treating victims insensitively. I was the reporter pursuing the story. The detectives were defensive and angry, and I was aggressive. Despite that inauspicious start, we eventually became friends, and I'm glad we did.

When Louise joined the force twenty years ago, women were not particularly welcome as Miami cops. A pioneer, she made life easier for those who followed. She remembers nearly drowning during the rugged underwater swimming test—one hundred yards, carrying a weight. But she passed it, and she uses that same grit and determination to solve more complex cases than any detective I have ever seen.

She never gives up. When a serial rapist she was stalking left a single clue, a key dropped at the scene of one of his crimes, Louise and a partner knocked on every door in a ten-block radius asking residents for permission to try the key in their locks.

It opened the front door of an elderly woman who lived alone. Louise showed her a police drawing of the rapist. "My son," the woman acknowledged, smiling, "where did you get his picture?"

Another rapist, shot by his victim's neighbor, fled barefoot and dripping blood. A police dog lost the scent after a block. No use, said the handler, the trail had ended. But Louise and another detective painstakingly tracked a nearly imperceptible trail of crimson droplets for six blocks. On hands and knees, they lost it, followed it, lost it, then picked it up again.

The specks became smaller and smaller and further and further apart. Paint spatters and cherry hedges lining the streets made the task more difficult. There were smashed cherries all over the sidewalk. The trail came to a dead end several times, with the detectives off in the wrong direction. The man they were following must have climbed into a car and vanished, they thought. But each time they were about to give up, they spotted another tiny spot or slight smudge and continued on. They traced the circuitous trail until they came to a house. A single drop of blood glistened on the front-door sill.

The man inside matched both the blood and the fingerprints at the scene of the crime.

Unassuming and modest, Lousie is no prima donna, she just uses common sense and gets the job done. When she was named International Policewoman of the Year in 1983, she was showered with long-stemmed roses, a hotel suite, baskets of fruit, a complimentary hairdo, and a manicure. Two days later, she was back to real life—and death—in Miami, behind the wheel of the trusty Honda she drives thirty thousand miles a year and wearing the sensible shoes she wears when working around-the-clock to catch killers and rapists.

Though not flamboyant, she is a fighter. When her seven children grew up, the house was too quiet, so she and Eddie adopted a little boy named Joey. Adoption authorities, armed with their bureaucratic lists of rules and regulations, insisted she quit work for a year. It was their policy. Louise battled the bureaucracy and won. She had proved she could combine both policing and parenting. Joey is now a husky and happy junior-college baseball star. Her oldest son, Chris, was a college football hero. Not one of the kids followed Louise into police work, but when Chris fell in love, it was with a girl just like his mother: He married a cop.

Most men are not secure enough to love a woman who packs a gun, wears a badge, and can put people in jail. Unmarried policewomen tell me that the men with courage enough to ask for a date often prove to be weirdos with strange ideas, some of them relating to handcuffs and uniforms.

Consider Christine Echroll: tall, blond, and beautiful, with the Nordic features and green eyes of a Viking princess. A witty and well-read world traveler, she is also a police sergeant, assigned to Metro's rape squad.

On a New York–Miami flight, an attractive man sat next to her. Sparks flew, the chemistry clicked, and they talked through the entire trip. She did not reveal her occupation. But as the jet circled Miami for a landing and he was enthusiastically discussing where they would dine Saturday night, she thought it might be safe to tell him. So she did. He reached for a magazine, buried his face in it, and never said another word, not even goodbye.

Think a cop's life is tough? Try it if you are a woman.

Though the specter of violence is ever-present in the lives of cops, some wear badges for twenty years and never fire a weapon except at the pistol range. Others watch too much television, itch to play *Miami Vice*, and get in trouble. Then there are those who possess the uncanny knack of being in the right place at the right time.

How do you explain a cop who goes to lunch, hears his radio broadcast the description of a bank robber's car, and watches it ease into traffic directly in front of him? How do you explain it when incidents that will never happen to others in an entire lifetime occur again and again to the same few cops?

Coincidence cannot explain a Sherwood Griscom.

Buck Griscom was Dirty Harry long before Clint Eastwood ever thought of him. When this loner turned in his badge to retire in 1986, Miami Beach city fathers breathed sighs of relief, mingled with regret. He was the best, yet he made them nervous. They live in fear of lawsuits and bad press, and Griscom made them sweat. They never knew what he would do next or if they would somehow be criticized for it.

He was South Florida's most deadly cop, quite extraordinary when you consider that his beat, Miami Beach, was the Playground of the World, a resort city where there is comparatively little gunplay. Yet in an eighty-eight-block-long beachfront community with no ghettos and no riots, largely populated by senior citizens, Griscom fought so many gun duels he cannot remember them all. He has shot eight men, killing four.

A slow night on *Miami Vice*—heavy-duty in real life.

A soft-spoken and prolific—though unpublished—poet, Buck Griscom nurtured no childhood dreams of being a cop. Upon discharge from the Navy, he needed a job. He applied for both the police and the fire departments because the work was steady. The police called him first.

Yet he was the cop you wanted on your side if trouble came. The first Griscom shooting I covered was for the *Sun*, on July 20, 1966. He, Emmett Miller, and a rookie named Pete Corso shotgunned a robber during a stakeout. Both Emmett Miller and Corso eventually became Miami Beach police chiefs.

Griscom became a legend.

This was during an era in which Metro and Miami cops were indicted for wrongful shooting deaths. Each time Griscom fired his weapon, his decision was a split-second one. Each man he shot was a total stranger and a dangerous criminal. Each shooting was thoroughly investigated, and as their numbers increased, so did the intensity of the probes by peers, prosecutors, and grand juries. Each was ruled justifiable.

When adrenaline is pumping and there is no time to think, cops often shoot the wrong person. Some have even shot their partners or innocent victims. When a Beach supermarket was robbed, police arrived to save the day and in the excitement shot dead the assistant manager. Guns are tricky devices. Even in trained hands there are accidents. Lots of them.

A member of the Miami Beach task force picked up a machine gun at headquarters, then dropped it. With reflexes fast as lightning, he caught it before it could hit the floor—caught it by the trigger. The wounded included a fellow officer in a squad room down the hall and a secretary in a nearby office.

Mistakes are easy—and deadly—when it comes to guns. That makes Buck Griscom's record all the more astonishing.

The men who worked with him suspect that Griscom had something besides fast reflexes and deadly aim: a sixth sense. They think he knew when something was about to happen.

Take the time he and his wife, Fran, were about to depart on a long-planned vacation. It was his last day of work, and she was busy packing so they could leave early the next day. But something was wrong. "I don't think we're going to get to go," he told her. All he knew was that "something bad is going to happen today." He was right.

A few hours later, he steered his patrol car south on Collins Avenue through heavy Sunday-afternoon traffic. A flashy, open Cadillac convertible with a young man at the wheel passed him, headed north. Griscom and the driver exchanged glances. He had "a fish-eye look," Griscom recalls. "A guy gives you that look and you know he's nervous about something."

He popped his patrol car into a U-turn. The young driver floored it and fled, dodging other cars. When the Caddy got caught in traffic, Griscom braked alongside and yelled, "Freeze!" The driver nodded, as if to obey, but his hand came up clutching a gun. He fired, point-blank. The bullet crashed into the window frame, inches above Griscom's head.

He drew his own gun and emptied it. The Caddy hurtled forward and slammed into a taxicab. Griscom ran up, dragged the man out of the car and then saw he was bleeding. "Poor guy. I didn't think I had hit him," he said.

The wounded man was twenty years old. The Cadillac was stolen, and he was wanted by police in Michigan. His spinal cord was severed. He only lived a few weeks.

Another time, about to leave for work on a midnight shift, Buck Griscom suddenly wanted his "speed-loaders," devices which snap six bullets into the cylinder instantly, making it possible to reload a revolver in a single motion. He never had the need to carry them before. This night, he felt he had to have them.

He and Fran and the kids searched under beds and through closets. The household was in an uproar. By the time he put on his uniform and left for work without the speed-loaders, Fran was in tears.

Uneasy, he asked another cop to ride with him. The jitters were contagious, and the cop declined, saying, "You're gonna get involved in a shooting."

He made it halfway through the night. At 4:20 A.M., Griscom spotted three people in a dented rental car. Thinking it might have been in a hit-and-run accident, he signaled the driver to pull over. Instead, the driver stomped on the gas, and they were off.

The chase led across the MacArthur Causeway, the southernmost span linking Miami to Miami Beach, then back, then into another U-turn. During the second U-turn, a gunman jumped out, unseen, into the shadowy bushes and trees lining the wide median. As Griscom slowed to a few miles an hour to make the same turn, he drove into an ambush. The gunman loomed suddenly at the patrol car's passenger side, shoving a weapon in through the open window. "Don't move," he said, "or I'll kill you."

Griscom bailed out of his patrol car as the gunman fired and missed. The car was to be his cover, but still in drive, it rolled away and slammed into a pine tree at the water's edge.

Griscom ran for the tree line, returning fire. He rolled through the bushes and scrambled beneath the heavy branches of a sea grape tree, as the car he had been chasing roared up onto the median and the driver tried to run him down. He fumbled to reload in the dark—wishing he had his speed-loaders.

The gunman was wounded, and the occupants of the car captured, after a chase by fifty squad cars from four police departments. The wounded man was an escapee from prison where he was serving life for murder and bank robbery. A few days later, he used a ballpoint-pen refill to unlock his handcuffs and escaped from Jackson Memorial Hospital.

Some people Griscom shot didn't even hold a grudge. A beaming stranger vigorously pumped his hand in a coffee shop. "I finished my education, got straightened out with my family, and I've got a good job," he announced.

Griscom congratulated him, then asked where they had met before. The young man rolled up his trouser leg. "I remembered when I saw the scar," Griscom says. The young man was a robber he had shot after chasing him into an alley behind a synagogue.

He chased one burglar from rooftop to rooftop, across the city skyline. They "went to knuckle city" atop a bank, in a struggle that ended when the burglar plunged off the roof.

He arrested beachboy jewel thief Jack "Murph the Surf" Murphy so often that Murphy and his beachboy buddies yelled foul, complaining that Griscom was "bothering them." Murphy peevishly told a judge that the detective's persistent presence was so alarming that when fellow beachboy and jewel thief Allen Kuhn heard Griscom was looking for him, "he swam underwater to the beach and went home in a friend's car."

Buck Griscom took his job seriously, and he took it home. Fran Griscom, for whom I have the highest respect, recalls seeing her husband happy only "when he has caught somebody." He even maintained a "fink phone," a private line at home for informants to call day or night, at his own expense.

He began writing poetry shortly after Hurricane Donna blew him and a partner down a street, still clinging to a large board they had been trying to nail over a shattered storefront. His poems are odes to his wife and dramatic verses about neglected orphans, injustice, and fallen heroes.

On the job, he has plunged into the ocean to save midnight swimmers swept away by the tides; another time, he delivered a baby on a South Beach bus bench. He has saved more lives than he has taken, but the American Civil Liberties Union still sought for years to pull his badge. It sounded bad—all those people shot . . .

His sixth sense, or else the countless coincidences, built Griscom into a legend over the years. When he routinely stopped a car that somehow drew his attention, he noticed a purse on the front seat. At that precise moment, his radio burst to life with a description of the same purse, taken minutes earlier by thugs who knocked down and seriously hurt an elderly woman to steal it.

When a busy bandit spent an evening robbing the desk clerks at several hotels, Griscom and a partner conducted a manhunt. They checked a bar, then stepped out onto the street. A pair of approaching headlights cut the darkness. "That's the guy doing the robberies," Griscom said flatly.

They flagged down the car. The robber was behind the

wheel, his disguise in the backseat. The bandit was bewildered. So was Griscom's partner.

One night as they rode in an unmarked car, his partner signaled to turn left at Seventy-first Street. "No," Griscom said suddenly, "let's go to Seventy-fifth Street and catch a guy in a stolen car." At Seventy-fifth Street, a motorist had flooded his engine at a red light. The car, of course, was stolen.

Once I asked Griscom what crime angers him most. "People who rape little old ladies, that irritates me. That really irritates me," he said. "Not just raping, but brutalizing them. Little old ladies. There's no excuse for that." I quoted him in a magazine article.

Shortly after, a seventy-two-year-old widow was raped and murdered in her South Beach apartment. A copy of the magazine lay on the dead woman's coffee table. She had been reading my story about Sherwood Griscom and the crime that angers him most when her killer interrupted. Buck Griscom happened to be the detective assigned the case. I happened to be the reporter sent to cover it.

Coincidence explains away many things, but how do you explain a Sherwood Griscom?

Miami's most successful supercop does no shooting or chasing and he makes no arrests: Dr. Joseph H. Davis, Dade County medical examiner for thirty years, works quietly among the dead. His office has been the last stop on the way to the cemetery for a hundred thousand people, but far more important are the people who do not have their toes tagged at his morgue.

They are still alive, thousands upon thousands of them. Joe Davis has saved more lives than any police officer, lifeguard, or fire fighter. He has engineered out traffic traps that kill motorists and pushed through laws against drunk driving and hazardous pesticides. He has forced changes in the designs of dangerous home heaters and electrical appliances and in the code of electrical standards for commercial swimming pools.

Joe Davis started out equipped with a fly swatter and an office in an abandoned garage. His morgue was a rented, refrigerated truck.

In the years 1980–81, when murder in Miami broke records and made headlines nationwide, Davis's antiquated morgue, conveniently adjacent to the emergency room at Jackson Memorial Hospital, was literally overwhelmed and stacked with corpses. I arrived one day on a story and found half the precious few parking spaces out front swallowed up by a huge, humming, refrigerated trailer. It had been leased from Burger King to handle the overflow of bodies.

The story was picked up everywhere, and soon even the BBC was calling transatlantically for interviews. Irate county officials said the story damaged Miami's tourist image, and the staff at the medical examiner's office was furious—at me. The story was absolutely accurate, and in fact, the trailer is still in use. But not for long; the appalled politicians have managed to find the money for a brand-new building for the medical examiner. Construction is under way.

I can live with that.

The building will be named for Joseph Davis, whose imagination enables him to see what escapes others. His ability to reconstruct a baffling homicide in a matter of seconds is astonishing. When Davis took over as medical examiner in 1956, Mike Gonzalez was already a Miami homicide detective. They met over a skeleton found in a mangrove hammock. A young mother had been missing for weeks, and foul play was suspected. It seemed doubtful, however, that the scattered bones could ever be identified as those of the missing woman. She was known to wear three distinctive rings on one finger, but no jewelry was found. In fact, no fingers were found.

Joe Davis was new to Miami and curious. He asked the cops about all the little holes in the ground around the skeleton. The work of land crabs, Gonzalez told him. The detectives soon decided that the doctor had lost interest in the investigation and was "playing with the land crabs."

Actually Davis was speculating: If the dead woman's jewelry was not stolen by her killer, perhaps it was carried away by wildlife, possibly the land crabs.

"If I were a land crab and found a rotting finger with rings on it, what would I do?" Davis mused. "If I stayed, somebody might take it away. If I dragged it toward the road, I might get run over. If I took it home, other land crabs might snatch it." If he were a land crab, he concluded, he would sneak to the nearest secluded spot for a leisurely lunch.

The nearest secluded spot for a leisurely lunch was under an old stump nearby. Davis found a piece of wood and began to probe.

As the detectives silently pondered the sanity of this new doctor from out of town, he returned, carrying a stick. Clinging to it was a land crab, a finger bone tenaciously clutched in its claw.

The finger bone wore three rings.

One 3:00 A.M., twenty-five years later, Davis was summoned from his slumber to the scene of a baffling case—another uncounted night among thousands similarly interrupted. He climbed the stairs to a third-floor apartment in an old wooden building. If he was surprised that it was me who answered the door, he did not show it. I happened to be out riding with the detectives that night.

A woman sat dead on a sofa in her living room. Her skin was horribly burned and falling away from her body in transparent, tissuelike sheets. Her boyfriend had found her and called police. Eighty percent of her skin was burned off, from her neck to the soles of her feet. Her clothing, however, lavender slacks and a knit vest, was dry and undamaged. Nothing else in the room was burned. There was no smell of smoke.

There were no clues in her tidy kitchen or neatly kept bathroom, no caustic fluids that could have inflicted the fatal burns. The telephone, in working order, appeared untouched. Nothing in the modest flat seemed out of place, except an iron skillet askew on a countertop in the kitchen. The detectives and an assistant medical examiner were perplexed.

Davis brushed briskly by me, lifted the white sheet, shooed an irreverent fly from her cheek, and studied the woman briefly. Then he stepped into the kitchen, glanced at the skillet, and checked the tiny bathroom. Probing the bathtub drain with tweezers, he withdrew shreds of human skin. He tested the faucet's water temperature with a thermometer. It was scalding.

Then he told us what happened.

The woman and her boyfriend drank and quarreled. He struck her with the skillet, and she fell, unconscious. He picked her up and carried her into the bathroom to revive her. Placing her in the tub, he plugged the drain and turned on the faucet, full blast. In his drunken state, it did not occur to him until too late that it was the hot-water tap. When he realized what he had done, he emptied the tub, dried and dressed the burned woman, and carried her into the living room, intending to take her to a hospital. When he saw that she was dead, he wandered off to consider the matter over a few more drinks. He returned later to "discover" the corpse.

Confronted, he admitted that was exactly what happened.

The cops who deal daily with what is happening in Miami must be among the best and most experienced in the world. Those experiences, however, are not easily shared.

Consider this real-life scene: A twenty-two-year-old Miami cop encounters a man strolling at dawn in a quiet neighborhood. The man is naked and carrying the severed head of a young woman. He throws the head at the cop—twice.

"I killed her. She's the devil!" the man shouts.

What does that young cop say to the people who ask how his day went?

What about the detectives who raced all over Dade County—which is larger than Rhode Island—for two weeks, trying to collect and piece together the dismembered murder victims who were surfacing piece by piece in the waters around Miami? A torso would bob up in one place; a hand would surface somewhere else. A leg washed up on the beach. What would you say if you were one of those cops?

How do you shoot the breeze with normal people? How do you casually confide how you spent the day? At least cops have each other. No wonder they feel better with another cop living next door.

I think I understand.

When I lived in an apartment with no washing machine, I lugged my clothes to the laundromat at two in the morning. It was partly because of my hours but mostly because the place is peaceful and unoccupied at that time. During the day, it is alive with chatty young housewives who talk endlessly, mostly war stories about how many hours they were in labor. If not that, it's a new recipe for meat loaf.

We have not a thing in common—nothing. When you have no babies or meat loaf, they ask politely about your work. They want to hear *all* about it. How could I explain what I do to these nice normal people?

I could say: "Guess what, girls? Guess what happened to me today? Know what that smell is?" How could I tell them what that smell actually was? That day I had broken a police seal on a door where a widowed laundry worker and her little girl died after the power company cut off their electricity.

The widow had fallen behind in her bills. Her service was shut off. She and her eleven-year-old daughter used candles for light, and in Miami's winter chill, they burned charcoal in a hibachi to warm their bedroom. It killed them of course: carbon monoxide poisoning.

The bodies went undiscovered for days. People at the laundry didn't check when the woman failed to show up for work at her $2.10 an hour job. Neither did school officials investigate why the little girl, a good student, was suddenly absent from sixth grade. A busy world did not miss them until that old "foul odor" reached the nostrils of neighbors who called the police.

The neighbors all told me what a swell little girl she was. I wanted to put her picture in the newspaper with my story. It would say more than I could write. The landlord said that the child's school picture was on a dresser in the bedroom where they died. He didn't mind if I borrowed it, but police had sealed the doors.

It was dark as a dungeon inside the apartment. I groped in the dark for a light switch. It didn't work, of course. That was why they were dead. I wanted to borrow a flashlight, but the queasy landlord had vanished.

The little girl and her mother had oozed into the mattress as they decomposed. Although they had been removed in polypropylene body bags, they would always be there. Nothing in that tiny apartment would ever smell the same. I held a tissue over my nose, tried not to breathe, and groped in the dark. Naturally, klutz that I am, I stumbled up against the bed—and got some of the mother and the little girl on my clothes. I also got it on my hand—wet and sticky. But I found the photo, took it to the office, and went home to change my clothes.

No, I had no small talk to share with the young wives at the laundromat. Alone and weary at two in the morning, my clothes sloshing around in the machine, I thought that this must be how police officers feel. Each day some of them live through experiences one does not discuss in polite company.

I think I understand.

The best cops I know love being cops and would never be happy doing anything else. They understand the streets and human nature and will probably never be chiefs. Those who do make it to the very top are usually the ones who know how to play politics, how to study textbooks and theories and score well on tests. Really great cops are too busy for all that; they are out there doing police work.

The very best seem to gravitate to the homicide bureau to investigate murders, the most challenging crime to solve. Some of them, like Joe Davis, are cops without badges, who do their detecting in the morgue, translating messages from the dead. I have been lucky enough to see them at work. Knowing them and learning from them has changed me and my career forever.

The very best cops are people who care—people like

Mike Gonzalez and Louise Vasquez—plain-talking men and women who listen. Street people, the hurt, and those frightened and severely disturbed feel comfortable talking to cops like them. For years I have seen Mike and Louise reach out to people who live on the edge. "If there is ever anything I can do to help you, give me a call," they say.

The offer is a perilous one, of course, because those people *do* call. They always need help, advice, comfort, and direction. Despite the stress, the pressure, and the long hours, Mike and Louise are there for them.

It always impresses the hell out of me.

Over the years, I have found myself doing the same thing; I am sure it is their influence. Like them, I meet a lot of people who may not be newsworthy but need help: problems as simple as referrals or as complex as battling the beast of bureaucracy and slashing at red tape.

The people only cops can help, I refer to Mike or Louise. The ones that only a reporter can help, they send to me.

It works for us.

You're mistaken if you think wrongdoers are always unhappy. The really professional evil-doers love it. They're as happy as larks in the sky.
Muriel Spark

SIX

Crooks

Bad guys are never boring, or all bad.

Like cops, they are human. That is what makes them so dangerous. Crooks can captivate you if you drop your guard. They can be dashing and daring, with a certain charisma. The charm is what undoes them—it makes it possible for them to get into big trouble without being stopped sooner.

We are always fascinated by bad and beautiful people who lack our built-in restraints. The romance is there, from Robin Hood and Jesse James to Willie Sutton and D. B. Cooper.

Writers have to work at not glamorizing them. Crooks may be colorful, quotable, and even likable, but they are not nice people. When you tell their stories, it always helps to give the victims equal space.

You should not pity most criminals, either; tie a tourniquet on your heart. Sad and sleazy losers are easy to feel sorry for, until you recall what they have done, over and over and over, and will continue to do, given the chance. They say all they need is a break, but if you check it out, you find they've used up lots of them.

Men in prison are magnets for otherwise intelligent women, who work endlessly to spring them. The reason for this phenomenon has always escaped me. A man in a cage is usually there for good cause. The only plus is that you never have to wonder where he is.

But there must be something else, because good and sensitive women show up regularly in newsrooms clutching voluminous legal files, trying to persuade reporters to take up the crusade, to help free her wrongly imprisoned man. She is never a long-suffering, true-blue wife or sweetheart, standing by her man; she is inevitably some stranger who met this criminal through the mail or a so-called friend and never even knew him before he was a convicted felon. Yet she invests her time, her talent, and her money, hiring lawyers, writing to politicians and parole boards, and pleading his case with journalists. If she succeeds, she will be lucky if all he does is split with whatever money she has left.

I am not saying that I have not known men who belonged in jail—but at least they weren't already there when I met them. Women in this world need rules of survival. One of them: Do not tell a bad guy your secrets or your home telephone number, and at all costs, keep him at arm's length.

I first knew Jack "Murph the Surf" Murphy as the clown prince of Miami Beach. He wore the costume of a jester and wowed the tourists, particularly the women, with a stunt-diving act that played the oceanfront hotel circuit.

His life changed course when he used his athletic ability and daring to invade New York's Museum of Natural History and steal the world's most fabulous sapphire, the centuries-old Star of India. He and his two beachboy buddies made off with the 565-carat gem, the size of a golf ball, in the dead of night. They also snatched the 117-carat Midnight Star and the priceless, 100-carat DeLong ruby. The beachboys were suddenly notorious.

Jack seemed to love the attention and the headlines. A former child prodigy, he had played violin with the Pittsburgh Symphony Orchestra. He was showy, humorous, and charming, also doomed and dangerous, and therefore, great fun. His style and free spirit attracted the press. He was certainly not a good thief; he always got caught. Despite his jokes, he did not leave those who loved him laughing.

Jack's bubbly blond sweetheart, Bonnie, faithfully attended every court appearance with him—until she committed suicide.

The beachboys, Jack, Allen Kuhn, and Roger Clark, served two years in prison for the Star of India caper. They were released in 1967, and I tagged along that first day to cover their homecoming for the *Sun*. Every convicted felon who arrived in town was required to register with the police, so we dropped by headquarters first. Then we visited the office of their attorney, the equally flamboyant, silver-haired Harvey St. Jean, and lunched at an outdoor café on Lincoln Road Mall.

The beachboys were treated more like local heroes come home than newly released ex-convicts. Strangers wished them good luck and stopped to shake their hands, old ladies waved, and young girls giggled. Everybody seemed to like Jack until later, when violence and murder ruined his image.

But that day, heady with new freedom, Murphy and his partners wolfed down fresh shrimp and key lime pie, talked about regaining their suntans, and boasted of a new lifestyle that would include a speaking tour to warn America's youth against lives of crimes.

The tour never quite did materialize, but trouble did. Allen Kuhn, often thought to be the brains behind the beachboy trio, bought a flashy Cadillac convertible. It was immediately torched in the night by unknown arsonists. Kuhn swore he knew who did it: the Miami Beach police task force. They patrolled the city by night in unmarked cars, engaged in a secret war. Their mission: to persuade known robbers and burglars to leave town. Members of the task force were enthusiastic and often unorthodox.

"I don't have any enemies in town except those cops," Kuhn told me.

Police denied burning his Caddy, but agreed that Kuhn should settle elsewhere, preferably in another state. The same night persons unknown slashed the tires of a flashy car owned by a thug known as Big Tony. His real name was Anthony Esperti and he was a suspect in some of the bookie-war bombings plaguing police. The crooks were furious and accused police of not playing fair.

"We don't call it harassment," the police chief said. "In our semantics, it's tight surveillance."

Police were also hoping that another unwanted local citizen would leave town. He was selling heroin from his South Beach surf shop, they said. Just before dawn an unidentified person hurled a bomb, apparently aiming for the roof of the surf shop. His aim was faulty, and the bomb bounced like a rubber ball along the common rooftop. It came to rest on the wrong target, an all-night restaurant, and exploded.

No one was seriously injured. Even the drunks, dozing in their coffee after a night of barhopping, managed to scramble to safety as the ceiling rained down around them. The damage was extensive. I shot photos of sad-faced employees cleaning up the mess, and the manager and a fireman inside, squinting up at daylight through the hole in the roof.

I called the *Sun* to keep my editor, Bob Swift, informed. It was a mistake; the less contact with editors the better. Bob asked if I had climbed onto the roof to shoot the damage. No, I said, there is nothing there, just the hole blasted by the bomb. The best photos were of people, action, and debris down where the impact was felt.

No, Swift insisted, he wanted a picture taken up on the roof where the bomb had exploded. I was wearing high heels and a miniskirt. I am not good at heights and have almost no sense of balance.

Bob *had* to have the picture.

Hoping they would say no, I asked the firemen if I could climb their ladder. Unfortunately, fire fighters rarely say no to anything. It must be all that heat and the smoke they swallow. They would be delighted, they said.

One fire fighter pushed me up from below, another tugged from above. A third held my camera. The others watched.

Descending the ladder was an even worse ordeal. But I got the picture my editor wanted.

Later, back at the office, he casually scanned the photos. "You were right," he said. "These others are better." Without looking up, he tossed the rooftop picture into the trash can.

Big Tony Esperti's trouble was soon more serious than slashed tires. A well-dressed Mafia hit man known as the Enforcer opened the door of a swinging North Bay Village night spot and looked around. It was Halloween. He had just returned from a business trip to California and had ten thousand dollars in the pockets of his natty silk suit. He never got to spend it. Big Tony lumbered out of the bar and riddled the Enforcer with bullets.

The fatal dispute was over turf. The Enforcer had ordered Big Tony out of North Bay Village. When Big Tony ignored the warning and partied with a girlfriend at a nightspot in the forbidden village, a bomb exploded. It seriously damaged the premises and blasted Big Tony's lady right off her bar stool. The incident led to other skirmishes. The climax came on Halloween. Big Tony and his girl just could not stay away. They were back in North Bay Village sipping drinks when the Enforcer strolled in. Big Tony saw him first and shot him five times.

It seemed like the right thing to do at the time.

Then Murph the Surf, who had hoped to set a wholesome example for the youth of America, got himself into even worse trouble.

Two pretty young women in bikinis surfaced in Whiskey Creek, a waterway named for the bootleggers who once used it. They were dead—strangled and slashed. The women were secretaries involved in a big securities theft from the brokerage house where they worked. The last time anybody saw them alive, they were with Jack Murphy.

There were rumors that Murphy might be indicted for murder, but weeks went by with no action. Then, on a sunny Sunday afternoon, a bombshell: Widowed socialite Olive Wofford, a regular in Maude Massengale's society column, foiled a spectacular daylight robbery attempt at her waterfront estate in Miami Beach.

A man said he had a package to deliver, pulled a gun on the maid, and forced his way into the Wofford mansion. Three masked bandits followed. Murph the Surf was one of them. He wore a pair of filmy black panties as a mask to hide his well-known face.

They tied up the maid and Mrs. Wofford's eight-year-old niece, then surprised the widow at gunpoint in her bedroom. They warned her to open the safe or they would torture the little girl with boiling water. The widow obeyed. She opened the safe—triggering a silent alarm linked directly to police headquarters. Two officers arrived within sixty seconds. A robber stepped outside to act as lookout and saw them. He darted back into the house, shouting, "The cops are here!"

The robbers scattered in panic. Murphy tried to escape

through a sliding glass door. It was locked. He blasted the bolt three times with slugs from his chrome-plated .45 caliber automatic. It held fast. The former stuntman made a desperate running dive through the door, shattering it. The jagged glass slashed his face and knee.

Moments later a cop on the far side of the house saw two men running along a seawall. One of them was Murphy. Cops and robbers exchanged shots, the cops firing low, afraid their bullets might cross the waterway to Collins Avenue where tourists strolled near the Fountainebleau Hotel.

Cornered, Murphy tossed his gun up onto a rooftop and raised his hands. The other robbers were hunted down. One was found crouched in a clump of mangroves on the old Firestone estate nearby. Another was hiding in the gatehouse of a mansion a block away. A third was collared as he tried to stroll out of the neighborhood looking casual.

They were still being rounded up when I got there. Other reporters began arriving. Everybody wanted to know about Murph the Surf. Police said he had been taken to Mount Sinai Hospital, but a friendly cop whispered to me that he was actually at St. Francis Hospital.

I found Murph the Surf shackled to a wheelchair in the emergency room. He wore a yellow hospital gown. It was not his best color. His right knee was bloodied, his face a mess. There was an open gash three inches long under his right eye and a deep cut on his lower lip. He was still jaunty. "Hi, honey," he said.

"Jack," I cried, "what happened?"

"I cut myself shaving," he quipped.

He waved as they rolled him to X-ray.

He would be behind bars for the next seventeen years.

Murphy was convicted in the robbery attempt and of murder in the first degree at Whiskey Creek. A prosecutor wanted the death penalty, but Murphy was sentenced to two life terms plus twenty years. The judge called him an "incorrigible criminal and a public enemy." He warned that Jack Murphy must never, ever be released into "the free world with a law-abiding society."

Murph the Surf found "sweet Jesus" in prison.

They usually do.

In 1985 he was released to a halfway house so he could preach the gospel. Working on a story about Murphy's imminent parole, I sought comment from those who knew him. Olive Wofford, his last victim, was dead, of natural causes. Harvey St. Jean, his lawyer, was dead, of unnatural causes, in an unsolved murder mystery. Emery Zerick, the veteran detective who spent some of his best years in pursuit of Murph the Surf, is alive and well. He has not mellowed. "If I see him, I'll put a bullet in him, and you can quote me," Zerick growled.

I did. Murphy was paroled in November 1986 and warned to stay out of South Florida. He was as dapper and well-manicured as ever, free at forty-nine. He talked of big plans, a book, TV and personal appearances—at twenty-five hundred dollars a shot—to warn young Americans against lives of crime. Even Murph the Surf had trouble keeping a straight face.

"God," he chuckled, "has a sense of humor."

*   *   *

One day about two months after I was hired at the *Herald*, Steve Rogers stopped at my desk. "We hear that Willie Sutton, the bank robber, is in Sarasota. Would you be interested?"

Would I be interested? Willie "the Actor" Sutton was a larger-than-life figure out of my childhood. I didn't need to read his yellowed news clips in our morgue; I had read and reread them all as a little girl.

Willie the Actor did bad things. But he did them so well, with such flair that he never hurt anyone and never fired his gun. His bank jobs were flawlessly planned and executed with style and precision. He was certainly no master criminal—he did get caught—but he was one of the dark and dashing princes of my childhood fantasies.

All we had was a tip picked up from a too-talkative TV reporter. Willie the Actor, newly released from Attica State Prison in New York, had retired to Sarasota to live out the remainder of his days in the care of a married daughter. The publicity-shy daughter had never been publicly linked to her notorious father. Her identity was top secret.

All we knew was the name of the Sarasota motel where a Miami TV news crew was to meet Sutton for an exclusive interview at 2:00 P.M. Photographer Albert Coya and I scrambled for a Sarasota flight, hoping to find him first. Cuban-born Coya had never heard of America's number-one bank robber, so I told him how Willie the Actor never broke into a bank. He boldly walked in, posing as an armored-car guard, an elevator repairman, a window cleaner, a postman, a fireman, even a florist's delivery-man.

He arrived early and often collected dozens of employees while awaiting the one who knew the combination. He flattered the ladies and told jokes, cheerfully pointing out that it was not their money but the bank's that he had come to steal.

In those simpler times robbing banks was considered a serious matter. Willie Sutton, a four-time loser, was sent to prison for the last time in 1952. The sentence: thirty years to life.

This Sarasota interview could be Willie the Actor's farewell performance. Humane judges had heeded the pleas of an old man who did not want to die behind bars. Nearly seventy, he was suffering from a bad heart, blocked arteries, and chronic emphysema that left him gasping. Prison officials hastily released him. Willie Sutton was now part of American folklore; he had embarrassed them by escaping frequently when he was a young man, now they feared he might embarrass them by dying in their custody.

Hunched over and wrapped in a blanket, he rode a wheelchair to freedom on Christmas Eve. Front-page photos showed him stooped and brittle, his hair snow-white. The one-time desperado was now "a subdued, frail, and wrinkled old man," according to a New York newspaper account.

We had to find him. Such a well-known character should be easy to locate. He was not. Small-town cabbies are usually a great help. Ours polled his colleagues by radio. No luck. I called all the local banks. They had not seen him either. Like Miami Beach, Sarasota required convicted felons to register with the police. An obliging records clerk at headquarters found Willie Sutton's registration card. Smiling with relief, I reached for the card with his address, but the clerk jerked it away from my grasping fingers. "Wait a minute," he said, scrutinizing it carefully. The felon's daughter, a local resident, had asked that no information be released, to anyone.

I could not persuade the clerk, his supervisor, or his supervisor's supervisor. Now I knew how J. Edgar Hoover felt when Willie led his most-wanted list. He couldn't find him either. How could I return to Miami and the *Herald* without this story?

One slim chance remained: the motel where he was to meet the TV crew. Willie the Actor was always early, I recalled. He always arrived at the banks before they opened. We loitered hopefully outside the motel. When a dark-colored compact car rolled up to discharge a passenger, the woman at the wheel spotted Coya's camera, threw a hand in front of her face, and speeded away.

The passenger stepped briskly to the curb. His hair was bright red. He wore a jaunty grin above a plaid jacket and a splashy tie. I would have known him anywhere. It was Willie the Actor, the same man who had huddled, white-haired, in a wheelchair on Christmas Eve.

I think he assumed we were the people he had come to meet. After all, we seemed to be expecting him. His handshake was strong. We invited him to join us at a coffee shop. A delightful sort of wizened Red Buttons, he happily agreed to be spirited away. He was eager to talk and indignant, he said, at the sad state of society.

"I don't want to brag," he said, adjusting his tie, "but I never hurt anybody. Today you have brutal crimes, naked hate. I never hated anybody." American family life had sadly deteriorated in his absence, he said. "Conversation has become a lost art. I blame television."

He was now gainfully employed by a credit-card firm, busy writing a book, and considering a lecture tour.

As I scribbled notes, I began to experience that old familiar feeling—deadline pressure. Without consulting my watch, I knew it was time to start writing for the early edition.

"Rumors," Sutton was saying spiritedly. "That's what worries me now. Rumors. If somebody pulls a big bank job, I hope I'm a thousand miles away."

We could have totally blitzed the TV crew, but they had made all this possible. We returned Willie to the motel, where the reporter and cameramen were waiting. They did not know me. They assumed I was Willie's daughter. Before we said goodbye, I asked one final question. All his talk about promoting prison reform, helping to beef up bank security, and saving the youth of America from lives of crimes—was it real, or was it only Willie the Actor's latest role? He looked shocked that I would ask.

"It's the real me," he insisted. He squeezed my hands in his, kissed me, and walked away. Then he turned, glanced slyly over his shoulder, grinned and winked.

The motel manager let me pound out the story on an old typewriter behind the front desk. Coya sent the film to Miami and I called in the copy, while the TV crew was still in the motel room interviewing Willie.

Their station had spent the day promoting their exclusive Willie Sutton interview. When the camera crew stepped off the plane in Miami, our early edition, with its front-page story and color pictures, greeted them from the newsracks.

Next time we met, the TV crew knew me.

Willie the Actor finished his book, starred in credit-card commercials, and played out his final role in his own inimitable style. His final curtain did not ring down until almost eleven years after his dramatic wheelchair ride out of prison.

Sociopaths like Murph the Surf and Willie the Actor always leave me with the impression that they lack something integral in their makeup: They have no conscience. They either lost it early or never had it at all. There are other criminals who seem to have something added, something evil.

Robert Carr is the most evil man I ever met. Red-haired and freckle-faced, with an engaging, Huckleberry Finn grin, he is flesh-and-blood proof that the monsters at large in the world never look like monsters. He kidnapped fifteen people. He raped and tortured most of them. He murdered four of them. They were women and children.

I sat alone with Robert Carr in a jail cell full of echoes for more than one hundred hours. I know more about him than I do about anyone else in the world. I wish I could forget his story, but it is a real-life nightmare that someone must remember for as long as Robert Carr remains alive.

In the early summer of 1976, a cop tipped me that a rapist caught in the act had confessed to four murders. Two Metro homicide detectives were about to escort the prisoner on a cross-country gravedigging trip to recover the bodies. He said he had buried them deep, in graves that he dug in Mississippi, Louisiana, and Connecticut. The investigation was being kept secret, because the detectives wanted to be sure the victims were really there.

Cops hate being embarrassed.

They were not convinced he was truthful, but I was, instantly. I knew it because I asked who the victims were, and my tipster said that one was a teenage girl missing from Miami for two months and that two others were eleven-year-old boys who had been missing for four years.

I had to sit down because my knees were suddenly weak. Mark and Todd: The policeman I was talking to did not know their names—but I did. Their files lay on my desk. I had been planning a magazine story about Miami's most baffling missing-persons cases. The two little boys had vanished as totally as footprints in melted snow. Initially written off by police as runaways, the youngsters were forgotten, filed away in dusty missing-persons records. Only their loved ones remembered. This rapist, described as a hard-drinking drifter and ex-convict from Connecticut, had to be telling the truth. How else would he even know that these two little boys from Miami ever existed—unless he was the one who made them disappear.

Two days later, in Hancock County, Mississippi, the killer led a caravan of cops deep into the wilderness of a dense forest. "Dig here," he told them. They did so, and unearthed the first body at that precise spot.

Robert Carr pinpointed all the graves, including the burial place of a Connecticut prostitute, with the same unerring accuracy.

When they returned to Miami, a medical examiner, a prosecutor, and a homicide detective, all members of the successful search party, suggested that I go talk to Carr in jail. They were fascinated by the man.

"You'll like him," they said. That seemed unlikely. His crimes were reprehensible. Then Carr himself telephoned to introduce himself. He had read all the news stories, he said, and mine were the only accurate accounts of what he had done. He wanted to tell me more.

He was not at all what I expected. I thought he would be a slick, fast-talking con man, the type who could lure unsuspecting victims into his car without a struggle.

Instead, he is soft-spoken, almost shy. He looks like somebody you grew up with: the next-door neighbor, the scoutmaster, or the auto mechanic down the block. He never hit anyone over the head or dragged them screaming into his car. All his victims stepped willingly, even eagerly, into his automobile. And once they closed that door behind them, they were trapped. He had rigged the passenger-side door handle—it could not be opened from the inside.

He wanted me to write his story, a book, he said, to

help keep such tragedies from happening again. He had nothing to lose; he was certain that he was going to die for his crimes. It seemed likely. He made other executed killers look like choir boys. I was not interested in writing more about Carr or ever seeing him again.

He wrote me long, persuasive letters on yellow legal paper, and he called so often that I began to suspect that he had a private phone in his cell. In one letter he wrote that he could not blame me for not wanting to become involved but, "I may die before anything is written and someone has to know this story."

He was right. I did not want to be involved. But what made this man what he is? All of his victims had a chance to escape. Why didn't they? Why did they go with him in the first place? And was his compulsion to rape—and then murder—really irresistible?

My curiosity won. I began to spend a great deal of time in jail. We started at the beginning. The man has a photographic memory. He swears he can remember being held in the arms of his father, who deserted him when he was nine months old. He clearly remembers killing all of his grandfather's chickens at age three and experimenting aggressively with sex when he was four.

He told me that whatever is wrong with him is something that he was born with.

At first, the jail guards kept close watch on us. Soon, however, I became part of the daily routine, a piece of the furniture. I often spent six or eight hours with Carr, tape-recording everything he could recall. I did not fear him, at least not consciously. But I was ready to leave one evening after five or six hours and found no guard in sight. I pushed a buzzer. No one answered. I rattled the bars and called. Still, no answer. Carr smiled and smoked his cigarette. It took twenty minutes before I could attract anyone's attention. They had forgotten I was there.

That night, by coincidence, I read Carr's psychiatric reports: highly dangerous, homicidal, unpredictable. One doctor urged that his jailers be warned never to turn their backs on him.

It did not worry me. I knew Carr was a coward and that all his victims were tied up and helpless when he strangled them. The next day, ready to drive to the jail, I caught my reflection in a mirror as I walked out my front door. I was wearing a blouse with a long trailing scarf.

I went back and changed.

Day after day we sat facing each other as he calmly told me his story. He left nothing out. Each time, I left with a throbbing headache. I would go home, take off my clothes, and step into a hot shower, as if to scrub away the things that made my skin crawl. In spite of that, I became as convinced as Carr that his story should be told. Never had such an articulate, self-analytical sex killer been so absolutely candid, so willing to expose the dark side of his own sick soul. Certain he was going to die, he gave me his death-bed confession.

Carr refused to cooperate with his own defense attorney. He warned from the start that he would turn against me, too. He knows himself well. It is his life's pattern, to turn on everyone close to him. He begged me not to let it deter me, and I gave him my word.

To everyone's surprise, Robert Carr did not die. A judge named Natalie Baskin sentenced him, instead, to more than three hundred years in prison.

The numbers mean little—he will be eligible for parole in fourteen years.

Now that he was no longer facing death, Carr began to think of his future and the day the parole commission considers his case. He wanted to change his story, about the murders, the rapes, and his past. He wanted to delete details that show premeditation. He decided that he committed his crimes during moments of temporary insanity and that now, of course, he is cured and has found religion as well.

He wanted to omit his recollections about killing the chickens when he was three and his earlier belief that he was born with the propensity to kill. He also wanted to take out the fact that he had been driving around Miami for days in search of a victim when he finally picked up Tammy Huntley, age sixteen—and that he already had the shovel with which to bury her in the trunk. Now he wanted me to change that to say that he never intended to kill her.

His original story was totally confirmed by lie-detector tests, physical evidence, and the stories of survivors. I was not about to let him tamper with the truth. He wrote me long letters from an upstate mental hospital, underlining his demands in red ink so passionately that his pen tore the paper. One night he called, long distance from Chattahoochee. "I could walk out of here right now," he bragged. In fact, he said, he would. He was coming to

Miami, he said, to kill his lawyer and the prosecutor, to "choke their tongues out."

I could not ignore him, since he had choked people's tongues out in the past. I called hospital administrators to ask why they allow the inmates to make long-distance, threatening phone calls at the taxpayers' expense and if he really could walk out of there.

His keepers were surprised. They said they would check. They did and found Robert Carr with wire cutters, pliers, money, a crowbar, and a supply of food. He was obviously planning a trip.

He is now in maximum security in Florida State Prison.

I think.

I finished the book, but I doubt that it is the end of Carr's story. His most recent letters to acquaintances and family are full of plans. He writes that he expects to be released shortly, within months. When I queried prison officials they denied it. Perhaps he knows something they don't.

If he is released, I know one thing for sure: He will hurt someone, most likely someone who was not even born when he went to prison.

Some criminals simply have no conscience. Others, like Robert Carr, have something extra that roams the wilderness of their minds.

Something evil.

Update: 2004

Robert Carr became eligible for parole more than two years ago. The parole commission heard his story and listened to some of his victims. He was not paroled. They added an additional fourteen centuries to his sentence instead. His tentative release date: July 30, 3414.

Makes sense to me.

Carr, however, remains optimistic as he busily exchanges love letters with lonely women and girls he meets through the mail and has announced future plans: A bus tour of the USA with the Manson family members when they are all free to travel.

Sex is the biggest nothing of all time.
Andy Warhol

SEVEN

Sex

Sex gets people into so much trouble it's a wonder more of them don't give it up.

I often joke that my job keeps me single and celibate. But actually, celibacy may not be so awful after all. Sex gets people killed, put in jail, beaten up, bankrupted, and disgraced, to say nothing of ruined—personally, politically, and professionally. Looking for sex can lead to misfortune, and if you get lucky and find it, it can leave you maimed, infected, or dead.

Other than that, it's swell: the great American pastime.

Every newspaper story has something to do with sex. Money, power, politics: Sex is always involved somewhere. Everybody wants it. Some like it risky. A lot of people could live without it—literally. Where are the cold showers when they are needed?

Not here. Miami is a sexy city. It is also a violent city. Maybe it is the climate; the soft, sultry evenings; the gigantic pale moon beaming shafts of silver onto shimmering water; or the aroma of night-blooming jasmine. It all contributes to a lot of craziness.

The first person a Miami rape victim met as she staggered for help in a desolate area was another young rape victim running for help from the opposite direction.

Police were skeptical when a high school girl insisted that the man who kidnapped and raped her was wearing a hat decorated with rainbow-colored lights that blinked on and off. At dawn, a detective noticed a motorist, driving near the scene of the crime, wearing a visor cap with flashing rainbow-colored lights. The batteries still worked at the time of the trial, and the little lights blinked on and off for the jury that convicted him.

After my *Herald* story about all the men—doctors, lawyers, engineers, even newspaper employees—who tried to pick up decoy policewomen on Biscayne Boulevard and got nabbed by "the John Squad," I found a note in my office mailbox, obviously from someone who works in the building. The writer called me a castrating female and did not sign his name. Perhaps it is perverse, but I was happy to see the horny rascals hauled off in the paddy wagon, just like the hookers. It made sense to me. The furor the story created, however, made the cops back off. Now they simply issue the men citations, as if they had been jaywalking. The prostitutes still go to jail.

Your sex life could and should be a private matter— but if it kills you, it will likely become a public matter, causing great posthumous embarrassment, if there is such a thing. I've covered the shootings of a priest, a bridegroom on his honeymoon, and one of my neighbors, all caught in compromising positions. You probably won't see it on a bumper sticker, but sex kills.

It can also be damned awkward. Prominent politicians die in bed with women not their wives; a respected judge is bumped off the bench because he can't keep his hands off a defendant's wife. Cops get in trouble for seeking sex from suspects, crime victims, and other cops.

What is unique about sex crimes is the silence that often surrounds them.

When killers left the body of a prominent cardiologist on an isolated back-road bridge, the medical community cried out for justice, funded memorials, and posted rewards. Then police solved the case, and the silence was deafening. It was sex that killed the heart doctor, in the form of a bullet fired into his head by a fifteen-year-old prostitute.

When my neighbor got shot, I met and skirmished with Miami Homicide Sergeant Russ Leasberg. I did not know the neighbor well. He was a plumber, and he was critically wounded. When I routinely investigated the shooting, Leasberg was evasive and would say nothing. I suspected some sort of a cover-up. The problem was that the detective is an old-fashioned sort of guy who believed some things were better left unsaid, particularly to female reporters.

In the official police account, the plumber was shot and robbed on the street. Not true—guys stick together— the detective didn't want the victim's wife to know he was flagrante delicto with a prostitute when wounded. I didn't want her hurt or embarrassed either. She figured it out herself. I met her later, after their divorce, and she brought up the subject. The hospital returned her injured husband's garments. She was washing them when she realized that, although there were a number of bullet holes in his body, there were none in his clothes.

At least he survived. The bridegroom didn't. He brought his new wife to Miami Beach, and when she fell asleep, he slipped off to continue the honeymoon without her. He found more action than he expected. A hooker he hired set him up to be robbed, and he was shot.

Looking for love, or whatever you like to call it, was fatal for a girl named Jeanie Rivera.

She took a stranger home from a South Beach bar. The only witness to her murder was her beautiful, snow-white, long-haired cat. It mewed plaintively around the legs of all the strangers—cops, detectives, and crime-lab technicians—who were crowded into the small apartment when I got there.

Jeanie Rivera lay barefoot on the living-room floor, beaten and strangled, a pillowcase over her head. Cops came and went, leaving the door to her second-floor apartment open as they completed their tasks. A small but frisky neighborhood dog joined the crowd, ambled upstairs, nosed his way into the apartment—and tried to attack Jeanie Rivera's already-traumatized cat.

The yappy little brown dog chased the terrified creature around and around and over her dead owner's body.

Policemen cursed and shouted as the animals raced back and forth across the crime scene they were trying to preserve.

A cop finally shoved the dog out the door, swatted his rump, and shooed him back down the stairs. Ten minutes later, while everyone was preoccupied, the persistent little dog trotted back up the stairs and barged, yapping, through the door. Cops screamed, shouted, and cursed as the dog and the cat skittered and scrambled around and over the corpse of Jeanie Rivera.

A furious lieutenant snatched up the dog, flung him outside, and began kicking at him just as a TV news crew came dashing up to the murder scene, camera rolling, to catch this obvious act of police brutality to a small and innocent animal.

As the lieutenant pursued the film crew, pleading his case, the medical examiner arrived. I stood in the doorway and watched him kneel beside the body for a preliminary examination. The doctor squinted at something he held up in his hand, and I overheard him inform a detective that "the killer is obviously an older person." He carefully placed a long strand of snow-white hair in a plastic evidence bag. With tweezers, he painstakingly began to pluck other long white hairs—and a few short, curly brown ones—from the body.

I stared at the detective who said nothing. The department already had a reputation for improperly maintaining crime scenes, due in part to a patrolman who not only picked up a murder weapon, but absentmindedly reloaded it while waiting for detectives to arrive.

I cornered the detective outside. "Tell him," I muttered, "or I will." He turned and marched back into the apartment, looking glum.

I heard him say, "Doc, about those hairs . . ."

I didn't want to embarrass him. But hell, Jeanie Rivera could have been any of us—looking for love. I just wanted to make sure that everything went right.

When sex got Jimmie Lee Wilson killed, a lot of people agreed that it should have happened sooner.

Jimmie Lee Wilson was on death row when I first heard of him. He had brutally raped two young migrant farm workers back in the days when rape was still a capital offense in Florida.

A high-powered defense attorney won Wilson a new trial. Both victims had married; neither they nor their husbands wanted to endure the ordeal of a trial. So after eight years, Jimmie Lee Wilson stepped off death row a free man.

Three months later, terrible sex crimes began to happen in South Dade. A killer was stalking young couples on dates. One couple was shot dead. Another was wounded and left for dead. The women were raped. The South Dade Rapist became the target of a major manhunt. The cops found him, surrounded his house, then crashed inside as he sat at the dinner table with his wife and family.

It was Jimmie Lee Wilson, of course. He had learned something from his unpleasant experience with the migrant women: Leave no witnesses.

By the time of this arrest, Florida had no death penalty; the state supreme court had ruled it unconstitutional. The most serious punishment Jimmie Lee Wilson could face now, for both murder and rape, was life in prison.

A tall and strapping fellow, he was feared and hated by other prisoners, a number of whom accused him of homosexual rape in the Dade County Jail. His presence became a handy tool for enterprising detectives. When they wanted a prisoner to cooperate or confess, all they had to do was to threaten to place him in a cell with Jimmie Lee Wilson. Everybody was relieved when he was shipped off to state prison for five life terms plus 160 years.

He did not serve even a fraction of it. Sex got him in trouble again.

His habits did not change, and his fellow convicts were now stuck with him, but not for long. Cell doors are swung open in the evenings for recreation. One night somebody decided the best recreation would be to stab Jimmie Lee Wilson with a sharpened spoon until he died. Ninety-five other inmates were present, but nobody saw a thing.

It was almost like being back on the streets of Miami.

The killing occurred during the Christmas season, and one reader, a sweet-voiced older woman, was overwhelmed by the spirit. She wanted to do something nice for the ninety-five men on that cell block. The cash she could send wouldn't be much, divided ninety-five ways. So she baked little individual fruitcakes. She telephoned to ask my help in finding the correct mailing address.

She got it.

*   *   *

When writing about a rapist who is still on the prowl, it is important to give him a distinctive moniker. That way the public, the police, and the press can get a fix on him and hopefully catch the SOB or at least make him notorious enough that officials will make the manhunt a priority.

We have had the Bandanna Rapist, the Flashbulb Rapist, the A/C Rapist, the Coral Gables Rapist, the Silver-Toothed Rapist, and the Umbrella Rapist.

We still have the Pillowcase Rapist.

The Flashbulb Rapist posed as a jogger. He carried his camera in a paper sack and a gun in the pocket of his sweat suit. He shot naked photos of his victims at gunpoint. The cops finally captured him, but before they could even question him, a judge released him to the custody of his wife. He didn't even have to post bond. Police were furious. The judge said he had no idea why they were upset. All police really seemed to have was the man's fingerprints on a flashcube dropped by the rapist and a prior victim who screamed and pointed him out as he jogged by.

The cops did not like the way that judge thought. Sometimes I don't like the way cops think. Cops have strange ideas about rape. They are to blame for much of the silence surrounding the crime. They usually like to keep it a secret; they prefer that the public *not* know a rapist is out there.

They kept the investigation quiet for two years while they tried to catch the Bird Road Rapist.

This rapist used a distinctive *modus operandi:* He

would drive by night and fall in behind lone women motorists, flashing his headlights persistently. Some thought
he was a police officer instructing them to pull over and
obeyed. Others believed he was someone they knew or a
good Samaritan warning that something was wrong with
their car.

He would trot up to the woman's car as she rolled
down the window and shove a .45-caliber automatic pistol in her face. He was responsible for sixteen known
rapes; police suspected there were others.

I heard about the rapist and began gathering information for a story. The cops were furious. Their lieutenant
even called my editor, insisting we keep it out of the
paper. Their reasoning was the usual: If the rapist is
tipped off that police are looking for him, they will never
be able to catch him.

I don't understand that logic. I never will. Someone
committing all these crimes obviously assumes he is
being sought, and if police had been unable to stop him
for two years, at least women motorists should be warned
to protect themselves.

Over police objections, the story appeared in the
Sunday paper. The rapist was in jail by the end of the
week.

Half a dozen new victims called police after reading
the story. Embarrassed, ashamed, or afraid, they had
never reported their encounters with the rapist. Each
thought she was the only victim, until she read the newspaper. Among them were women with more accurate descriptions of the man and the cars he drove. One had

even seen him in a gas station some time after the rape. Based on the new information, detectives were able to identify and arrest him.

He was sentenced to multiple life terms.

You would think that the detectives' thinking would change as a result. But no, the very next time I heard about another rapist who was eluding them, they were furious. They did not want the story in the newspaper.

Yet when information flows freely both ways, justice often triumphs. On two consecutive Saturday nights, young couples on dates stopped at the same downtown Miami traffic light and were abducted by ten men. The gang was led by an armed youth who fired shots. They robbed the couples, raped the women, beat the men, and stripped their cars. One woman was raped ten times, had her front teeth broken, and was sexually assaulted with a wine bottle.

I wrote the story. Police had no leads.

A reader called, angry and frightened. She lived in the neighborhood and saw the second crime. Afraid to talk to police, she did talk to me. She knew the street names and the addresses of several of the hoodlums and described to me what she had seen. I arranged for her to meet Sergeant Mike Gonzalez—on neutral turf, far from police headquarters and her own neighborhood. I promised her he could be trusted to protect her identity.

As a result, the attackers were arrested, their fingerprints matched those left on the victims' cars; the victims positively identified them. They were sentenced to thirty-year prison terms.

Except the man with the gun. He got ninety years. Sometimes it works.

It takes strong people like Miami Homicide Detectives Mike Gonzalez and Louise Vasquez to push for change and fight the silence. Roxcy Bolton has fought it even longer. She drew up the battle lines before the rest of us even thought about it.

Roxcy is one of a kind. And that is sad because we need more like her. She has done more to change things for women than anyone I know, and she is pure of heart. She is not promoting herself for public office, writing a book, or fueling a career. She fought for equal pay, though she did not enter the workplace. She fought for day-care, though she remained at home to raise her own children.

Straight-backed and sturdy, plain-speaking and formidable, she is a tall woman as comfortable in designer clothes as in overalls and sneakers. Her Irish blue eyes shoot sparks and she looks like a pioneer woman. She *is* a pioneer woman. From a farm family in Duck Hill, Mississippi, she became Florida's first feminist.

She can do more, faster—whether it be washing ten loads of dirty clothes or righting a social injustice—than a courtroom of slick city lawyers or a platoon of combat marines. Blessed with a big strong voice, she uses it and minces no words. She not only fights the silence, she shatters it. More than a nuisance, she can be downright pushy, reducing college presidents, politicians, and police to quivering masses and driving male chauvinist pigs right up the walls of their pens.

God bless her.

Some people might call her "strident": wrong word. *Stalwart* is the word for Roxcy.

Consider this scene at a Dade County Commission meeting:

MAYOR: We'll appoint the best man to this board . . .

VOICE FROM AUDIENCE: You mean "person." The best *person.*

MAYOR: Mrs. Bolton, you're disrupting these proceedings.

VOICE: Person!

MAYOR: One more word . . .

VOICE: *Person!*

She opened the "businessmen's grills" at big Miami department stores to women. Carrying sleeping bags and emergency rations, she and others stormed the office of the University of Miami's president to demand equal representation of women at executive and administrative levels.

Often a lone voice, she is never daunted. She founded Women in Distress, a shelter for homeless women. Because of her grit and determination, Miami has a rape center, the first established in the nation.

When the Downtown Rapist stalked city stairwells and women's rest rooms, the hardest hit were the low-income women who worked late, cleaning hotels and offices and waiting on tables in restaurants. They were often mothers who had to walk to desolate parking lots or wait at lonely bus stops, after working to put food on the table for their children. Concerned about the rising number of rape cases, Roxcy organized a nighttime rally and led a hundred businesswomen, political leaders, activists, and housewives down Flagler Street in downtown Miami, on what was probably the first March Against Rape.

She stood on the courthouse steps to demand sodium-vapor lights, court priority for rape cases, and the presence of policewomen during rape investigations. Noting that the Miami police chief had recently installed iron security bars at his house, she said, "If he feels unsafe in his own home, how do you think a woman getting off work at 9:00 P.M. feels in downtown Miami?"

If they could not stop the rapes, Roxcy suggested, police should enlist soldiers from Homestead Air Force Base to help them patrol. Both then and earlier, when she accused the cops of juggling rape statistics, she decried police attitudes toward the crime. Her point was well taken. Members of the all-male county rape squad playfully referred to themselves as the "Pussy Posse." National statistics showed that only one rape in three is reported. Roxcy blamed police attitudes for that.

Looking through papers at police headquarters one weekend, I came upon a police report I thought curious. Sometimes the most important detail is the one that is missing. You read between the lines and suspect the worst.

A frightened young woman found running naked down a Miami street said she was raped by five men in a white van. At the very bottom of the narrative, in a small postscript, the officer noted the victim claimed that the men who attacked her were city employees.

What city employees cruise Miami's mean streets at night in a van? Cops on stakeouts and surveillance. Sure enough, it was five cops who sexually assaulted the victim, a teenage prostitute named Wanda Jean, a runaway from her Kentucky home.

The police department had her stashed away. I suspected that the girl would be encouraged to drop the allegations and leave town.

Before that could occur, Roxcy Bolton just happened to somehow hear about Wanda Jean. She also managed to learn the name of the motel where police had her hidden. The state attorney knew nothing of the case; the cops were keeping it under wraps. Roxcy steamrolled into that motel. A hefty plainclothes police officer was patrolling the hall, a newspaper under his arm. This had to be the right place, but she didn't know the room number. Roxcy marched down the hallway booming in that big voice: "Wanda Jean! Wanda Jean! This is Roxcy!"

The policeman nearly had a heart attack. He tiptoed off to a pay phone, trying hard to look casual.

As Roxcy shouted her name, a door cracked open and a small, frightened face peeped out.

"This is Roxcy. I'm a sister."

The girl swung open the door. Inside, Roxcy announced, "Wanda Jean, we're going to the state attorney's office."

"Okay," the teenager said, and they left, as the policeman watched helplessly.

"I am here with Wanda Jean and we want to see Ed Carhart," Roxcy announced at the state attorney's office. Detectives Mike Gonzalez and Louise Vasquez were already there. They were not happy. They investigated rapes, and Roxcy's prior allegations had reflected on them—now this.

Louise asked Wanda Jean if Roxcy had intimidated her. No, said Wanda Jean. "But she frightened you, didn't she?"

Wanda Jean said no. What frightened her were the five cops who attacked her. Carhart, a chief prosecutor and a sensitive man, listened. His parting words to Roxcy that day were "Let the system work."

And it did. The cops were convicted.

They served time—the greatest tragedy that can ever befall a police officer. Five minutes in jail is too long for a cop. One of the convicted cops still calls me from time to time when he's depressed and needs a shoulder. He says that I am the only person who treated him fairly. I had written about those same five cops before, when they came to the rescue of a young English girl, a tourist attacked by a maniac in a Miami bus station. Whenever I wrote about the sex charges against them later, I always included the commendations, the awards, the things they did right, the fact that all had families and were human. They were good cops who were not properly supervised, out there in the night, working the seamiest side of town, undercover, on their own. Not the sort of assignment conducive to character building and sterling behavior.

Sex got them in trouble.

Undercover work, especially narcotics and vice, often ruins good cops. By the time you get down to the same level as the bad guys and successfully convince them you are one of them—sometimes you are.

Roxcy and Ed Carhart sat together at Wanda Jean's high school graduation. Wanda Jean hoped to go on to college and become a social worker.

I hope she did.

Roxcy lives in Coral Gables, known nationwide as the City Beautiful. When a rapist was afoot in their affluent residential community, city officials were loath to admit it. But the news got out: three rapes and one attempt—women attacked at home, in their own beds. Roxcy was irate. She announced plans for a Women's Walking Patrol. Groups of three and four women would patrol, each woman would be armed with a flashlight, and a family dog would accompany each group.

The city fathers were apoplectic. Police warned that it could be dangerous and anxiously tried to dissuade Roxcy and the women who flocked to volunteer. The officials seemed most concerned about the publicity. To call Coral Gables image-conscious is an understatement. Tree houses are forbidden, pickup trucks cannot be parked in residential driveways overnight, and the city even tried at one point to legislate the numbers of dogs and cats permitted per household.

Detectives let it slip that they had a composite drawing of the rapist and a good description of a distinctive shirt he wore. Terrific, I said, asking eagerly for both. I was told they would not be released to the public.

That drives me crazy. You almost wonder which side they are on. I usually lose patience and mutter something derisive such as "Why? Are you afraid you might catch him?" Which, of course, does not endear me to their hearts. But it all seems so insane. I confess, my greatest fault is impatience.

The same old argument, over and over: If the shirt is distinctive and we describe it, someone may recognize it—perhaps the girlfriend who bought it for him, or a co-worker who saw him wear it, or his dry cleaner, or a neighbor who saw it hanging on his clothesline. The *Herald* has half a million circulation. Isn't there more chance of identification if half a million people know what the rapist and his shirt look like, rather than just the handful of secretive cops on the case?

No, they said, the information was classified—for their eyes only. I mentioned that in our story. Women were furious, and the next day, beleaguered police released the composite and a description of the shirt, which had JOU JOU written in large letters across the front. We put it in the newspaper.

At 7:00 A.M. a man walked into Miami Springs police headquarters, miles from Coral Gables. JOU JOU was written in large letters across the front of his shirt. During the night he had stolen the purse of a woman he met in a bar. He wanted to confess. The desk sergeant's graveyard shift was ending; he turned the man over to an officer to take the report, went home, sat down, and opened his morning *Herald*.

Moments later, he leaped to his feet and raced back to headquarters, taking his newspaper with him. It was the same man, same shirt. It worked again.

From the detectives: no comment.

Roxcy, Louise Vasquez, and I are all friends now. Roxcy and Louise were at odds in the beginning, but Roxcy says, "She saw that I wasn't there for myself. I was there about social change. We made peace and that's the best kind of sisterhood in the world."

It sure is. They are both tough; they both have the same Irish blue eyes, and if I were in trouble, they would be the first people I would call.

They know how to handle trouble—Louise knows how to stop it in its tracks. She arrested a married couple on sex charges. The husband had raped the stepdaughters; the wife did nothing to stop him. It was the first case in Miami in which the mother went to jail along with her husband. The victims were nine, eighteen, and twenty, and the parents' arrests left the two older girls with five small children to care for.

Linda, a teenager, is fighting to keep the family together. "I feel like I have an obligation to my sisters," she told me. The rapes took place over six years and were never reported to the police. Each girl said she told her mother and begged for help.

When I met Linda she was eighteen, the mother of a two-year-old daughter and an eight-month-old son, and worked at a McDonald's for $3.35 an hour. A trophy-winning honor student with a perfect high school attendance record, she had once hoped to win a college scholarship. Instead, she dropped out of school, pregnant at sixteen. Before fleeing the family home, she talked heart-to-heart to her little sister. Their stepfather had "no business in your room," she warned. "If he comes into your room, tell me, because if you tell your mother, she won't do anything."

It happened anyway. When she found out that the little girl had been raped too, she told me: "I was so angry at myself for not doing something about it. My little sister is the shy type, like me. She's really like my own daughter. I'm obligated to show her the right way."

At first the teenager did not know where to turn or what to do, so she dialed information on the telephone and asked the operator. The operator, bless her, gave her the number for Miami police and told her to use it.

Once the parents were arrested, thieves looted their apartment and stole all the little girls' clothes. Linda had moved to Broward County to be as far away as possible from the stepfather she feared. There was no telephone or electricity in her tiny apartment because she could not afford the deposits. She rode four buses, then walked a mile—each way—to get to her minimum-wage job every day.

I drove her home a few times and brought her clothes and shoes from Roxcy. The spunky teenage mother fought obstacle after obstacle. The bank directly across the street from the McDonald's where she worked refused to cash her paycheck or even allow her to open a checking account. I called to ask why and bank officials said it was because she lacked identification. All they would accept was a driver's license, and she did not have one. The bank is in Miami Beach. Obviously the accounts of well-heeled retirees are welcomed whether they have a driver's license or not. Obviously the real problem was that Linda is young, poor, black, and a woman. I suggested that to bank officials, who denied it and opened the account.

Nothing comes easy for a kid with so many strikes against her.

Some good people at St. Thomas University became interested in her after I wrote a story about the case. They gave her a job at the school and may help her dream of an education come true. I was recently sent a copy of her newly acquired high school equivalency diploma.

It was the best news I'd had in a long time.

Good news or even hopeful endings are rare when covering sex crimes, especially in Miami. The two most elusive rapists in South Florida have thumbed their noses for years at the police, the press, and the community. One man, the Gentle Rapist, is perhaps the most prolific rapist in state history. Police say they have identified him, but he was never charged with a single case. The other, the Pillowcase Rapist, is still at large, his identity a mystery, despite the most intensive manhunt of its kind ever conducted in Florida.

I was new at the *Herald* when I became aware of the Gentle Rapist. He was not called that at the time. When he first surfaced, in 1971, he was called the Coconut Grove Rapist. Distinctively kinky, he stalked that shady

Miami community of huge trees and old houses favored by young people.

He wore a costume: purple leotards and a leopard-skin cape. He also wore a rape kit: a homemade belt with pouches to hold his wig, a can of Mace, a starter pistol, masks, towels, a lubricant, and spermicidal jelly. He was later seen wearing black tights, Earth shoes, and masks fashioned from support hose. It was believed that he changed into his bizarre costumes in the bushes or shrubbery before confronting his victims. He liked to force them into lewd dress and order them to pose in obscene scenarios. He told them he did not want to make them pregnant and often lectured them on proper attire and morality.

He committed a number of double rapes on roommates, sisters, and mothers and daughters. He seemed to have no trouble finding and clipping their telephone lines in the maze of apartment-house wires.

They nearly caught him once; a Miami police officer got close enough to almost touch him. He even dropped his rape kit that night, but he slipped away and won a footrace down an alley. He eluded fifty officers and fire trucks with spotlights.

Mike Gonzalez and Louise Vasquez were the first to try to track him down. Unlike most detectives, their approach was original. In 1973, they dictated to me an open letter to the rapist, hoping to start a dialogue with him. They wanted to gain insight; they wanted to help him—after arresting him of course, though we did not dwell on that in the letter. They gave a telephone number where he could contact them.

We published the letter to the rapist in the newspaper. Rival Metro detectives hooted and jeered at the idea, probably regretting that they had not thought of it first. It bore fruit. A number of sex offenders called, wanting to talk out their hidden passions and problems with the detectives. The man they were seeking did call once, they believe, but he quickly hung up and never called back.

Mike and Louise became so interested, however, that they met with psychologists and psychiatrists. On their own time, they organized a series of rap sessions with men, many of whom they had arrested, in a sex-offenders program at South Florida State Hospital. They went on to become consultants for a crime-prevention film produced by a governor's committee, they have lectured widely, and Louise was twice named to advisory committees on criminal legislation.

The rapist stayed out of their jurisdiction, but it eventually became apparent that he was not only Miami's problem. We all soon began to realize that the Coconut Grove Rapist was known in another jurisdiction as the Bicycle Rapist, and in Boca Raton, thirty-five miles north, as the Cape. They were all the same man.

Investigators from each police department had initially suspected that the rapist was home-grown. He slipped so easily in and out of their neighborhoods, always choosing homes where young women were alone. He seemed to know his way around—everywhere.

Because he spoke courteously to his victims, he became known as the Gentle Rapist. When police reluctantly admitted that the same man was responsible for about forty-five rapes and that they had no idea how to stop him, Roxcy called a group of women to her home. They would organize the Vigilantes, a massive, county-wide neighborhood watch to fight the rapist and combat crime by becoming the eyes and ears of the community. The aim was to make people more aware and to alert them to everyday crime in their neighborhoods. Roxcy turned her brainchild over to Betty Ann Good, one of the women at that first meeting. She took it from there and sought a liaison with police. They were wary, but hopeful. The very word *vigilante* made them extremely queasy. At their suggestion, the name of the organization was changed to Citizens' Crime Watch.

It grew, was successful, and is now more than a million strong.

There is no accurate accounting of the Gentle Rapist's crimes. By early 1978, they numbered approximately two hundred. No one will ever know how many assaults went unreported. By then the rapist had been sought for seven years. A city police major, weary of the embarrassment of failure, ordered the men and women of his department not to talk about the case, warning that discipline would be swift and severe if they did.

You would think that a man who wears a flower-embroidered rape kit strapped around his waist and a leopard-skin cape would not be difficult to locate. But he was.

Three years later, police say, by the simplest of accidents, he was identified.

He was featured in *Cosmopolitan* magazine.

Jesse Patmore, a county rape-squad detective, had given up on Miami and police work after the 1980 riots. Now he operated a little country store in North Carolina, and there he sat one day, idly thumbing through his wife's *Cosmo*. He paused at an article about a criminal they called the Superthief. In prison, serving a fifteen-year term for burglary, robbery, and grand theft, he bragged that he had grossed $133 million in two thousand burglaries. He was shooting for early parole, another convict eager to launch a nationwide speaking tour to tell people how to protect themselves from thieves like him.

The former detective began to read the story, then suddenly snatched up a pen and began to underline passages. Similarities between the Superthief and the Gentle Rapist leaped out at him from the slick pages. Superthief used police scanners to monitor patrols; so did the rapist. Superthief came to Florida in 1969, shortly before the costumed rapist's first appearance. Superthief was a locksmith and an electronics expert; locked doors had never stopped the rapist, who always knew which telephone line to snip.

Superthief owned a helicopter, two small planes, a van, cars, and motorcycles; the rapist's mobility had always confused police. Superthief emphasized his nonviolence; the Gentle Rapist comforted his victims by demonstrating before departing that the gun he had pointed at their heads was a fake. Superthief vacationed annually in Maine; Florida police had long speculated about the rapist's summer hiatus.

Superthief's photo was a dead ringer for a police composite of the rapist.

Patmore dialed long distance and reported his hunch to old friends on the force. They compared fingerprints left behind by the Gentle Rapist to those of the Super-thief, John MacLean.

They were the same.

Victims were willing to testify, including a Chicago business executive who had been a University of Miami coed when raped nine years earlier. MacLean's fingerprints had been left in her bedroom. Others had married and moved out of state but said they would gladly return to testify against the man who attacked them.

They never got the chance.

Police jubilation faded fast when it became clear that most of the rape cases could no longer be prosecuted because of the four-year statute of limitations in force when they occurred. In the remaining cases the evidence was not strong enough. MacLean, now thirty-five, a model prisoner, seeing the possibility of his early burglary parole wane, would admit to nothing.

He refused to talk to police, but Mike Gonzalez and Louise Vasquez went to the prison hoping for an interview with the man they had sought for so long. It was nearly nine years after their open letter to the Gentle Rapist won national attention.

When he heard their names, the man who had haunted them for a decade agreed to see them.

Face to face, at last.

"It was very dramatic," Mike said. "All those years . . . it was like dealing with a phantom."

Many of their theories seemed accurate. "He looked

like I thought he was going to look and he acted like I thought he would," Mike said. "He came from the kind of background I expected. And I expected he would be involved in all that police gear. I just didn't expect he would also be a jewel thief."

John Arthur MacLean, known to police as the Superthief, the Gentle Rapist, the Cape, the Bicycle Rapist, and the Coconut Grove Rapist, was cordial, but he never admitted a thing. He has never been charged with a rape. He will be released soon.

How sad for the victims, who still remember and wanted to testify, to be told that according to the law it's too late. "He outsmarted us all," Louise said.

There was one positive result: Former detective Patmore realized that once a cop, always a cop. He sold the country store, returned to Miami, and reclaimed his badge.

South Florida police are just as baffled by the Pillowcase Rapist. It is always something. The most sophisticated and intense manhunt in state history has brought an army of police no closer to collaring him today than they were in 1981.

Like the Gentle Rapist, he also started out with a different moniker: As the Alisian Lakes Rapist, he attacked six women in that West Dade apartment complex. The rapes were the secret of both the police and the management of the sprawling Alisian Lakes Apartments.

What women residents did not know *did* hurt them. The rapist easily pried open the sliding glass doors of their two-story townhouselike apartments. Had the women been warned, it would have been a simple matter for them to secure their doors, yet neither police nor management cautioned anyone after the rapes began. Chatty monthly newsletters from the management shared social news and recipes and admonished tenants about illegal parking.

Not a word about a rapist.

Curious tenants who occasionally questioned the presence of police cars and detectives were told it was nothing, just a family quarrel. Traumatized and terrified, the sixth victim called me. She and her neighbors had heard whispers, rumors of other rapes. I confronted the police. It was true.

Women were furious at the management. Police were irked at the publicity. Now the rapist knew they were looking for him, they grumbled, and if it drove him to rape elsewhere, their chances of catching him were reduced. They had been hoping to catch him in the act, even though the rambling Alisian Lakes complex was a maze almost impossible to surveil. In other words, police hoped to get lucky, using the women tenants as sitting ducks.

I argued that if the publicity forced management to beef up security, alerted the women who lived there, and spared other victims, I could live with that. And if the rapist was forced to stalk a new neighborhood, maybe it would be one where he did not have the advantage and would make a mistake. I could live with that, too.

Victim number six filed a million-dollar damage suit against the firm that owns the complex. She charged that they failed to protect or warn tenants out of economic self-interest and that she was raped as a result. Even after the attack on her, management still did not inform other tenants of the danger. "I feel like going door-to-door telling everybody myself, just for their own protection," she wept to me.

We still talk often. She speaks of little else: justice. An arrest, a trial, and a conviction might have helped her recapture the scattered fragments of her own life, but there has been no justice. She moves frequently and often calls police to say she has seen her attacker, or someone who could be him, in traffic, in restaurants, or on the street. Hospitalized by ulcers, distraught, and ill, she settled her civil suit on the eve of the trial, unable to relive the crime in a public courtroom, although she does so in private every day of her life.

At the height of the publicity, the management at long last took action. They quietly changed the name of the apartment complex, took down the sign, and replaced it with a new one. A TV reporter who lived there was embarrassed because he had been unaware of the rapes until he read about them in the *Herald*. He was even more embarrassed the night his news director called him out on a breaking story and his car was in the repair shop. The reporter telephoned for a taxi. The cab never came. He called again and was told the driver could not find the complex. The reporter kept repeating, "the Alisian Lakes Apartments, you can't miss it."

The driver never found it. Alisian Lakes no longer existed. That was the night they changed the sign.

No more rapes took place there, although police say the rapist may have telephoned the manager's office. The caller was angry, defiant. Publicity, he vowed, would not stop him.

It didn't. Four years later, a sergeant decided to go public with the Metro Rape Squad's most frustrating manhunt, the search for the Pillowcase Rapist: a young, white American who stalks career women in the world of comfortable upper-middle-class apartment complexes from South Miami to Deerfield Beach, across three counties. It is the same man who began at Alisian Lakes. Now he has raped forty-four women, probably more. Until recently his face had not been seen. It was always covered by a towel, a hood, a mask, or his own T-shirt. He might as well have been invisible.

His victims are an artist, an architect, an engineer, a model, a publicist, a student, a health-spa instructor, and several schoolteachers, nurses, airline attendants—all young, slender, and attractive. He almost always slips into the woman's apartment through an unlocked sliding glass door or an open window. Sometimes he returns weeks later, to scrawl an obscene greeting on a victim's bathroom mirror, to masturbate on her lingerie, or to rape her again.

In Coral Gables, the City Beautiful, he raped a woman in a fashionable palm-shaded apartment building, returned four weeks later, and attacked her neighbor. A newly hired security guard saw the second woman park her car and enter the building. The rapist was following, trailing about fifty feet behind. From a distance, he looked quite ordinary.

Police moved victims out of their apartments and replaced them with policewomen doubles. The rapist ignored the bait. As many as one hundred detectives at a time have worked on the case. It has cost taxpayers close to a million dollars and police untold thousands of hours, with more to come. Tens of thousands of apartment dwellers have been issued warnings at civic, tenants', and Citizens' Crime Watch meetings. More than six hundred men have been investigated and eliminated as suspects. State and FBI resources as well as computerized manhunters have joined the pursuit.

Law-enforcement agencies in Dade, Broward, and Palm Beach counties have met for hundreds of strategy sessions. They know a great deal about the man they are seeking:

In his mid-twenties to early thirties, he is five feet eight to eleven inches tall and about 170 pounds, with a slim, muscular build, and fair skin. His hair is dirty blond or medium brown, and he is tanned, neat, and clean. He dresses for prowling in blue jeans, a T-shirt, and sneakers, size 10½—and sometimes wears a black plastic digital watch. His hands are not those of a laborer, neither rough nor callused. The most curious detail is his blood type. It is common—type O—but with a rare subgrouping characteristic found in only one percent of the population. He rapes women on every day of the week, but most often on Wednesday, Thursday, and Friday. He has a problem maintaining an erection.

Sergeant David "Spiffy" Simmons has been tracking the rapist, on twenty-four-hour call, since 1983. A fastidious and dapper man with clear eyes and a clean, boyish look, Simmons, thirty-six, is known to his colleagues as Spiffy because of his well-tailored wardrobe. He is equally meticulous about the manhunt he is conducting.

Notable changes in the rapist's pattern concern him. At the outset, a victim would be awakened in the dark before dawn when a pillow was placed over her face. Then bolder, the rapist began taking chances, arriving earlier in the evening to stalk women still awake in their own homes.

He hid one woman's telephone in her refrigerator, where police found it later. He slices telephone cords with a knife that he also uses to torment his victim with minor wounds or to slash off her undergarments. He says little except to warn her to "shut up" and not to look at him. He sometimes forces her from room to room, spinning her about dizzily to disorient her. He always covers her face, with pillowcases, pillows, blankets, or bed linens, as well as hiding his own. The great care that he takes led Sergeant Simmons to suspect for a time that the face of the rapist might be marked by an unusual scar or deformity.

Women who dwell on upper floors should not feel safe. The rapist has scaled third- and fourth-floor balconies. A noise on her second-floor balcony startled one young woman. A sliding glass door was open, but the screen was locked. She saw a shadow. "You better get out of here!" she cried, "I'm calling the police!" As she ran to her telephone, the man on the balcony pulled a knife, slashed the screen, and dashed inside. He caught her before she could dial 911. She never saw his face. It was covered by his T-shirt.

Another woman was refinishing the woodwork in her apartment and left the sliding glass door open for circulation. When he grabbed her around the neck from behind, the can of brown paint stain in her hands flew into the air, splashing over her attacker.

After the rape, bound hand and foot, her face covered, she could hear him in her bathroom trying to scrub off the stains. Police checked every store that might sell thinner or paint remover. No one recalled a customer who could be the rapist.

The rapist used to bind his victims' wrists and ankles with pillowcases, but now he is more imaginative. He tied up one young woman with a satin sash from the formal gown she planned to wear at a wedding that weekend. Sometimes he playfully jingles her car keys and scrutinizes her driver's license. Later she will receive telephone calls from someone who does not speak. He steals cash and jewelry, saying that he needs the money. It may be true. To rape forty-four women, detectives believe he has stalked hundreds. They suspect it has become his career and that he devotes all of his time to his obsession.

"He's putting in a lot of hours," Simmons said. "He either parks in the complex and sits in his car for long periods of time, watching women as they arrive home, or he's hiding nearby." He may be out there, watching, every night. He asked one victim who her visitor "in the brown Pontiac" had been five days earlier.

Police questioned the usual suspects—the known sex offenders—and then utility company workers, mail carriers, cable TV installers, roofers, pool and lawn maintenance workers, and newspaper delivery men. They pored over tenant lists and even consulted the Boy Scouts of America, seeking a clue in the knots used to bind his victims.

They found none.

At the time of the initial story, police opened a twenty-four-hour hotline for tipsters. In the first few hours after the *Herald*'s Sunday edition landed on lawns with the hotline number, one hundred people called with clues. None bore fruit. It would not be that easy.

Simmons even employed the tactic hooted at when Mike and Louise thought of it more than a decade earlier. He invited the rapist to get in touch.

"I'd welcome a call from him, to open a dialogue," the detective said. "He's a troubled person. We might explore ways in which he can surrender peacefully and stop traumatizing others."

They think he did call once, his curiosity piqued by news of the rare and identifiable characteristic he carries in his blood. Two days after it was reported in the *Herald*, the police hot line rang at 7:26 P.M.

A man, talking fast, asked about the rapist's unusual blood, what it meant. "Tell me quick or I'll hang up," he warned. The cop who answered was asleep at the switch. He simply said that the information could not be released, and the caller hung up.

Scientists at the FBI Academy in Quantico, Virginia, produced a five-page psychological profile of the Pillowcase Rapist. You don't have to be an FBI scientist to deter-mine, as they did, that the man is a loner who fantasizes about sex. Or that the man we know to be tanned and muscular is a "body-conscious person who spends time in the sun and conditions himself through . . . hobbies such as weightlifting and jogging."

He probably rents and has neighbors who see him come and go at odd hours, the profile suggests. Since we know he is familiar with apartment complexes and that the rapes occur at odd hours, that takes no genius either. If he lives with anyone, the scientists say, it is a dominant woman—a mother, a wife, or an aunt—with whom he has problems.

That stress, the FBI theorizes, is in part responsible for the crimes, which he commits "to tell himself he is in fact 'a man,' and sexually adequate"—which of course he is not. He probably stole panties and was considered more nuisance than menace as a child, the report continues. He collected *Playboy*, then *Penthouse*, they say, dreamed of rape, and then slid over the threshold of his fantasies. His victims are not in "high-risk" occupations; nothing they do in their daily lives places them in particular jeopardy. They are selected because they fit his profile of preference. The report suggests there was a link to Alisian Lakes: that he lived, worked, or visited there. His employment record is "spotty." He may be a lifeguard, bellhop, or in some service-related field: a route man or taxi driver and an average employee at best. He probably drives an older model car with high mileage.

After a crime, he "is very smug" that he was not caught. A man overlooked in crowds, he wants very much to be noticed. He may have talked about his problems, without divulging their precise nature, to a friend, therapist, or minister.

That is the best the FBI could do. Most of us could have put together the same profile. It fits a lot of people.

Luckily, few of them are rapists.

Even IBM joined the manhunt. Experts from New York and Miami brainstormed for days with police computer operators and data processors. At a secret operations center established away from headquarters, detectives and computer experts studied charts, aerial pictures, maps, and plat photographs of neighborhoods stalked by the rapist.

They set up five data bases, a system similar to the one Georgia police used in the Atlanta child murders. The information included:

- Victim surveys: where they shop, work, have their hair done, their cars serviced, and whether they take part in exercise or aerobics classes.
- Thousands and thousands of names: witnesses, suspects, and occupant lists, cross-filed and cross-referenced. If a name appears more than once, police want to know why.
- All the leads and the results of each follow-up investigation: Each is numbered, and none can slip through the cracks, they say. The computer should tell detectives, for example, if a car description, license tag number, or partial tag number ever appeared before in the investigation.

- All the case documents: thousands and thousands of pages fed into the system by data processing employees working overtime.
- Details on more than ten thousand field interrogation cards: reporting police contact with suspicious persons or vehicles.

Volumes of case files that stretch the length of two desks were entered into a system that can scan the equivalent of the Library of Congress for a specific word, phrase, name, or piece of information within seconds. It can spit out instantly the names of all suspects with a certain description, accent, or characteristic.

It has all produced—nothing. The rapist remains an elusive enigma. His luck has got to run out, Simmons insists. "It's the law of averages."

The failed manhunt did yield unexpected bonuses. One was the long-sought A/C Rapist. He stalked apartment dwellers in 1980–81, posing as an air-conditioning repairman sent by the management. Oddly enough, he had regressed from rapist to exhibitionist. Officers caught him sprinting naked through an apartment complex after residents complained of a flasher. His aging brown Monte Carlo was backed into a space for a quick getaway, with the ignition key on the left rear tire.

The cops suspected he might be the Pillowcase Rapist. He insisted he was only an exhibitionist who preyed on walking women. He would park ahead of them, strip off his jogging shorts, and crouch in ambush. "Some screamed bloody murder," he told the detectives, others just turned away; one, he said, "invited me into her apartment." If a woman screamed loud enough, he jumped into his car and drove away naked.

At the time of his arrest, he lived at the complex that was formerly the Alisian Lakes—with a woman. He had cautioned her about the Pillowcase Rapist. Not only that, his brother lived in another apartment house visited by the rapist. The suspect was even the correct blood type, minus the rare subgrouping. He was not the Pillowcase Rapist, but something about his face sent the detectives digging into old files. An L-shaped scar on his neck and a pockmark above his left eyebrow were identical to those in a police artist's sketch of the A/C Rapist, drawn four years earlier. Questioned, he confessed that five times he had clipped a leather tool set to his belt and knocked on doors between 8:15 A.M. and 5:00 P.M., posing as an air-conditioning repairman. He attacked women he found at home alone.

After raping a fifteen-year-old, he considered suicide but reverted instead to exposing himself. Both he and the Pillowcase Rapist had stalked young women in some of the same complexes since 1981. Both roamed about on foot, lurking in laundry rooms and hallways. It is almost certain that they passed in the night. Maybe they even bumped into each other.

What seemed to be a real break in the case came when an ex-cop in trouble claimed to be the Pillowcase Rapist. I had written about this cop before; in 1982, he was sent to investigate a loud music complaint at a party and shot the host to death. The noise complaint was phony, called in by a relative angry at not being invited to the party, a backyard family barbecue.

The cop was fired. Miami's police chief said it was all a mistake. The cop should have been fired sooner, after a prior shooting incident; it was an oversight that no one had dismissed him. Now this young ex-cop was in new difficulty. He had killed again; this time it was his girlfriend. Cops who arrested him on the murder charge found a bloodstained pillowcase and a black hood in his car. They began to look harder at this suspect.

After his badge was yanked for killing the party host, he had gone to work as a security guard at a big oceanfront Miami Beach hotel. He bragged to a co-worker there that he was the Pillowcase Rapist, South Florida's most-wanted fugitive. The co-worker did not report it to police.

The ex-cop had also told his sweetheart, the girl he later killed, that he was the Pillowcase Rapist. When she didn't believe him, he "proved" it by scaling a balcony, opening a sliding glass door, and appearing at her bedside wearing a Halloween skeleton costume. Terrified, she now believed him and told the secret to friends. But nobody told police. One night he showed up at his sweetheart's apartment, brushed by her roommate, took a policeman's stance in the bedroom doorway, and shot her five times.

Simmons interviewed the jailed ex-cop at length: five days of cat-and-mouse, that old game-playing love of intrigue. During questioning the prisoner would reach a crucial point, stop himself, and smile furtively. Slyly, he would go into detail—but never quite specific enough detail.

He did say he had never really injured any of his victims and had made it a point to tie the knots loosely so they could free themselves. He said he often drove by the crime scenes when Simmons and his men were still there, to gloat at the stupidity of the police, especially Miami police for firing him. He wanted to show them how smart he was.

His story was plausible. He fit the rapist's general physical description. He was agile enough and even had a motive. He raped, he said, as a result of the stress built up when he was a police officer. He accused superiors of pressuring him and the cops he worked with of skimming confiscated drugs and stealing money from drunk drivers. It wasn't fair, he said bitterly, that they all still wore uniforms and he had been fired.

Smirking, he tantalized Simmons and his partners, saying "you guys have overlooked one important detail in all the cases. If you ever find out what it is, you'll be able to bury me."

The quickest way to find out if this man really was the Pillowcase Rapist, of course, was a blood test. He agreed to submit but kept stalling. He loved the attention, swaggering from his cell for daily meetings with detectives. Simmons worked three days on just five hours' sleep.

Employment records showed the suspect logged in on his guard job at the hotel, or on duty as a police officer at the time of nine of the rapes. But—perhaps he could have slipped away.

What disturbed me, however, was that all the victims said the rapist has no accent. The ex-cop was born in

Puerto Rico, and I had read in his police personnel file that he rated poorly in evaluations because of an apparent inability to communicate with English-speaking citizens.

The blood test was the key. He continued to play coy, until exasperated detectives went to a judge who gave them the authority to take blood and saliva from the suspect—by force if necessary. A jail nurse drew a blood specimen from his arm and gave him a wad of cotton to chew on. The test tube of blood and the cotton went to the crime lab. A serologist, summoned on his day off, performed the tests.

Within minutes he knew that the ex-cop's blood is type O—like the rapist and like half the male population.

He knew after thirty minutes that the ex-cop is an O secretor, which means that the type can be discerned in his body fluids, such as saliva and perspiration. Eighty percent of the people with type O are secretors. The rapist is one of them.

The detectives' pulses quickened. The more sophisticated tests that break down subgroupings take three hours. We all waited. At long last, word came from the lab: The ex-cop's blood did not have the same rare characteristics present in the blood of the Pillowcase Rapist.

He had obviously pulled the scam hoping to build a strong insanity defense in the murder, police said. I suspect it was also wishful thinking. He delighted in the limelight; rather than just a security guard who killed a girlfriend, he wanted the braggadocio role of Florida's most-wanted sex criminal.

His mother called me later that day, hysterically begging for help, claiming that her son had sworn to her in tears that he was innocent of everything. Not only was he framed for the murder, now detectives were trying to blame him for the rapes. I tried to explain to her that the murder was eye-witnessed and that the detectives were proving—despite his own claims—that her son was *not* the rapist.

People had always picked on her boy, she said, insisting that her son never had mental problems. She pointed out that when he was hired, not so long ago, by the Miami Police Department, he passed all the psychological tests they gave him.

It was a true and sobering thought. So is the number of sex offenders unmasked when they surfaced as suspects in this case. Each was a deviate, but not the right one.

A young woman in a complex where the rapist has twice struck saw a man crouched on her second-floor balcony watching her undress. Coolly, she switched off her light and dialed 911. He was still masturbating when police arrived. College-educated, twenty-four, the manager of a popular restaurant, he lived in the complex and fit the description. Even his shoe size was correct. He had moved to Miami in May 1981, the month the Pillowcase Rapist first struck. The woman he was watching fit the profile of victims.

He looked good, and he admitted to climbing onto the same balcony to watch her disrobe four times in the past two weeks and to peeping in the windows of a dozen other women. But he denied being the rapist. The serologist was called out in the middle of the night. Test results proved the peeper was not the Pillowcase Rapist.

A real break came when the rapist showed his face for the first time. On Tuesday, February 11, 1986, a frightened rape victim, a thirty-six-year-old business executive, tricked him into exposing what he had always so carefully hidden.

Something, more an instinct than a sound or a movement, woke her at 12:45 A.M. A man was standing quietly in her bedroom, gazing out a window. She screamed, startling the rapist, who had not yet covered his face. He lunged onto her bed, slammed a pillow over her head, and vowed to kill her if she did not obey.

He ordered her not to look at him. Thinking fast, she mumbled that she is as "blind as a bat" without her glasses. He kept warning her. She pointed to her spectacles on the night table. She kept repeating that she could not see without them and acted the part, blinking and peering blindly about. Her performance convinced him. He did not cover her face—or his own.

She was lying. She could see him just fine. Lighting outside her window enabled her to study his features during the ten- or fifteen-minute ordeal. He tied her up and fled with her purse. She heard him run and a car door slam. He drove away.

She was victim number forty-four.

At her office the next day, she received a telephone call. "I want to make love to you again," the caller said. Stunned, she hung up. Police believe it was the rapist.

After years of frustration, this was a major development for the detectives; the victim worked with police artist John Valor to reproduce the face of the rapist. It was bland and unremarkable. It would become one of the best-known faces in Florida. The police sketch was reproduced on half a million fliers. Bag boys stuffed tens of thousands into supermarket sacks. Posters were tacked up in stores, shopping areas, and malls. Youth groups ranging from juvenile delinquents performing penance to high school service-club volunteers helped distribute them. Printers donated their services. It was a community effort.

The rapist resembles many men. A number of people tipped police to a waiter at a well-known restaurant. Wives brought in their husbands, and girls brought in their boyfriends, all dead-ringers for the suspect. The embarrassed men were all cooperative, if for no other reason than to assure their loved ones of their innocence. A Broward County woman called me, convinced that the rapist was a man she had lived with for two years. She sounded as if she had a strong foundation for her suspicions. And she seemed genuinely anguished, reluctant at first to even divulge the man's name. I asked questions and took notes—until she confided something else in a tearful whisper. Not only was her former lover the Pillowcase Rapist, he was also the killer who put the cyanide in the Tylenol capsules.

Even Sergeant Simmons's former fifth-grade teacher came forward. She had no suspect to offer, but recalled fondly that the veteran detective was always one of her "favorite students," a little boy who could play rough-

and-tumble on the playground but still come back to class neat and clean. He was "Spiffy," even then.

Jail and prison inmates also wrote and called Simmons with leads. Half a dozen psychics went into trances and offered their help. Police did not lack suspects. The sketch generated four hundred leads.

None led to the right man.

The wanted poster was taken a step further when police commissioned a well-known sculptor to create a life-size bust of the Pillowcase Rapist. They found Tony Lopez in the yellow pages of the Miami telephone book. They liked his ad. Among Lopez's distinguished works are the Torch of Friendship in Bayfront Park, a sculpture of Cuban General Antonio Maceo y Grajeles in Little Havana and the bust of Andrew Jackson at Miami's Jackson High School. This was the artist's first rapist.

The victim agreed to assist, and as the face of her attacker began to emerge from red clay, she fled the sculptor's studio in tears.

The bust was unveiled with great fanfare. Police emphasized that in no way did they intend to glorify the rapist. They simply felt it in the public interest to present his face in three dimensions, in the hope that someone would recognize it.

What followed was inevitable: the Pillowcase Rapist T-shirt. WANTED: PILLOWCASE RAPIST is lettered across the chest. Below that are four faces of the rapist: the police sketch with a small mustache, a version that is clean-shaven, one that is bearded, and the fourth—a hooded figure with a pillowcase over his head.

The businessman selling them called it public service. The wearers would be walking wanted posters, thereby aiding in the manhunt, he said. The price: six dollars.

Despite all the excitement, the rapist remained unidentified. Perhaps the likeness is not a good one, and the image now seared into the minds of South Floridians bears little real resemblance to the rapist. The room was dark. The woman was not wearing her glasses. But even so, it is astonishing that he remains unknown. The man has prowled South Florida for at least six years.

Someone who knows him must suspect.

Why hasn't he been turned in?

I think he has been—that his name is there, somewhere, in those thousands of calls, thousands of leads compiled by police, that he has been overlooked, checked out, passed over somehow. If so, we will not know until he is caught. That is how it was in New York, with the Son of Sam. Once the killer was arrested on a fluke, because of a parking ticket, it was discovered that his name did indeed appear in the gigantic police tip file on the case. Several good citizens had dutifully reported their suspicions, that David Berkowitz was the Son of Sam—and he was. But their tips were lost in the shuffle, overwhelmed, drowned in the sea of information on thousands of other, more likely suspects.

Publicity does not always work. It hasn't in this case. Not yet. Most of the time it does. And perhaps it has, in one respect. It appears at this writing that the Pillowcase Rapist has not struck since he attacked the quick-witted woman—victim number forty-four—who tricked him into showing his face. Perhaps that error panicked him into lying low, seeing a shrink, or joining group therapy.

Maybe he is in jail for some other crime, or dead, a suicide, or hit by a truck.

Maybe the sight of his own face staring out from every storefront drove him into relocating, to live out his dark fantasies in some other city.

If drugs are the answer, what's the question?
Anonymous graffito

EIGHT
Drugs

Miami is a city tainted by the illegal drug trade and awash in its riches. The product tumbles in jettisoned bales and bundles from the sky. It washes ashore on dawn-streaked beaches. It is smuggled in by air and sea and in human bodies. Illicit cargo is flown boldly over and under and through the radar. When I lived on a man-made island three minutes from downtown Miami, the soft and silent nights came alive with the sounds of low-flying planes, sudden splashes in a velvet bay, and the powerful roar of high-speed Cigarette power boats. The highs, the wealth, the adventure—they make people crazy. There is no effective way to patrol South Florida's thousands of miles of coastline, airspace, and internal waterways. Many enforcers quit trying and switch sides. Drugs have made criminals out of police, big businessmen, and politicians alike. Drugs are the great corrupter, and Miami's largest growth industry.

Since I began covering crime—in just a generation— the drug scene has burgeoned from kids jailed on felony charges for possessing a joint to major cartels and billions of dollars. The metamorphosis and its sweeping panorama of greed, self-indulgence, and corruption is almost too vast for the mind to grasp. Dizzying cycles have swept us from the internecine cocaine wars, the invasions of Colombian "cocaine cowboys," the Cuban connections, and the body-packers, to the crack and get-off houses that thrive on inner-city blocks and the cocaine labs that periodically explode in suburban neighborhoods.

The stories about drugs in Miami are also larger than life. So many are true that even the myth of the dead baby has become accepted as modern Miami-American folklore.

Let's get this straight right here and now: There is no cocaine-stuffed dead baby, at least at this writing.

The dead baby resurfaces frequently, reported as fact in otherwise responsible and prestigious—and some not so responsible and prestigious—publications. It has appeared on the front page of *The Washington Post,* in *Life* magazine, and in the *National Enquirer*. The story, with minor variations, is that an alert customs official, or airlines employee on a Colombia–Miami flight, noticed that a baby in the arms of a woman passenger did not look well. Closer scrutiny revealed that the baby was dead and its body stuffed with high-grade cocaine in an attempt to smuggle the drug into this country.

The dead baby is reported at least once a year. Each time, I am one of the many reporters assigned to check it out. It is fiction. It did not happen. I have laid the dead baby to rest so often that I can now see its poor little pasty face in my mind's eye.

The dead baby will not die. But men do.

They are called mules, the human pack animals of the drug trade. They force down last meals worth fifty thousand dollars or so—meals that kill them. In the last, terrible moments of their lives, they learn something that smart women already knew: Condoms can break, they can leak, they can get you in a lot of trouble. In their cases, it is fatal.

One body-packer died in a Miami Beach hotel room. In his stomach was a pound of cocaine, in eighty-two double-wrapped condoms. Fourteen had ruptured. Leaking cocaine paralyzes the intestinal tract and prevents the packets from passing through the digestive system. Surgery is the only answer. In an attempt to expel his deadly cargo, this man had purchased at a nearby drug store two enemas, an entire shelf of laxatives, and a package of pitted prunes.

Others die when their balloons burst. There were 110 brightly colored plastic balloons—green, pink, blue, and orange—in the intestines of one man when he arrived at the morgue. Surprise, surprise, for the medical examiners who conducted the first few such autopsies. Later it became routine.

Body-packers usually swallow the cocaine-loaded condoms or balloons, washing them down with a quart or so of milk, just before boarding a flight to Miami. Some make it; others collapse before they even check through customs, or they die in lonely hotel rooms with a fortune they can't touch in their gut. I wonder what the fast-lane crowd would say if they knew how some of the stuff they snort came here from Colombia.

As a rookie reporter, drugs meant heroin: covering the deaths of young people, curled up in dirty bathrooms with needles still stuck in their arms. Now, we see professionals—lawyers and businessmen—who rampage violently in the streets, often naked, as they experience the febrile death of cocaine intoxication. Their body temperatures skyrocket, still registering at the 107-degree mark on rectal thermometers hours after they arrive at the morgue. They are joined there by the victims of more outright drug killings, sometimes six people at a time gunned down in a house or apartment, or three or four bodies found stacked in a car trunk. Deranged dopers suffering from cocaine paranoia will turn on anybody: friends and loved ones, each other, themselves.

Profit-conscious drug traffickers—ruthless businessmen—will coldly kill a stranger, or even innocent picnickers, who happen upon something they should not have seen. They are a new breed of cruel and merciless criminals. The Mafia got bad press, but by comparison they were somewhat circumspect and kept within certain unwritten guidelines when disposing of an associate: Usually, they did not molest the victim's wife and family or kill off innocent people.

But many Miami drug traffickers, especially the initial wave of Colombian cocaine cowboys, showed little finesse. It is not surprising; one day they were thundering on horseback through the wild mountains of their own backward country. Next day they were thundering through city streets, turned loose in Miami behind the wheels of an expensive Audi or Mercedes, armed with high-powered weaponry, killing anybody or anything in their way.

Some of the Rastafarians, a Jamaican religious sect into ganja and guns, show the same lack of discrimination. When the shooting starts, everybody is a target. If the Avon lady rings the doorbell, she goes too. If they want to murder a man who flees into a crowded shopping center, they don't wait to catch him later in private, they go in shooting, never mind who might step in the way.

Law-enforcement agencies announce record-breaking seizures of vast illegal shipments so often now that it no longer even seems newsworthy to report the kilos, pounds, tons, truckloads, and shiploads confiscated. It is almost meaningless. There is always more where that came from—lots more.

It was not that way when I first joined the *Herald,* in the days when marijuana by the pound was still news. That is when I went on my first drug raid and learned to be cautious about sharing information with co-workers. A new police chief was hired in Opa-Locka, a small northwest Dade city of minarets and streets with exotic names out of *The Arabian Nights.* The chief was a former federal narc who had worked in New York City, and he confided to me that the film *The French Connection* was based on his undercover exploits. Two other former narcs have confided the same thing since, but I was duly impressed at the time.

Opa-Locka, with its Sharazad Boulevard and Ali Baba Avenue, is small-time compared to New York City. It didn't have much of a drug problem then, but what there was, the chief vowed to clean up. He suspected drugs were being used and sold at a neighborhood poolroom and invited me to join the raiding party. I told the night-slot editor, and he assigned a curly-haired young intern named Herb to monitor the police radios and pay special attention to that channel. Herb would notify the city desk if a shooting went down or anything happened to make it into a bigger story.

I went out there with the chief and his men, and we all crouched in the bushes, watching the poolroom, waiting for the suspects to arrive. Back at the office, Herb kept his ear to the radio. He heard nothing. New on the job, he feared that somehow he had missed it. So he began calling the Opa-Locka police, to ask if they had raided the poolroom yet. Police are somewhat paranoid about that sort of thing. They didn't know who he was, and they wouldn't tell him a thing. Meanwhile we were still hiding in the bushes, waiting, watching, and swatting mosquitoes. Herb got desperate. He was afraid he had missed it, so he called the poolroom—and asked if the police had arrived yet.

We were still crouched in the bushes, when suddenly, people began to barrel out of the pool hall. They came out the doors and windows and scattered in every direction. From inside came the sounds of toilets flushing, again and again. The chief and his men moved in fast when they realized what was happening. They found small bags of narcotics on the floor, but they couldn't arrest anybody because they couldn't prove who dropped it.

The police never did find out how they made us. But I asked Herb, and he confessed.

Less than a decade later, in July 1979, Miami was the battlefield in a cocaine war, and the police had a whole lot more than poolrooms to worry about. A major skirmish took place when cocaine cowboys in an armored "war wagon" invaded the Dadeland Mall, the county's biggest and busiest shopping center, at midday.

Women and children ran for cover as high-powered submachine-gun slugs shattered plate glass, slammed into parked cars, and spilled gasoline from riddled fuel tanks into the parking lot.

A teenage stockboy eating his lunch in a liquor-store backroom heard an odd sound, stepped out, and saw a man spraying the store with a submachine gun. The boy dove under the counter and scrambled to the front door on hands and knees. He ran into the parking lot seeking cover; the killers pursued him, still shooting. The teenager tried to hide under parked cars, screaming, "Why are they shooting at me? I didn't do anything!"

Yet the gunmen pursued him, firing out a window of their customized armored van, finally wounding him in the ankle. They were trying to kill him. A clerk inside the store had been hit in the shoulder and chest.

People who ran out of a nearby restaurant to see what

was happening tried to run back in, but the terrified proprietors had locked the door. Thirty people took refuge in a beauty shop. A shopper who had been walking to his parked car ran in panic, saying a bullet whizzed by his ear so fast "that I could hear it."

Two shoppers were killed and two store employees wounded by the gunmen who got away. The men who were killed had parked their white Mercedes and stepped into the liquor store to buy some Chivas Regal. The first was a kingpin in one of the five Colombian narcotics rings then operating in Dade. The other was his bodyguard. Their assassins were seeking revenge for the murder of another ring's leader.

The store was left with the liquor bottles all smashed, bullet holes in the ceilings, in the walls, and in cases of wine and whiskey. The two dead men were riddled. "They looked like Swiss cheese," said Dr. Charles Diggs, a medical examiner. "I started counting bullet holes in one of them—and gave up. I have never seen a shoot-out like this in my life. This is another Chicago."

The gunmen who escaped the Dadeland shoot-out were part of the throwaway Dixie-cup generation. They not only threw down their weapons, discarding them when they were empty, they also abandoned their new armored Ford step-van. To them expensive equipment was as expendable as people.

The van had only 108 miles on the odometer. Its contents astonished and sobered police, who were undoubtedly imagining what could have occurred had any of them attempted to pull over the driver for a traffic violation. It had gun ports, one-way glass, and HAPPY TIME COMPLETE PARTY SUPPLY lettered on both sides. It also had two fuel tanks and was equipped with eight bullet-proof vests, more than a dozen guns, including submachine guns, silencer-equipped automatics, and thousands of rounds of ammunition, including deadly, homemade shotgun shells fashioned from ball bearings.

The van bore the emblem of the automobile dealer who had sold it. I called him as soon as I got back to the newsroom from the mess at the mall. The friendly manager, who had not yet been contacted by police, said that the customizing had not been done by his dealership. "Hell, no," he said, "we're not in the armament business. They didn't tell me they were going to have it customized." He obligingly gave me the name and address of the Colombian who had paid cash for the van.

I rushed right out to find the war wagon's owner. An editor stopped me, his face serious. "This could be dangerous," he warned. "Don't go alone. You need protection, take a photographer."

He called photo and asked them to have a photographer meet me downstairs at once. As I fidgeted impatiently, a summer intern arrived on the run—ponytail bouncing. The delicately boned eighty-five-pound college girl who stood about five feet tall did not laugh when I explained to her why I thought this was very funny. The situation did not strike her as humorous at all. We found the right building, the right apartment, and listened warily at the door. There was movement inside. We knocked, standing prudently on either side of the door instead of directly in front of it. No one opened fire. I looked at our photographer as the door swung open. Holding her breath, her eyes were squeezed shut, her camera forgotten. A pretty young blonde opened the door. She wore a swim suit, had a towel over her shoulder, and was on her way to the pool. She had just moved in and did not know the former occupant.

The landlady gave us the forwarding address of the man who bought the war wagon: Dade County Jail. He had been in jail for weeks on rape and kidnap charges along with gun and immigration violations. He had obviously purchased the van for someone else.

No one has ever been charged with the Dadeland shootings.

That wild era slowed to a simmer as the cocaine cowboys began to become aware of public relations and the inconvenience caused them by publicity. The spotlight is focused now on the more recent phenomena of crack houses. They are killers; their real victims are not the rich or the famous or the talented who succumb to drugs. I don't feel sorry for them at all; they make their choice and they have to live—or die—with it. Nobody forced them to use cocaine. The people who wrench my heart are the low-income mothers, the children, the disabled, and the elderly, who live in ghetto buildings converted to crack houses by greedy pushers and landlords. And people like Louis, who was crying, wandering in the lobby of the Miami police headquarters when I first saw him.

A bright young black man, he had a future once; now

tears mingled with the perspiration that streaked his face and his eyes were red-rimmed. He had spent the past several days in a crack house. Out of money, drained of all hope, he wanted desperately to break the cycle somehow, to save himself and others. With nowhere else to turn, he went to Miami police headquarters. The cops at the front desk were sympathetic but could not help him. Rehabilitation programs are expensive and overcrowded.

There are thousands like Louis.

Crack houses stay full twenty-four hours a day. The centerpiece is a mirror, taped off in sections of varying size, marked $5, $10, $15, $20, and $25. The proprietors can sell a mirror load of cocaine for $5,000 to $6,000 in an hour or so.

Any child old enough to talk can direct you to the crack house in his building or on his block. Preschoolers run with warnings if they spot a police car in the neighborhood. The houses, usually just one-bedroom apartments, are crowded. You tap once on the door. Inside, there is a gate of ornamental iron. The operators carry walkie-talkies and frisk you, just like the police. There is usually a line waiting, like a grocery store. One customer uses a pipe, the next picks it up and sucks on it. It might be a prostitute who just turned a trick to pay for this. You don't know if he or she has AIDS or herpes or hepatitis. On some blocks there are four houses. A lot of people are carrying guns. Ask seven or eight customers at any free-base house and they can each tell you where there are fifteen other houses. It's so easy. It's money.

"There is poison in me," Louis said, the first time we

met. A native Miamian, he is the fifth of twelve children, from a family that did not drink or smoke. "My mother sheltered us a lot," he says. "A lot of parents just turn their kids loose. My mother wasn't like that. As a kid I said, 'Not me, no way to get me dependent on drugs.' You are the person in control. When I was thirteen or fourteen I had surgery on a kidney, they gave me an anesthetic to put me to sleep. I tried to fight it, I didn't want drugs. I wouldn't shoot a needle in my arm. Liquor or beer, I never had a taste for it. Eggnog in the house at Christmastime, that was it."

His life changed after an encounter with a childhood friend he had not seen in years. The man can neither read nor write, yet he had prospered. He was wearing expensive clothes and jewelry and owns both a Jaguar and a Mercedes. "The man is illiterate. I can read and write and finished two years of college," says Louis, who is married, with five children.

The man offered him a job and a chance to share his secret of success:

He showed me what cocaine was, how to stretch it, how to make free-base coke. He was a smuggler and a dealer, and he urged me to try it so I could recognize quality stuff from garbage. That was my mistake. It sexually aroused me. I've always been shy, but it made me know what to say to the ladies. I was a Don Juan. A quarter-piece of cocaine, and you get a woman and a five-dollar room for an hour.

When you run with free-base people, you lie, you

cheat. It's a terrible world. You see a lot of guns flashing. You have to expose yourself. You see the terror. It's depressing. Some coke out there is cut with speed—you know it when it starts to affect your nerves. You get all jittery. It makes you feel like a different person, sensations you never had. It has me very paranoid.

I don't know anymore where I fit in in this world. I have five kids. Most of my wife's relatives are in the drug business. She sees them with expensive houses and cars, and she pressures me. She keeps threatening to leave me. People I went to school with are quick successes. They make a lot of money. People see this, they want to have something for themselves in life too. They work legitimate jobs forty hours a week, they don't make much money. They see it going for taxes, the cost of living is so high, they got kids to feed. By the time you get through paying bills and buying kids' shoes, day in and day out, you get frustrated, especially if you watch TV. You see people on there with new cars, fancy this, fancy that. Your wives see it on TV. They start fantasizing. "Why can't my husband be like these guys?" They see *Lifestyles of the Rich and Famous*. When they see that they really go crazy to be like those people on *Dallas* and *Dynasty*, those soap operas you see on TV. Everybody wants to be Superfly.

With my brother and sister-in-law and other relatives—alcohol used to be the sociable thing. Now they're free-basing—all of them. And their house is a shambles, the living room and the bathrooms are dirty. My brother is a diabetic and takes insulin shots, and he's free-basing on a regular basis.

Louis worked at a state hospital as a behavior specialist, and he is a talented musician. His intelligence makes what is happening to him and the people around him more painful.

Education opens things up to you. The ones without any education can't see anything beyond the ghetto. They go ahead and die. They die with a pipe in their mouth. You walk into a free-base house, there are bars on the windows. If you see a white face on the outside, you suspect it's a police officer or an informant. Inside, you see them pick up a submachine gun. I've seen old guys and girls so young in the base houses . . . This morning I saw a girl so young that her breasts were not fully developed.

People in the black community are treating each other dirty and nasty because of cocaine. Three guys were walking down the street the other day, kind of high, making a lot of noise. The guy in the middle, he fell in the street. They started slapping him and dragging him, trying to make him walk. One said, "I'm going to call an ambulance!" and ran. The other one ran after him, hit him, and took the phone and wouldn't let him call.

A white guy named Michael, me, and this girl went to buy at this house where they have bigger pieces, better protection. In a trash pile outside, I saw something move. I looked, and a guy was lying in the trash pile, foaming at the mouth. People were standing around watching. My friend got hysterical and started taking boxes off the guy. My friend started screaming and a crowd gathered, but nobody called or reached down to help him. They were just looking. If somebody has a convulsion in one of these houses they carry him out and throw him in the trash.

I have a beautiful thirteen-month-old daughter, I don't ever want her to know her father was on this stuff . . . They say it takes five days to get it out of your system. I did stop, the bills were paid and I was doing fine. But one day I had ten or twenty dollars and went back, it turns to forty, a hundred, three hundred dollars. It turns into a whole day. You are supposed to pick your wife up at six o'clock. You call her and say you have a flat tire. It turns into a lie. Then I see all these sales coming on TV, wishing I could buy things for my daughter, and it's too late, I gave it all to the dope man.

I got depressed and saw the 1-800-COCAINE number on TV. I listen to Don Johnson on TV about drugs. Whoever wrote that script knows it's true. It never works out. They say in the free-base house to come "suck on the devil's dick." It's true. It's terrible. It's a good way to destroy America. There is nothing going on in the black community but drugs.

On my last job, I was doing drugs and taking days off. It caused me to lose the job; I wanted to get high more than I wanted to work. Depression, mood changes, it takes the strength from your body, it takes the ambition out of you, except thinking what you can do to get more. You go in a normal person, and you come out thinking you will do anything to get some more, go as far as killing somebody. It gives you courage where you didn't have courage before. It takes the fear away. You're not afraid of being arrested. You're not afraid of dying. Lord, how close I am. It's slowly creeping everywhere. It's a booming business.

The last time I spoke to Louis, he wanted money for a tip that photographers could catch a national sports star in a free-base house he had just left. I told him we didn't pay for news tips. He said he was going to call *Sports Illustrated*.

When I hear talk about free-basing, I think of Emilio. I don't even know if he is still alive. The last time he called, he did not sound like himself. He said he had been free-basing cocaine for seventeen days straight. Then loud voices and the thumps and crashes of a struggle erupted in the background. I heard somebody yell, "Get the gun!" and Emilio hung up abruptly.

That was our last contact, more than a year ago. His future sounded uncertain. But Emilio has been in tough spots before, and he is always a survivor.

If something serious did happen to him—if he was hurt, dead, or in prison—I probably would not know, even if it made the front pages. His name has been changed so many times, for undercover work and for his protection, that I could easily read about him in the newspaper and never know it was him. Unless, of course, I recognized his distinctive style, that certain panache. The government surely wouldn't tell me. It would embarrass them.

Emilio is dashing, spirited, and flamboyant—and too dangerous to stand next to in public. His last call probably came from Virginia or Washington, D.C., the last place he was relocated to under the federal witness protection plan.

His life and times stretch the imagination, and I know only a small part of the big picture. At fifteen, he fought in the Sierra Maestra mountains at the side of Fidel Castro. After the revolution came disillusionment and a falling out. He fled a Cuban jail, flew to this country, and joined the army, expecting an early return to his homeland. At the time of the 1962 missile crisis, he and a fellow exile feared that President Kennedy had struck a deal with Nikita Khrushchev at the expense of a free Cuba. They protested by going AWOL and fleeing to Miami to try to recruit volunteers for a Cuban invasion of their own. When the effort failed, they returned to their army base and surrendered. Emilio was discharged for "hardship" reasons after thirty-seven days in solitary confinement.

He became a dope peddler quite by accident. His old army buddy resurfaced after a few years and urged him to quit his factory job to join him in drug trafficking. The profits were to be used to buy guns and train soldiers for the liberation of Cuba. A passionate patriot, Emilio embraced the effort enthusiastically. Like so many similar schemes, it was a farce. There was nothing for Cuba. The conspirators got fat, buying expensive houses, suits, and cars.

Emilio was disillusioned again—but not enough to throw away his chance to get rich. When he did throw it away, it was for love. The romance was with the wife of an accomplice; they eventually married, and he was forced out of the business. He continued to traffic in drugs on his own, vowing privately, he said, to inform on the others "and put them all in jail," if he was ever caught.

He was, and he did.

The feds busted him in New York with a kilo and a half of heroin. He pleaded guilty, told them everything, and went to work for them as a flashy, free-spending drug-world spy. He did it, as he does everything, with exuberance and energy. After he made several excellent cases for the government, the agent with whom he worked told Emilio, who had a wife and children, that he was free of the bargain and could go his own way. But Emilio loved working for the government—it fed his own wacky sense of patriotism. He hit it off with another Drug Enforcement Administration agent, and they began to work together. But government money was tight, and the DEA paid him only a few hundred dollars a month. In order to cover the major deficit in his household income, Emilio moonlighted by committing drug rip-offs. The robberies were patriotic, he insists, because he only robbed people who wished to buy drugs.

He says he never told the agents with whom he worked about his moonlighting. If they did not suspect, they soon found out—the hard way. Emilio and an accomplice robbed two would-be drug buyers of $11,500 one spring day. It did not go down as easily as they expected. The victims were unexpectedly desperate as they struggled for their money. Both sides started shooting. It ended in a running gun battle through South Miami, with bullets shattering store windows as passers-by ducked for cover. Emilio and his partner barely escaped, their red Cadillac riddled with bullets. They split the cash and parted. The story of the gun battle hit the front page of *The Miami Herald* the next morning. Emilio was stunned.

The men he robbed were federal narcotics agents.

He called the DEA at once to apologize profusely. He offered to pay back the money. It would have to be in installments, since his partner had already departed with half. He also pointed out, somewhat indignantly, that the DEA was to blame for the entire unfortunate incident. The agents he worked with should have told him that their colleagues had a deal in progress. Had he known they were federal agents, he swears, he would never have taken their money and tried to shoot them. He was never prosecuted, and the feds quietly accepted his offer of restitution. They even gave him receipts, signed by a DEA supervisor, and stamped PARTIAL RETURN OF FUNDS SEIZED FROM U.S. AGENTS.

They could not afford to hold a grudge. Emilio's natural-born street-smarts, combined with a free-wheeling and gregarious charm, made him the best they had. His work led to hundreds of arrests and huge seizures of cocaine and heroin in New York, California,

Mexico, and Miami. He testified in a number of cases; in many others the feds never surfaced him. He was their pride and joy. He even foiled an alleged plot to kidnap Richard Nixon's pal C. G. "Bebe" Rebozo. The plan, hatched by a group of radical exiles, was to snatch Rebozo off his yacht at sea and hold him captive in a waterfront home for $5 million in ransom. Emilio reported it to the U.S. Marshal's Service.

When drug-world figures plotted to kill him, the feds relocated Emilio to Orlando on the witness protection plan. The move was unfortunate. Some of his government-shipped furniture vanished forever. His wife and children were unhappy. They were lonesome. They bounced back to Miami, where the action is, making the government extremely nervous.

A car crash during a DEA chase in California had left Emilio with a painfully herniated disc. Workmen's compensation was denied him on the grounds that undercover drug informants are not covered. He began to suspect that, deeply in debt, in pain, and in need of back surgery, he was about to be abandoned by the government. He was feuding with the feds when we met. He gave me a photo of himself in happier days, grinning behind a DEA supervisor's desk, flanked by flags and stacked high with sacks of seized cocaine. I checked him out. He was everything he said he was.

"If he gets killed, we're stuck with it," griped a government official out of Washington. Despite the annoyance he called Emilio a "brilliant, first-class informant. The guy would walk into a place and in fifteen minutes know everything that's going on." Emilio, he said, was "a helluva nice guy, sincere, but dangerous to himself."

It was true; his cover was blown and since his return to Miami there had been two serious attempts on Emilio's life.

All he wanted now, he said, was a job and a normal life with his wife and children; the beach on weekends—maybe a little fishing.

But he had trouble finding a job, and his life was hopelessly complicated by paperwork, or the lack of it. He was neither a citizen nor a resident. He claimed the government had promised to unscramble it all for him. But after three years of requests, the government still failed to provide him with earnings statements for his income tax returns. And he needed job training: He wanted to learn the advertising business or commercial art, even a six- or eight-week course would have made him happy.

Job training for protected witnesses is out, the man from Washington told me. It is too difficult to control. "Say you spend five hundred dollars to train a witness to be a meat cutter, for example, and then he decides he doesn't want to be a meat cutter and wants to be trained as an auto mechanic. Where do you stop?"

The only job the government offered was washing dishes for a hundred dollars a week. The job market in Miami was terrible, they said, "especially for a Cuban whose only training is as a guerrilla, a drug peddler, and an informant."

He insisted that Miami was not a safe haven for Emilio, who was creating his own problems by returning to a dangerous area.

A spokesman from the U.S. Marshal's Service denied ever promising to straighten out his papers, saying that it must have been the DEA or the FBI. The problem was really one for the Immigration and Naturalization Service, he said. The INS, in turn, said that to make Emilio a citizen would require a private bill in Congress and that it was impossible to change his alien status to that of permanent resident.

Emilio was chagrined. He knew how to handle life and death situations in the shadowy drug world, but the federal bureaucracy was an impossible maze to him. "If I get killed, I am not so afraid," he told me earnestly. "You only die once." Slow death by red tape is far more difficult to deal with, he said. "I am not afraid of the criminals who want to kill me—I am afraid of the U.S. Justice Department."

Life became more complicated when he was arrested. When men with guns tried to abduct him from a Little Havana nightspot, he successfully escaped out a washroom window and dashed down a nearby street, where he was stopped by Miami police. He was glad to see them until they took away his .38-caliber revolver and arrested him for carrying it. He explained the situation, saying that he worked for federal agents, his life was in danger, and he would be killed in jail. The officers listened, then added another charge: giving false information to police.

The judge did not believe his preposterous story either. Then federal agents showed up. They asked for Emilio's release. They said he worked for them, his life was in danger, and he would be killed in jail. The state attorney's office, feuding with federal agencies at the time, grudgingly released him into the agents' custody but refused to drop the gun charges. The feds were now alarmed. If Emilio was convicted in state court it could damage his credibility as star witness in a major, still-pending federal drug case in New York.

Emilio took his wife out to dinner to cheer her up, but two men recognized him as an informant and remained lurking outside the restaurant. He dialed the DEA for help and police were sent to the rescue.

His wife got a job as a waitress, but a man Emilio had testified against strolled into the restaurant where she worked, and she hid in a back room, then ran in terror.

Emilio now feared the feds were going to drop him from the protection program altogether. Perhaps if he went public it would embarrass the government into extending him the help he felt they owed him. His career and his troubles with the feds made an intriguing news story.

I wrote it. The reaction was immediate. The government was furious. "It's like saying, 'Here I am. Shoot me,' " said the man from Washington.

Publicly, they announced that Emilio had been dropped from the program. Privately, they quietly agreed to reinstate and relocate him once more, with another new identity. He was bursting with anticipation, like a kid cast in a class play. "Who am I going to be?" he kept asking me. "Will I be American? Cuban?" He was sternly instructed to sever all old ties and maintain no contact with anyone in Miami. We said goodbye. Forever, I thought.

He called almost at once from his new home, outside of Washington, D.C. His cover was a job selling vacuum cleaners at Sears. One day he called bubbling over with pride and patriotism. He had sold a vacuum cleaner to Henry Kissinger's wife, Nancy. It made him very happy.

He called me often, both at the office and at home, sometimes several times a day, to chat at length. I wondered who was paying his phone bills. It was probably all of us. He missed the excitement and intrigue of Miami— and he remained an amazingly good news source. A thousand miles away he still knew first what was happening in Miami's Cuban community and in the drug world. If I was not at home, he played exuberant Latin music into my telephone answering machine. Sometimes when I did answer, he simply played music and did not talk. When he did, he was fond of saying things like, "Money, baby, it's only green paper."

I began to suspect he was doing more than working at Sears. He began to slip in and out of Miami. I never knew if he was calling from the phone booth in the lobby or from a thousand miles away. I soon got the impression that he was making cases, working for the government again. He could not resist the lure of his love affair with the feds. His luck could not hold out forever. Each time we talked, I urged him to live the life he said he wanted, with his wife and his family, and quit the dangerous games that would only lead to trouble.

He said he had invested in a pig farm and was settling down to learn the business. I hoped it was true. Then his stepdaughter, age twenty-one, got in trouble in Miami.

She was charged with murder by heart attack. She and two other young women got into a fight with a seventy-two-year-old man outside a gay night spot. He walked away with minor bruises, but collapsed and died moments later of a heart attack.

The medical examiner called it murder, because the women knew the old man had a bad heart when they scuffled with him. She fled home, to her mother and Emilio, outside Washington. He called me with the news, put her on the telephone, and she described what happened for my story on the murder. Then he brought her back to Miami to surrender to police. His attorney, Bill Cagney, a former federal strike force prosecutor, won her an acquittal. We all breathed easier. She was a nice girl, just mixed up.

Some time later I would receive another long-distance call from Emilio about his stepdaughter. This time she was dead in Miami. He was so distraught and emotional that I could barely understand him. I hoped it wasn't true, but checked the morgue, and there she was. Her small car had slid sideways into a concrete pole on a slippery Miami street in the rain. She was twenty-six.

When I had to make an overnight trip to Washington, I suggested to Emilio, whom I had not seen for some time, that we meet at the airport for a drink before I left the capital. It would be good to see him again, and standing next to him in a crowd that big, and that far from Miami, would probably be safe. Just before I left my hotel, he called and offered to drive me to the airport. Sure, I said. That was my mistake.

He looked fine, the same old Emilio, as handsome and robust as ever. He wanted to show me the sights and we had a little time. We drove by the White House and the Washington Monument in a light rain. Same old wacky patriot, he was so proud, his eyes welled. I had to smile to myself. Then we swung by the Cuban embassy, and he fell into a bitter anti-Castro tirade. He stepped up the speed and seemed to be driving much faster, dangerously fast. Then he really hit the gas, but too late. The cops standing at attention on the security detail outside the embassy had spotted his car. One shouted, pointing at us, and they scrambled. Two ran for their motorcycles. Emilio floored it. They were chasing us!

The road was slippery, clogged with heavy, rainy afternoon traffic. Emilio was shouting, cursing in Spanish at the sirens that were gaining on us. I was screaming: Why are they chasing us? What have you done? What are you involved in? What am I involved in?

We skidded, cut corners, ran two red lights, and somehow lost them. I had no idea where we were.

I wanted to go to the airport—*now.*

Emilio wanted to show me the mountains, his mountains. It was fall. They were so beautiful.

I wanted to go to the airport—*at once.*

Now we were somewhere in Virginia or maybe Maryland. Emilio's mood had swung, he was sentimental. Suddenly, dramatically, he was in love.

I wanted to go to the airport.

He clutched my hand, passionately pressing it to his lips as he steered with his other hand. I suggested he watch the road. He begged me to stay with him. Don't be ridiculous, I told him. Take me to the airport. He pleaded, he cajoled, he made long romantic speeches. He missed me. He missed Miami.

I vowed to never, ever get in a car with this man again. I promised God that if I ever got back to Miami I would never leave it again. The airport! The airport! I shrieked.

Reluctantly, he took me there, grieving all the way. He accompanied me to the concourse, though I insisted it was not necessary. We sat and waited. I kept saying good-bye, but he did not leave. Instead he took my hands in his, pleading with me not to go, not to leave him. For God's sake, I had never even seen this man before outside of the *Herald* newsroom, a courtroom, or his lawyer's office. A stranger would have thought we were star-crossed lovers.

He begged so pitifully and brokenheartedly, that other travelers began to stare accusingly. One nicely dressed motherly lady even mouthed a single word at me: *Stay.*

I explained to Emilio that we were not even friends really, only acquaintances. He began to cry—real tears. "Don't leave, don't leave me, baby," he pleaded. It was time to board at last, but my relief was shortlived. If I would not stay, he announced emotionally, he would go to Miami with me. He actually had one foot on the plane when they turned him back in a noisy commotion.

I did not see him again, but he continued to call and to slip in and out of town. One day he called when I was on deadline at the *Herald.* He was in trouble, somewhere in Miami. He was upset; he had shot someone, he said. I hoped he was hallucinating—or that I was. The man he shot tried to shoot him first, he said. It was self-defense, a deal, a double-cross of some sort. He got away and did not know if the man was still alive.

He told me the man's first name, the time, and the place. I checked it out. It was true. The shooting victim was in intensive care but would survive. This was serious. I urged Emilio to surrender. He said the man he shot would never tell police what really happened and would not identify him or prosecute.

Emilio was right. The wounded man did lie to the cops. He told them that a young black man whose face he did not see tried to rob him, then shot him down.

I swore to Emilio that if the man died, I would tell police the truth, whether they believed it or not and despite the fact that I wasn't sure what Emilio's last name was anymore.

The wounded man made a full recovery.

We talked a number of times after that, long distance. Mostly he talked about politics, his pig farm, and his young son's soccer trophies—until that last, unsettling call.

I hope Emilio is straight now, living normally with his family and going to the beach on weekends—maybe doing a little fishing. Wherever he is, I know that no one is ever bored, life is not simple, and nothing is ever black-and-white.

Update: November 2003

I heard nothing from Emilio for more than a decade. Did he still live life on the edge? Did excitement and danger still trail in his wake?

As a reporter and a novelist, I always want to know how

the story ends. Emilio was one of the most unforgettable characters I've ever met. I always feared that if something happened to him, I would never know, even if he made the news. His name had been changed so many times that I could easily read about him and never know it was him—unless I recognized his distinctive style, that certain panache.

Was he still dashing, spirited, flamboyant—and too dangerous to stand next to in public? His government handlers had warned him many times that Miami was too dangerous a place for him to visit.

They were right.

A Miami Herald *headline caught my eye one September morning in 1996. A spectacular daylight shooting in Miami Beach. One dead, another wounded.*

The dead man's name did not appear until the eleventh paragraph. Emilio Martinez. My heart stopped. That was a name Emilio used. Somehow, I knew instantly. I hoped I was wrong. The name is common. There are nearly seven thousand listings for the name Martinez in the Miami telephone directory.

I read on. The Martinez killed was age fifty-two, a visitor from Virginia.

That would be Emilio's age. Virginia was the last place he had been relocated to as a protected federal witness.

The daylight shooting was bold, on a busy Saturday afternoon in front of dozens of weekend strollers and tourists sipping piña coladas along Ocean Drive in South Beach, described by publicists as the most exciting few blocks in the world.

A homicide detective described it as "like something out of *Miami Vice*."

Sounded like Emilio to me.

I prayed to be wrong but knew in my heart I was right.

The detective confirmed it. Ironically, Emilio's violent death had nothing to do with his past as one of the most successful and flamboyant drug world spies ever to work undercover for the U.S. government.

The man who killed him did not know him or his history.

Emilio was simply in the wrong place, at the wrong time, with the wrong woman. The man who had survived shootouts, shadowy plots, international intrigue, and attempts to kill him while he worked major cases in California, Mexico, Miami, and New York was killed by somebody's irate boyfriend.

During a brief visit to Miami, he and a friend had met a woman with a nasty ex-lover, a Cuban rafter in Miami only a year. She had left him after a fight over money. He was riding a bicycle in South Beach and spotted her in Emilio's car. Enraged, he threatened to kill her. The terrified woman pleaded with Emilio to drive off, and he did, bumping the ex-boyfriend's bike. The infuriated man threatened to kill him too.

Emilio's luck began running out later, when his car was towed from a Miami Beach parking spot. He called home and spoke to his wife. It was the last time she heard his voice. He reclaimed his automobile, then called the police to report his wallet missing from the car. As he, his friend, and the woman waited on Ocean Drive for a police officer to come take a report, the ex-boyfriend spotted them and *leaped from a car. The frightened woman screamed for Emilio to get her out of there. As he pulled away from the curb, the boyfriend fired three times at point-blank range through the open car window. Emilio was hit in the chest and arm. His male passenger was hit in the leg.*

The car careened for two hundred feet with Emilio slumped over the wheel. Witnesses screamed and ran as he fell dead into the street. The woman was not hurt.

The killer was arrested days later on first-degree murder charges.

Emilio was not afraid to die. He once told me, "You only die once."

Slow death by red tape, he said, was far worse than the life and death situations he faced in the shadowy under-cover world of drugs.

For decades, Emilio had tried to unravel the maze of red tape, the frustrating lack of paperwork that complicated his status and first brought him to me, when he turned to the press as a last resort. He never succeeded. His dreams of citizenship and a normal life never came true.

The young son whose soccer trophies made Emilio glow with pride is now a college graduate, successful in business, and a father himself.

Emilio's widow, the love of his life, still lives in Virginia. She has not remarried and she still seeks citizenship.

Agents of the DEA, the U.S. Marshals Service, and the FBI had threatened, warned, admonished, and pleaded with Emilio to stay away. He couldn't.

Miami was his fatal attraction.

I know the feeling.

NINE

Missing

One misfortune is worse than murder.

It is to lose someone you love, without ever knowing that person's fate. In such a life of uncertainty, the heart pounds each time a doorbell rings, and it is impossible to see a crowd without scanning faces. Dead or alive? Coming home or gone forever? After time in limbo, any news is welcome, no matter how searing.

Anything is better than endless waiting and searching.

Some people suggest that the source of my empathy for lost people must be personal experience: the childhood disappearance of my father, who left no forwarding address. It is true that missing persons and misplaced corpses intrigue me. It excites me to bring them home or to restore their names to the dead, but I am also fascinated by murder mysteries, and no one ever murdered my father.

In addition, I didn't love him. I hardly knew him. He

was not a nice man, a drinker, a gambler, a philanderer. He was also an abandoner of women and children. I admit that for nearly all my life I wished to meet him, to see his face and hear his voice, just once. It was curiosity. I had some questions. But he died before I ever got the chance to ask them. He died of natural causes.

The telephone rang one Saturday afternoon at the *Herald*. The caller said that my father had been found, and as my heart leaped, asked what I wanted done with the body. A strange expression must have crossed my face, because an editor asked what was wrong.

"My father died."

At once warm and caring, he said, "Go home. Take all the time you need."

I took no time at all. I didn't even go home early that day. Why should I? The man was a stranger.

The work I do is motivated more by a love of mystery, the challenge of trying to piece together life's riddles and fit the proper endings to unfinished stories. I don't try to solve crossword or jigsaw puzzles; I never had much time for games. If difficult, they are frustrating, and what do they accomplish? Life itself holds enough frustration and stress—why create more? If you love a challenge, why not take on one that matters, a real-life puzzle. People's lives—sometimes scattered over thousands of miles in as many mismatched pieces—are far more interesting to try to piece back together.

Thousands of people are reported missing in Greater Miami every year. More than ninety percent return safely on their own, many wearing silly grins. Nearly all of the others surface in hospitals or morgues, victims of accident, sudden illness, or murder. A small number are never seen again.

It must be terrible to be lost forever. It can happen easily in Miami's sprawling metropolis—the dropping-off place for refugees of all kinds, the jumping-off place for Latin America and the world. It is a community with few deep roots, few historic traditions, and hundreds of thousands of transients and travelers. Police and the keepers of the morgue perform the task of sorting out the missing and the dead and sending lost people home at last. They take it seriously, and they do it well, but sometimes even their most extraordinary measures fail.

That is why missing-persons stories can be a joy to write. They can reunite families, end uncertainty, and deliver the dead to their proper resting place, or they can disturb your dreams forever.

Like the story of Amy.

On my desk at the *Herald* is Amy Billig's dental record, precise and impersonal, from the files of a Miami dentist. It charts the silver fillings in three premolars and porcelain fillings in two upper front teeth.

At age seventeen, she vanished like footprints on a sea-washed beach. No day passes that I do not think of Amy. When unidentified bones or a skull is unearthed somewhere, I photocopy the dental chart and mail it for comparison purposes to the police or medical examiner in that jurisdiction. Then, I wait.

It was thirteen years ago that Amy disappeared off a sun-drenched street. She was beautiful, though she did not yet know it. She was warm and talented. She wrote playful, pretty poetry, dabbled in watercolors, and excelled at the flute and guitar. She was a practicing vegetarian, a budding feminist, a voracious reader. She loved Sylvia Plath, Chinese food, clothes from secondhand stores, babies, little children, and her family. She had a tenderness for animals, swam with dolphins, and worked on a project to save them.

If Amy is alive now, she is a woman of thirty. It is more likely that she is dead, that she died a teenager, probably on the day she disappeared, the victim of a Theodore Bundy, a Christopher Wilder, a Robert Carr, or some still-unidentified serial killer. They are always out there, twisted men who stalk women like animals. Police say that must be what happened to Amy. Logic says it is so. Sometimes I believe it myself, but then I speak again with her mother and come away, heart pounding, mind reeling, thinking, "My God! Amy is alive, and we have got to find her."

Susan Billig's obsession is contagious. The belief shines out of her blue eyes with startling intensity. Her voice sure and determined, she says, "I know she is alive. I know it. I would feel it if she was dead."

She continues to question. She keeps looking. She does not surrender. "I'll go to my grave looking for her," she says. "I can never give up until I see her—or bury her. I am her mother. I owe it to her to find her."

Her interminable and lonely search has taken Susan

Billig from the ornate lobby of the Fontainebleau Hotel to topless bars in strange cities. It has taken her into the company of killers and fugitives and sent her on coast-to-coast forays into danger, financial ruin, and desperation. I know no other mother who has endured what Susan Billig has endured searching for her daughter.

Amy did not like ostentation: flashy, showy things or flashy, showy people. Her diaries and poetry reflect the image of a gentle, happy girl, discovering life and herself:

> And so taking this book down from
> the shelf, I said to the elf with
> silver slippers and golden gown
> Tell me these secrets of old,
> of beauty, of life . . . take me
> away in . . . a sailboat with
> tall lofty white sails that catch
> the breeze and shadow the sun
> on a dark, dusty sea. Let me
> drown in the sound of the petals
> falling to the ground
> on the street where Amy lives.

> Amy 2/5/74

This portrait of Amy makes her mother's obsession all the more horrifying. Sue Billig clings to the belief that Amy was abducted, beaten, raped, and is still held captive by a motorcycle gang.

Amy was born January 9, 1957, in Oyster Bay, New

York, long-awaited and much-loved. Susan and Ned had been married for ten years. Four earlier pregnancies ended in miscarriages.

Amy was a miracle.

"I would look at her and think, what did I do to deserve such a beautiful thing?" her mother says.

Joshua, their only son, arrived on Valentine's Day the following year. The good times still live on the glossy pages of the family album. Amy and Josh frolicking with Ned on the grass in Central Park, brushing their teeth, splashing in a bubble-filled bathtub. Amy, in a sparkly pink tutu, prancing delicately through her ballet lesson.

There was no hint of disaster. Sue Billig was no overprotective mother beset by shadowy or silly fears. Her babies were good, they talked and read early, played Scrabble with their parents, and acquired voluminous vocabularies.

In May 1969, the Billigs left New York, "because of the violence." They had fallen in love with Coconut Grove, a suburb of Miami. Ned opened an art gallery, and Sue, a talented interior designer, pursued her profession.

They came to Florida to live their lives peacefully forever. That peaceful forever ended on March 5, 1974, a sunny, warm, typical day. Amy gulped her juice and rushed off to her senior high school classes. Ned drove to his art gallery. Sue's mother was visiting from New York. The two women tidied the house and went to the beach just before noon. Amy breezed in from school ten minutes later, telephoned her father, and asked to borrow two dollars for lunch with friends. He agreed. Amy nibbled at some yogurt and changed her blouse. She wore a short denim skirt and cork platform sandals. Her thick, brown waist-length hair hung loose and flowing. Slim and leggy, Amy had a distinctive walk, described by her mother as "a happy, lifting gait. I could tell three blocks away in a crowd if that was my daughter walking."

The route to her father's gallery was three-quarters of a mile at most, a short block down Poinciana onto Main Highway, then a half-mile to the gallery.

Amy Billig walked her happy walk into a sunny day at noon and disappeared.

She hitchhiked, her mother says. She believes that's how Amy got into trouble. "She hitchhiked because all her experiences were so pleasant. Experiences with people she knew, Coconut Grove people who make that same trip down Main Highway." Dinner hour came and went, and Amy wasn't there. No one in the family had ever failed to call if late for a meal. Ned said Amy had never come for the two dollars. He thought she had changed her mind. Her friends said Amy had never arrived.

Detective Mike Gonzalez, a friend of the family, came to the house. He asked Josh if his sister would run away. "Never," the boy said.

Of the tens of thousands of youngsters reported missing by anxious parents each year, more than ninety-nine percent return home quickly and safely, on their own. "Don't panic," said Gonzalez, the father of teenagers himself. "Call again if Amy isn't home by morning."

Sue called by 6:00 A.M. "I am now panicking," she said. "Amy is missing."

The police machinery cranked sluggishly into motion.

"I am very resentful, to this day, that they didn't do a more in-depth investigation," Sue Billig says. "I wanted helicopters in the sky. I wanted policemen walking hand-in-hand through vacant lots. Our friends did it—not the police. All our friends got together. They looked under every bush, every tree in the neighborhood." Police did talk to Amy's friends and slowly began to suspect something more serious. On March 10, five days after she disappeared, the first news story appeared:

GROVE 17-YEAR-OLD

MAY BE KIDNAPPING VICTIM,

POLICE SAY

That night, a benefit concert raised $850, and a fund was established at the Coconut Grove Bank to help pay expenses. The search for Amy Billig had become a community project. The offer of a thousand-dollar reward brought tips that Amy had been seen in a jeep, a Cadillac, on a bus, in a store. None were true sightings. The Billigs hired a high-priced private detective and pleaded for FBI intervention.

Her sleep haunted by dreams of Amy crying because rain was falling on her, Sue sat up and stared out a window each night. Her weight dropped from 110 to 92 pounds. Brief businesslike entries of precise, controlled handwriting tell the story of Sue Billig's search for the elusive shadow of her daughter—one notebook for each long year.

On March 16, 1974, eleven days after Amy vanished, a telephone tip came from a girl who called herself Susan Johnson. The Outlaws motorcycle gang had abducted Amy, she said.

A bail bondsman whose daughter went to school with Amy brought two Outlaws to the Billig home. "They were very rough looking," Sue Billig said, "with funny hair, leather jackets and boots, and wallets attached by chains to their belt loops." They telephoned their Florida "boss."

"If she is in the Outlaw Nation, we'll return her," he promised. They called back days later, no longer helpful. They advised the Billigs to "forget the whole thing."

On March 18, Amy's camera was found near a south-bound lane of the Florida Turnpike. The Instamatic with her name on it contained exposed film. One frame developed clearly, showing a vine-covered building with a white truck in the background. The vine is not native to South Florida; the building is unfamiliar to the Billigs. They think Amy dropped the camera that day as a clue. Police say it may have been lost or stolen before Amy disappeared. "But," asks Sue Billig, "if someone stole it, wouldn't they have taken Amy's name off it?"

Susan Billig's dreams grew violent: Amy hurled from a car, crumpled by the roadside.

On March 19, a Baltimore friend telephoned to say he knew a lawyer who represents the Pagans motorcycle gang, and there was talk a girl had been taken from Miami.

Bikers had rumbled through Coconut Grove on the day Amy vanished. On their way to the annual bike races in Daytona, they had congregated in Coconut Grove.

"Everybody in the little restaurants along Main Highway saw them, riding five abreast," Sue Billig said.

On March 20, the fifteenth day, at 9:00 A.M., the first ransom call came. The second came at 2:45 P.M., a muffled voice in the background saying, "Mama, Mama, please . . ."

Sue was instructed to wear red, white, and blue and bring thirty thousand dollars in a black attaché case to the Fontainebleau lobby. She was told to come alone, with no police.

She obeyed all the demands but one. Plainclothes cops mingled with tourists as Sue drove up with a policewoman who posed as her neighbor. The money, begged and borrowed from friends and relatives, was packed in a wired tan briefcase borrowed from a detective agency and hastily painted black. Ned and Sue hired extra investigators to insure Amy's safety, brought their private eye, Frank Rubino, and rented a helicopter and sophisticated electronic equipment.

The two women sat on a lobby couch, the briefcase between them. "I was so nervous about losing that money. I knew we had to get it back to where we borrowed it. They had to pry my fingers open later." Her grip was so powerful that black paint came off on Sue's hands.

A boy with acne and a ponytail under a green baseball cap told them, "Give me the money, and Amy will be home at six o'clock." They wanted proof he had Amy. All he could recall was "her long brown hair." They balked. He led them to an elevator. On the fifth floor they found the boy's brother—his identical twin—waiting.

The policewoman arrested them. Asked who pretended to be Amy and cried out "Mama," one pointed at the other and said, "He did."

The culprits, two sixteen-year-old Miami Beach High School sophomores, lived in a townhouse with their divorced mother. She wept at the hearing. They did not. A judge released them to her custody. The day had cost the Billigs nearly two thousand dollars and a delay at a time crucial to the investigation, Sue Billig says bitterly. "We were on the right track and they pulled us away." The boys won probation after Sue Billig spoke up for them in court. They never apologized. Sue wrote a letter to their well-to-do parents, asking if they would reimburse the search fund for the cost of their sons' extortion attempt. It was never answered.

The Billigs' twenty-seventh anniversary was on March 26. If she was alive, they felt, Amy—who always fussed with presents, poems, and handmade cards—would reach them somehow. They heard nothing.

Commercial pilots and stewardesses distributed posters in dozens of cities. Interpol sent her description across Europe and investigated a tip that she had been seen in Lebanon.

On March 31, Amy graduated from high school, in absentia. More than five hundred young people jammed a Coconut Grove park for Help Find Amy Billig Day. Conceived by Amy's classmates, the event raised $1,561. Ned attended and tried to smile. Sue waited by the telephone. When she could stand it no longer, she joined the young people who were handing fliers to motorists at intersections.

Ned became depressed. "I was a manic-depressive, I think, for a period. Sitting and waiting is the worst kind of thing to do." Both he and Sue saw a psychologist provided by the Jewish Federation. "We had no money at the time, and it helped keep us functioning."

Satan, the Pagan chieftain, reported to the Baltimore attorney that if Outlaws had Amy, they were most likely trading her. A Hells Angel told Sue the same thing. "They trade young women for another girl, money, a credit card, a bike."

Hopes soared when the Baltimore contact relayed a cryptic call from a gang member.

"You know that business we were talking about down south?"

"Is she alive?"

"Yes."

Hopes foundered four days later. "The Outlaws left Fort Lauderdale with her," the caller said.

The heat was on. The weighted bodies of three rival Hells Angels bobbed to the surface of a Broward County rock pit May first. Each was shotgunned in the head.

Sue Billig wrote then-President Nixon to plead for FBI help. Then—FBI Director Clarence Kelly replied. The FBI could not investigate because there was no proof that Amy had been abducted, he wrote. However, a missing-persons notice had been posted at FBI headquarters in Washington. He urged her to "have faith in the local authorities."

A $25,000 ransom call came the next day. It was traced to a retarded black teenager. He said a white man put him up to it. He was not prosecuted. "He was a sick boy," Sue Billig says wearily. "All these kids are somebody else's children. I don't believe in an eye for an eye and a tooth for a tooth."

There were others. Each was checked out.

A woman who worked for the Treasury Department said that in June she had seen Amy "looking very out of it, in a bar in Fort Lauderdale, with bikers." Sue Billig found the bar. The owner remembered the obstreperous gang. He had to put them out at gunpoint. He saw their colors. They were Outlaws, from the Orlando area.

Sue Billig followed the Outlaws to Orlando, where two Pagans had been shot in warfare between the gangs. She searched Orlando and nearby Kissimmee for a clue and found one. The manager of a Majik Market said a girl of Amy's description had come to the store, always with two bikers. The girl was very pretty, very quiet. She always bought Campbell's Vegetarian Vegetable soup and crackers.

Amy the vegetarian—Sue's heart leaped.

She found the Outlaws' deserted, filthy clubhouse. She took photos and rummaged in the garbage. She found a phone bill listing one frequently called number. It would later lead her to Big Jim Nolan, leader of the Outlaws in the Southeast.

But first she returned to Miami, marched into police headquarters on July 30 and became hysterical. They had instructed her five months earlier not to touch Amy's records and personal belongings until they sent someone to dust for fingerprints. She had called and waited; no one had ever come.

Crime lab expert Al Heath, whose daughter had been a school chum of Amy's, came to the house and tried to lift prints. By then, they were unclear. He laments that not a single perfect fingerprint left by Amy Billig exists. Had there been one, it could have been sent throughout the country by computer, to compare with those of unidentified young women—arrested, sick, or dead.

Heath did take strands from Amy's hairbrush. He compared them to hairs in a discarded brush Sue found at the Orlando Outlaw headquarters. The result was not yes or no, only "could be."

Heath's daughter never believed Amy ran away. Neither did he. "I have bad feelings about Amy," he told me. "I just don't feel she's alive."

Neither does Rubino, the detective. He eventually dropped the case. "Lots of people die," he said, "and their bodies aren't found, a body here, a body there. Out in The Everglades, it rots and is never found."

A biker became Sue's "snitch." He said an Orlando Outlaw told him Amy was sold in Fort Lauderdale in June, when a number of bikers had been arrested. Sue went to Raiford prison and the prison at Belle Glade to talk to other gang members. "Wherever I went, I got additional information that fit in. A lot of people were reticent. Bikers consider themselves brothers. They won't tell on each other."

Bikers looked at Amy's picture and said they'd seen her five weeks earlier, at a meet near Chicago.

Two ex-policemen volunteered to bring Amy back. All they needed, they said, was three thousand dollars. All

Ned and Sue could raise was fifteen hundred. She told them to call collect from anywhere. They never called. They later claimed they had searched Ocala, Orlando, Gainesville, Atlanta, and Chattanooga, Tennessee.

Sue Billig doubts they left Miami.

A doctor she consulted about her missing daughter told her that life with bikers would be a "contradiction of personality" for Amy, but that she would draw strength from "her psychological need to survive under any circumstances."

Other doctors talked about a possible "memory block" and the "Stockholm syndrome," named for the bank personnel in Sweden who began to sympathize with the robbers who held them captive.

In the fall, the Billigs' closest friends came from New York to comfort them. Sue and her friend sat talking and crying. The men were in another room when a young girl's screams rang out, "Help me! Help me! Somebody help me!"

Everyone but Sue Billig froze. "It was Amy calling me." She threw herself out of the house into the dark, across the street to where screams still came from the bushes. Sue Billig, less than one hundred pounds, tore apart the two people: a battered, bloodied young woman and a husky, enraged man. She pushed him, shouting, "Get away from her! Go away!"

He fled. She took the girl into the house and called police. The young woman had been baby-sitting. Her attacker was an old boyfriend. Later Sue trembled uncontrollably. "It was Amy calling me. It was my daughter, somebody else's daughter. I hope somebody will help Amy under the same circumstances."

Now, when she sees a young girl hitchhiking, she pulls to the curb, in tears. "I beg them not to hitchhike." She shows them posters with Amy's picture. "I beg friends not to give hitchhikers a lift. It gives the child a false sense of security. Everybody's not nice. People are evil."

For a long time, police called Sue Billig each time an unidentified young woman was found dead. After she was told of a human skull found in the Keys, the ghastly image haunted her, and she asked them not to notify her again before dental comparisons were made.

Determined to try every avenue, Sue consulted psychics. So did Josh and several friends. "All said more or less the same thing," Sue said, "that she is alive."

On the first anniversary of Amy's disappearance Ned and Josh went to the annual bike races at Daytona. "There were lots of bikers and lots of Outlaws, but they were behind some kind of chicken-wire fence, and they had guards with guns. There was no way for Ned to go in and the local police weren't about to go in either," Sue says.

Using the telephone number she found in Orlando, Sue contacted Big Jim Nolan, valedictorian of his high school class and a thorn in the side of police ever since. She rode a bus to Hollywood, Florida, where he picked her up in a van.

"He had long hair and was gigantic. He took me to his house where there were other bikers and girls and big dogs. It was an awful place. I said, 'I don't want to put anybody in jail. I just want my daughter back.'"

Nolan said he would try to help. He and three gang members were later indicted for the rock-pit murders. At the time of the indictments, Big Jim was behind bars for threatening a policeman. A co-defendant was in prison for savagely beating a woman. A third was serving life for kidnapping. One had already served time for his part in an Outlaw atrocity in which an eighteen-year-old girl was nailed to a tree.

The search stretched from months to years. Sue Billig's dreams were transformed into sweet sanity-saving memories: Amy growing up. Amy the child, dancing in the street. Amy the bright and beautiful toddler. Amy as a baby, an infant in her carriage.

Then the dreams change. The carriage is suddenly empty. And in her dreams, Sue Billig runs frantically, peering into baby carriages in search of her stolen daughter.

It seemed the nightmares would finally end when a biker named Paul saw a news story with Amy's picture. He called to say he had once "owned" Amy in Orlando. He lost her when he was arrested. It seemed to mesh with earlier information. Paul said he had "bought" Amy badly beaten, drugged, and confused. He described her precisely, even to a small scar the Billigs had kept secret for positive identification.

Convinced, Sue rushed to meet the stranger at a remote gas station. She had never ridden a motorcycle, but rode off on the back of his. The thought flashed through her mind that, like Amy, she might never be seen again. She dismissed it. "I was not frightened. I can do anything when it comes to Amy. I feel that somewhere she is saying, 'My mother is going to find me.' "

At the biker's trailer he looked at Amy's picture and swore it was the same girl. Sue Billig memorized the tag number on the car of another man at the trailer and gave it to Miami police. It was registered to a man wanted in Virginia for three counts of murder. Over her protests, police raided the trailer and arrested him.

Officers showed the fugitive Amy's photo. "My buddy's old lady," he said. "In fact her mother has been here looking for her."

Paul said Amy was now in Tulsa, and they could find her. The search seemed almost over. Amy's room had been preserved just as she had left it. Sue bought new linens, a calico print, a blanket for Amy's bed. "I wanted something to be new and fresh when she came home."

That was in June 1976, two years after Amy vanished. Sue flew to Tulsa—and waited. Paul arrived five days late. He had been in jail. He called her hotel room, said "Get ready to leave," and told her to wait for his call. It never came. He vanished. Frantic, she went to police. They heard rumors he'd been killed. She stayed in Tulsa for five weeks. She spent the nation's bicentennial alone in a hotel room. At local bars and bike shops, she talked endlessly, showing Amy's picture to anyone who might help. She found a girl who looked like Amy, only heavier. The girl said she had seen Amy at a bikers' swimming party in Fort Worth, Texas. "It was like looking in a mirror," she said. She asked her look-alike where she was from. "I don't know," the girl had replied. "Maybe here—or Miami."

Sue returned to Miami alone on July 15. She wrote hundreds of letters. If Patty Hearst was found alive, she thought, Amy can be alive. She wrote to Catherine Hearst, asking for help. A secretary replied. Mrs. Hearst could do nothing.

A girl named Barbara Stevens vanished in South Dade. If she is alive, Sue assured herself, Amy can be, too. Barbara Stevens was found in a woods. Her killer was never caught.

Then Paul resurfaced, he was alive but both his kneecaps had been broken. He had a final tip. Amy was in Seattle, working in a place with other bikers' girls, two blocks from the ferry, along the strip. "She's burned out, looks old," he said. "Don't look for anybody who looks under thirty."

Amy would have been almost twenty-one. Sue Billig caught a plane. A young man, the husband of one of Amy's closest friends, accompanied her. It was November 16, 1977, three and a half years after Amy disappeared.

Seattle police said they knew no bikers. Sue found them herself, wearing their colors—Florida Outlaws. They searched her. "I'm not heat," she told them. "I just want information about my daughter."

"Why do you want her back?" one asked. "She's not like you anymore. She's like us. Let whoever has her keep her."

She persisted and won him over. "You're a nice lady. You're spunky," he told her.

"They told me they'd get her back for me even if they had to blow somebody's head off," she said. "If bikers can ever be good guys, they were." They searched. So did Sue.

A drug deal went sour as she tried to talk to people in a bar. "An Indian broke a bottle and went for a black man." Shoved out of the way, she stumbled out the door as police cars converged. In a topless joint, men she talked to were dealing bags of marijuana on the bar as they spoke. "I showed her picture to hookers, Indians, bartenders. The few who recognized her were frightened and didn't want to be involved." People in a bookstore recognized her picture and said they had seen her. They described her walk, her teeth. "Either it's Amy, or a girl I've been following for years who looks just like Amy."

The Outlaws found a girl who could be Amy. They dressed Sue's companion in biker's clothes and offered him a gun. He declined but went with them. The girl said her name was Willow Treeland. She was pitiful, spaced out.

She wasn't Amy.

At Outlaw headquarters a car crunched into the driveway and the bikers "all grabbed guns from behind a potbellied stove and ran to the windows." But there was no shooting, and Sue stayed for Thanksgiving dinner.

A friendly biker "begged me to go back home. I think he got to care about us." As Sue checked out of her hotel, on her way to the airport, a breathless call came from a man she had talked to in a bar. He had spotted Amy on the street, he said, and was holding her at the Blue Eagle Bar.

She rushed to the bar. The girl was beautiful, a runaway. She wasn't Amy. She and Sue talked for hours. If she had a mother like Susan Billig and a family who loved her, she said, she would go home. But the girl refused Sue's offer to fly her home. She would not even reveal where she was from. "It's no use," she said. "My mother doesn't want me."

Sue returned to Miami without her daughter.

Again, a new lead. A Miami attorney said he had information that Amy was in New Jersey with bikers. "Be prepared for the worst," he warned. "She's a biker's girl now. We'll have to bring her back by force, in chains."

Horrified at the thought, Sue went to court. Emergency commitment papers were drawn up, so Amy could be immediately hospitalized until she was herself and able to travel. When the papers were ready, the attorney was not. He backed out, and stopped returning Sue Billig's phone calls.

The nadir of her ordeal came when the house where they lived with Amy was sold. Ned lost the gallery, all but ignored in the early years of Amy's absence. They sold everything they had of value and moved to a smaller home.

Sue walked Amy's dog back to the old house one day, to show the new occupants her daughter's picture, in case Amy came home. "The house was gone. It was the most devastating thing . . . It was the most destructive thing that ever happened to me. I never wanted to leave there. It was Amy's home," Sue says, choking back tears.

"I packed all her lovely little things: all her books, her stuffed animals, all her clothes, all the things that meant so much to her. I couldn't seal them. I just couldn't put that heavy tape on them. It was my daughter's whole life, there in those boxes." Josh finally taped them and put them in the attic.

"Sometimes," Sue Billig confides, "I want to go up in the attic and open them and look at them. But I don't let myself. I don't want to get sick and have them have to take care of me."

On Amy's twenty-first birthday, Sue Billig wrote in her notebook, "I'm so unhappy. It seems like a milestone. She is no closer to me now than she was four years ago."

A TV station updated the case, and a viewer walked into Metro police headquarters saying he had seen Amy. His car broke down in Ocala, he said. The mechanic had a girl with him, a girl the mechanic said he had "taken" from Coconut Grove.

A TV reporter tipped Sue. Police acknowledged that the man had been there, but the officer had mislaid the slip of paper he had written the information on and could not remember the man's name.

Sue's worst fear is that Amy is dead: "No matter how physically or emotionally sick she is, no matter what the situation, if she is alive, we can help her. If she is dead, it's forever. I'll never see her again."

From the day Amy disappeared, Sue has believed, "It was simply a matter of money, economics. I feel that if I had money I could have found her. But we don't have anything. We've lost everything we ever had."

More law-enforcement resources are now devoted to finding missing youngsters. "If Amy disappeared today," Sue says, "we would have found her. What I did, I did well, but I was alone.

"I only feel alive when I'm searching for Amy," she says, "when I'm running and looking." Her voice is strong and firm. "The worst time is when nothing is happening. I get desperate because I feel like people will forget."

Years in limbo have taken their toll. "I look in the mirror and I don't recognize myself." They have all changed. Ned's face is deeply lined. "We're torn apart," Sue says. "We still love each other, but we're a different family than we were. Sometimes we're afraid to talk to each other out of fear of causing pain."

"I feel as strongly as Sue," Ned says, "that there is still an Amy somewhere. Until we know something, neither of us has any intention of stopping. We've gotten so close, so many times. It's so frustrating. We've got to make our own lives livable. We have a son we love as dearly as we love Amy. He went through incredible trauma the first year or two. Sixteen-year-old boys have a lot of problems of their own. He was in a sense ignored."

Leads still come, but less frequently now. Sue works and tries to stay busy. It helps, because she fantasizes about Amy when she is awake. In her waking dreams the scenario changes, but always, Amy is coming home. She is walking in, thin and sick, pale but alive.

"Wherever she is, she's in bad shape," Sue says. "They say there is such a thing as strong vibrations. I need help. If we all just keep thinking about how much we love her, it will carry her through these hard times."

When Amy had been gone for five years, I wrote a magazine story about her for *Tropic,* the *Herald*'s Sunday magazine. It brought a welter of new leads, dead ends, and more crank calls.

When the movie *Without a Trace* opened in Miami,

Sue called, sobbing, about the film. It is based loosely on the true story of a little boy who disappeared in New York City. I thought she had seen it and been overwhelmed, but all she had seen was the ad, a trailer for it, on TV. It focused on the agony of a mother's search for a missing child, and it devastated Sue. Yet she felt compelled to see the film. Definitely not, I told her. I would go see it on my day off and then we could discuss whether she should. Of course she did not wait. She couldn't. Emotionally drained by the film and its contrived Hollywood-style happy ending, she stumbled into the lobby, leaned over the water fountain to drink, and collapsed.

Doctors found a heart problem.

Sometimes I am afraid that her parents may not live long enough to find Amy.

A fresh lead, in the fall of 1985, took a Miami homicide detective and a dentist, a forensic odontologist, to Texas, where the body of a young girl was exhumed from her grave. The girl had died in Texas eleven years earlier, four months after Amy disappeared. Dark-haired and leggy, she looked about eighteen and was beautiful. She and a man came to town with a traveling carnival. When it left, they stayed on at a remote farm in Mundy, Texas. The sheriff went out there several times to settle disputes between the couple. The girl was apparently abused. Eventually she got sick, and the boyfriend took her to a hospital. Her legs and breasts were bruised, and she was dying—natural causes, they said: a brain abscess.

On her deathbed the girl told a nurse she was part Indian and had grown up on a reservation in North Carolina. She said her name was Terri Ann Warner. She also used the names Terri Wild Feather and Terri White Horse. In three days she was dead. The boyfriend left town. No one claimed the body, and after a month she was buried.

Eleven years later in Pennsylvania, the boyfriend, now thirty-three, saw a poster of Amy, circulated by a missing-children's organization. He walked into a police station. The girl on the poster is not missing, he said, she died in Texas. He left without answering any other questions.

Texas officials were reluctant to authorize exhumation of the body. Susan Billig had to call upon Florida's governor to intervene. It was the first time she had seriously considered the ugly thought that Amy might be dead. She had to know. So did I.

I made plans to go to the small-town cemetery in Vernon, Texas. I would follow the hearse to Dallas where the remains were to be examined. Before leaving, I made a dozen phone calls to Texans who had seen the girl, both dead and alive, then I canceled the trip. I knew it was not Amy.

The Billigs welcomed the news as good, though Sue wept for "somebody's daughter." So did I, especially after hearing what the experts discovered upon examining the teeth and bones. The dead girl was not eighteen as had been believed. She was about twelve or thirteen years old. She is still unclaimed.

I checked missing persons in North Carolina and on every Indian reservation and registry I could find. The mysteries remain. Who was the girl who called herself

Terri Wild Feather? What was she running from? Why did no one look for her?

And God help us all, *where* is Amy?

The Billigs' ordeal is no easier after all these years. "Amy was a child when she was taken," Sue says. "Now she's a woman, and the things that may have happened to her keep me awake in the night.

"Sometimes Ned and I are in a restaurant, and a family walks in with a daughter, and something about the girl— her walk or her laugh—reminds us of Amy, and we can't even eat. We love her and we miss her. There isn't anything we wouldn't do to find her and make her safe. What keeps us alive is the thought that we will someday see her again."

Susan Billig's obsession is more than a story to me. I, too, dream about Amy coming home.

Sometimes I am afraid that I will not live long enough.

Update: 2004

Susan Billig has kept her promise. Now widowed, age seventy-eight, with four inoperable tumors in her lungs, she is still searching for Amy. Her husband Ned died in 1993, without knowing the fate of their only daughter.

On a recent trip to New York, Sue, as always, studied the faces of passing strangers.

"Our family tends not to change much as we age," she said. "Amy would still be Amy. She would look older, but she would still be Amy."

Paul, the biker who led Sue on a fruitless cross-country

quest to find her daughter twenty years ago, died on New Year's Eve, 1996. A woman who lived with him later claimed that on his deathbed he told her that Pagan bikers had picked up Amy the day she disappeared. She was drugged and gang raped during a party at their remote clubhouse. She fought back, and to subdue her "they kept injecting her with drugs" until she died, then disposed of her body in the swamp.

Sue was badly shaken, but doubts it's true. Miami police also spoke to Paul shortly before his death. He told them no such story.

I don't believe it either. The woman claimed that a number of bikers and young women were at that fatal party. Biker chicks grow up, become wives and mothers. People change. They talk. Some even develop a conscience.

With all the nationwide publicity Sue's search has generated over all these years, it seems inconceivable that not one ever picked up a telephone to tell her the truth.

The story makes no sense. If Amy was at their mercy at a remote clubhouse, bikers didn't need drugs to overpower her. Bikers will often kill for drugs. Why waste their precious stash to subdue a defenseless girl? And bikers are not adept at concealing bodies so well that they vanish forever. They tend to dump the dead into rockpits or leave them where they fall. The bodies of their victims have a history of turning up.

I never bought the biker theory from the start. I suspect Sue did because it offered the most hope that Amy was still alive, held captive.

I believe only one person knows the answer to the mystery of what happened to Amy: the man responsible for her disappearance.

Years ago, I wrote about the still-unsolved murder of a millionaire banker from Las Vegas who was found garroted in a stairwell at Miami Beach's Fountainebleau Hotel. His family said they consulted a renowned California psychic who shunned publicity and refused money.

She named the same suspect the police were investigating but could never charge for lack of evidence.

The dead man's brother gave me her telephone number. Her name was Mary. We talked about the millionaire's murder. Then, because Amy never strays far from my mind, I suddenly asked, "Where is Amy?" I divulged nothing more. For all the psychic knew, Amy could have been my cat or a canary.

In a heartbeat, without hesitation, this woman thousands of miles away, replied, "Lost. I see her bones scattered on the sand."

"Where?" I gasped. "We have to bring her home."

"Underwater." She apologized for not making it more clear that the sand she saw was at the bottom of a body of water.

"What happened to her?" I asked.

She said Amy died in a rape gone wrong. Her attacker did not intend to kill her, but a struggle got out of hand. In a fugue-like state at the time, he disposed of her body. According to Mary, the murderer has committed no other crimes, still lives in Miami and, haunted, tries to convince himself that the fatal encounter never really took place. Like Sue Billig, he tries to believe that Amy is still alive.

I did not tell Sue. God knows she has been through enough, but I share my own chilling theory, based on what Mary said, with Mike Gonzalez, the Miami homicide sergeant who investigated the case from the start.

What if the man who took Amy is among the cruel cranks, the would-be extortionists and obscene telephone callers who have tormented Sue for decades? Some call in the dark of night and ask for Amy. Others demand ransom. Sue speaks to them all, hoping against hope that one might actually know something that will bring Amy home. Could one of them be the man the psychic saw?

Police had long tried to identify one caller who had stalked Sue for almost two decades, beginning shortly after Amy disappeared. He said he had Amy, that she was his sex slave and ranted on with obscene descriptions of what he was doing to her missing daughter. He said his name was Hal Johnson. Occasionally he'd give an address where he said Amy could be found. Sue and Ned would rush there, but find no such address.

The caller taunted Sue when her mother died. When she arrived home from Ned's funeral, her phone was ringing. "I know you're alone now," he told her.

Amy had been taken to Canada, he said, then to London and Saudi Arabia. He said Amy's tongue had been cut out. Sick and in despair, Sue would hang up. He'd call back, sometimes six or seven times a night, demanding she join him in sex games with Amy.

The calls always came from telephone booths. Police never arrived in time. He'd change locations, always a step ahead of them. When Sue asked for proof that he had Amy, *he gave details he could have learned from newspapers or television. He arranged meetings, to show Sue a photo of Amy, or a sample of her handwriting. Desperate, fearless, she went and waited. He never showed up.*

Then he'd call to demand why she was not there. He became more and more threatening. But in 1993, he made a mistake. He began using a cell phone. At first, police could not trace the number. After another failed midnight meeting, monitored by FBI agents, detectives went to the Billig residence to install a new state-of-the-art cell phone tracer. They were still at the house when "Johnson" called again. Police and prosecutors zeroed in on the number. But again, they were frustrated. The cell phone was registered to a nonexistent Miami company. The "company" proved to be a U.S. government mail drop, a front for a federal undercover operation. Investigators finally matched the number to U.S. Customs. A Customs supervisor insisted it was none of the detectives' business who used that phone.

Not until police went to Customs and played a tape of his calls for shocked supervisors did the agency admit the identity of the familiar voice on the telephone.

The obscene caller who had stalked Sue for years claiming to have her missing daughter was Henry "Hank" Johnson Blair, forty-eight, a decorated U.S. Customs squad leader with twenty-four years of law-enforcement service. Married to a South Miami hospital administrator, he had two daughters, one of them seventeen, Amy's age when she vanished.

Blair was led away in handcuffs, charged with three counts of aggravated stalking, each punishable by a five-year prison term.

When Amy disappeared, Blair was twenty-seven, a newlywed recently returned from his honeymoon. He was a Customs officer, assigned to drive around, patrolling Miami's waterfront.

Just prior to that he had been an armed sky marshal, protecting commercial flights to the Caribbean and South America from hijackers.

A man named Hank was mentioned in Amy's diary. He had invited her to travel with him to South America. She had passed it off lightheartedly. The name was a mystery; there was no Hank among Amy's schoolmates or known friends. But police have never been able to link Hank Blair to Amy's disappearance.

Blair pleaded not guilty, posted bond, and left the courtroom hand-in-hand with his wife.

He derived a strange sexual pleasure, he admitted, from making cruelly obscene calls to women who were victims of tragedy. Police said Blair had also called the mothers of murdered or troubled girls he'd read about in the news. Psychiatrists call it telephone scatologia. Using obscene phone calls for sexual arousal is one of the deviant urges included under the broad category of paraphilia, which describes those who achieve arousal and orgasm from socially unacceptable stimulus.

Blair's lawyers tried to quash his confession saying paraphilia made him unable to understand his own actions. Blair claimed alcohol and stress brought on his sick urges.

Dade Circuit Judge Alex Ferrer didn't buy it. He did not allow paraphilia as a defense and refused to throw out Blair's confession.

Out of fifty potential jurors, only seven were unfamiliar with the case.

Blair testified and blamed Sue. If she didn't like it, she shouldn't have listened to him. The woman was obsessed, he said, and added, "Maybe we should both be locked up."

Unable to reach a verdict on the felony charge of aggravated stalking, the jury did convict on two misdemeanor stalking counts.

Judge Ferrer sentenced Blair to two years behind bars followed by five years probation and refused to allow him to serve the time in a work release program.

Since released, Blair has never apologized.

Sue still dreams about Amy, but lately her dreams have changed. "I couldn't see her face before, but now in dreams I can. She walks in the door looking just as she looked then."

If she is alive, Amy is forty-seven years old.

Not all missing-persons cases are mysteries without end. People do fall through cracks. Sometimes they can be fished out by a reporter whose story catches the right eye. It almost always works.

It did for Eddie Rosenman.

The seventy-five-year-old World War I veteran put on his jaunty red-banded straw hat one Sunday afternoon and stepped out of his small South Beach apartment for a stroll. A stroke had impaired his speech, and Eddie, a diabetic, could not speak well, but he signaled to his wife Rebecca that he would return in five or ten minutes.

He did not. By ten o'clock that night she had called police. A week later he was still gone, and Rebecca, his wife of more than fifty years, sobbed in my arms. Eddie had not been seen at local hospitals, the airport, or the morgue. My friend Elayne, at the missing-persons bureau, had checked them all out.

Eddie and Rebecca had fallen in love in New York after he came back from the war—in 1919. They had never been apart since their wedding in 1923. "Without each other, we're alone," she told me. A son died in infancy. Their daughter died in 1935 at age eleven.

Rebecca had searched everywhere. Hundreds of volunteers from a veterans' group and from Kneseth Israel Congregation where the couple worshiped had combed the narrow streets of densely populated South Beach. They had fanned out across the green acres of nearby Flamingo Park. The entire neighborhood was on alert. But they found no trace of Eddie Rosenman.

"It's like the ground opened, and he fell into it," Rebecca said between sobs. Because he was unable to speak, she did not believe Eddie could have bought a ticket and boarded a plane, but perhaps, disoriented, he got on a bus. She even called the cemetery in New York where their little daughter is buried. He had not been seen.

"Somebody might take him in overnight, but they wouldn't keep him," Rebecca reasoned. "Nobody would kidnap him for ransom. We're poor. I just want him back, dead or alive."

Police could offer no clues.

It was time for the ultimate weapon: publicity—the power of the press—to ferret out Eddie Rosenman wherever he might be. Most reporters will not admit it, but we all love times like this. It makes me feel like Superwoman to the rescue. "We'll find him," I promised Rebecca. I had a gut feeling; I knew somehow we would. The story hit the morning paper, accompanied by the couple's fiftieth wedding anniversary picture—and we had him.

An off-duty nurse, sipping her morning coffee at home, saw the story, recognized Eddie and excitedly called her co-workers about "the man in the little straw hat." He had spent most of his missing week locked in the psychiatric institute at a Miami hospital. The attendants showed him the newspaper, and he pointed tearfully to Rebecca's picture. "Mama, mama," he said.

Rebecca caught a taxi to the hospital, where Eddie swept her into his arms, crying like a child. He still had on the same clothes he was wearing when he disappeared. A policeman had brought him to the hospital at 5:00 A.M., the morning after his wife reported him missing. Eddie had $172 in his pockets but no identification.

"He could not communicate," explained a hospital administrator. "It seemed like he was incoherent, so he was placed in the institute."

Rebecca and Elayne had made repeated calls to that very hospital, describing Eddie in detail and explaining his speech difficulties. But because he had been admitted as a "no name," hospital officials insisted each time that they had no such patient. By the time we found him, Eddie did have a name, but it wasn't his. He was now listed in hospital records as Harry Brotice. No one could explain it. Perhaps Eddie tried to tell them who he was and that is how it sounded to someone. Hospital officials were also vague about where Eddie had been found, the circumstances of his encounter with police, or even which of Dade's twenty-seven police departments had delivered him to them.

I wrote the story and we photographed the happy couple, together again. Next day, an angry administrator complained to our managing editor that the story was unfair, that it made hospital procedures appear sloppy, and I was counseled about striving for better relations with the administrations of our wonderful local institutions.

But Rebecca was happy. So was Eddie. Me too.

"I'm so grateful he's alive and I have him back," she said, as neighbors and friends joined in a welcome-home party. "We're both overjoyed."

Publicity can find lost people tangled in the hopeless maze of government and bureaucracy. A man called the *Herald* asking for help one Sunday night, something about a missing person. I overheard a city-desk clerk telling him to call back Monday morning. A long time ago I deliberately relocated from a desk in the distant back row of the huge newsroom to a spot that had become vacant, close to the city desk—the newspaper's nerve center, the center of action. When a big story broke and harried editors lifted their eyes in search of a reporter—they would see me first.

I butted in and took the call. I am a sucker for a missing-persons case.

The man was distraught. His grandson was missing; he had been gone three days. His name was Corey and he was four.

The caller, whose name was Sam, started to cry. A widower, he worked two jobs to support his two grown daughters and his little grandson. Corey's mother, twenty-five, had a history of mental problems. She was controlled by medication, but sometimes she didn't take it. Violent in the past, she had once set the house on fire.

Sam had gone to his job with a concrete company at 3:00 A.M. on Friday. When he got home late that afternoon, his daughter and Corey were gone. They did not come home, and later, two policemen knocked at his door. His daughter, they told him, had been found incoherent and wandering in the street. She had been committed to the crisis center at Jackson Memorial Hospital. He asked about Corey, and they said, "What little boy?"

Sam immediately filed a missing-persons report and gave the officers Corey's picture. Frantic, he searched all day Saturday. On Sunday morning he anxiously called police to see if they had learned anything. He was told to call back on Tuesday, that the officer who took the missing-persons report was off until then. At the hospital, a nurse told him his daughter had muttered something about the Yahweh Temple, headquarters of the black militant Hebrew Israelites. Perhaps she had left Corey there. Sam rushed to the temple but white-robed guards turned him away saying they had not seen his grandson.

Sunday night with nowhere else to turn, he called the *Herald*. "I got to have some help to find him," he told me.

There was desperation in the man's voice. It didn't sound good to me. I asked if his daughter, in her troubled state, might have hurt Corey. Children are most often injured or murdered, not by strangers, but by their own families. His voice broke; he wasn't sure.

I was due to be off in twenty minutes but forgot going home and settled down to work. The police confirmed the grandfather's story, a missing-persons report had been filed. But our police desk reporter who monitors police radio frequencies had heard no BOLO (be on the lookout) broadcasts for a missing four-year-old. That was puzzling, but the department's public-information officer assured me, "I'm certain the officers in Central are doing all they can to find him. The guys over there have done everything they can."

The little boy could be anywhere, and I was worried that the search was apparently confined to the Central District, the neighborhood where he had disappeared. Then I discovered that there was no search at all—anywhere. Central District officers were totally unaware of the missing child. "I haven't heard anything. What little boy?" asked the officer manning the front desk. The same response came from patrolmen in squad cars.

At Communications, a sergeant told me that the boy's description was broadcast over police frequencies on Saturday, but not again on Sunday because the officers in charge did not know whether the child was still missing.

I told them he was.

A hospital administrator told me the mother "definitely did not come in here with a four-year-old." I asked that the patient be pressed for details. "They can't get much out of her," he reported back.

The Florida Division of Health and Rehabilitative Services takes custody of children who are lost, abused, or abandoned. But they said they had no little boy named Corey.

His granddad gave me a good description and a picture of Corey smiling. He said the boy was wearing a Spiderman T-shirt, blue jeans, and tennis shoes. "He is very smart," Sam said. "He knows his name and he knows my name—he calls me Granddaddy. He knows the name of his school—Turner's Kindergarten—but he doesn't know his address. He's only four." Asked for more details that might help identify the boy, he said Corey "likes potato chips and cookies—and his bicycle." The bike, his toys, and all his clothes were left behind.

Once the story and the picture ran in the morning *Herald,* Corey was lost no longer. A reader who saw it had Corey. He had been safe with her all along. His mother had left him at the Catholic Family and Children's Service, saying she could not care for him. They took him in and sent him to a foster home.

Sam and Corey were reunited that day. There was a picture in the paper next morning of Corey in his grandfather's arms. Both were beaming. As they walked hand in hand out of the agency's office, Corey looked coyly at the photographer's camera and said, "Cheese."

Bringing them home, that is what counts.

For the people who do the job, success is sometimes a

personal triumph, even in the face of tragedy. That is the sort of success won by Elizabeth Everson. A divorcée raising a family alone, she labored for years in the morgue at the Dade County Medical Examiner's office. A tough, beautiful, and often-brittle woman, the mother in Libby Everson would not let her send a young girl that nobody knew to an unmarked grave.

During my second year at the *Herald* I heard about the unidentified girl at the morgue and how in this particular case Libby Everson was fighting the official policy that sends unclaimed bodies to a pauper's grave after three weeks.

The girl had been at the morgue for five months.

A narcotics overdose killed her in a Miami motel room, and the one key to her identity, the man who brought her there, ran away and left her. They had registered as husband and wife, from New York, they said. The name they used was phony. A maid found the corpse the next day. The girl lay on a bed, the left sleeve of her blue flower-print blouse unbuttoned, exposing the soft flesh around the site of the fatal injection. A syringe, foil packets torn in two, a venetian-blind cord used to tie off the vein, and her companion's fingerprints were the only clues.

The prints identified the man. He was twenty-eight, a fugitive sought on burglary charges. Police nearly caught him a few weeks later, but he exchanged gunshots with them and escaped after a high-speed chase. In the room where the fugitive had been staying, police found a young woman's wallet and identification. But she was found alive, a burglary victim whose purse was stolen.

It was February, and the unidentified girl was Dade County's seventh fatal narcotics overdose of the year. In her pocket was a blank postcard from a Miami Beach hotel. Libby Everson took pictures of the girl to the hotel hoping someone might know her. No one did. *The Miami Herald* twice published brief descriptions, but no one came forward to identify or claim the body. Russ Leasburg, the detective I had sparred with when my neighbor got shot, worked hard on the case. This time he was more talkative. He had contacted the parents of missing girls from as far away as Indiana, Maryland, and Ohio.

A woman in Akron was certain the dead girl was her daughter. Their descriptions were identical, down to a scar on the girl's foot, but the girl with no name had perfect teeth, the missing Akron girl did not. When Leasburg went to New York on other police business, he spent most of his time checking the fugitive's old addresses, seeking a clue to the dead girl's identity.

At spring break, the tall, husky, blond detective plodded up and down Fort Lauderdale beaches, displaying morgue pictures of the dead girl to the vacationing college crowd. It grossed out a lot of kids, but none recognized her. Fliers and photos, before and after embalming, were dispatched across the nation.

I went to the morgue, and Libby Everson rolled the body out of the refrigerated cooler. The dead girl lay in a metal tray on wheels, wearing a swirly, more sophisticated hairdo than she probably ever did in life. Libby had called in a hairdresser before allowing her photo to be taken.

It was my first glimpse of the softer side of Libby Everson. A tough cookie in a tough job, she was also the mother of a teenage girl. "It must be terrible for her parents not to know what's become of their daughter." When all the leads dead-ended, and she and Leasburg found no new ones, she nearly agreed several times "to let the little girl go, but I just can't. I absolutely refuse to bury one this young in the county cemetery." Her eyes glistened, and she turned away so I wouldn't see.

I wrote a story about Miss Nobody, used the picture, and described the petite hazel-eyed girl in detail, down to her Ladybug blue jeans, blue birthstone ring, size 34-C brassiere, and the possibility that her name was Lisa. A paper valentine addressed to "Lisa" and signed "Will" was in the pocket of her expensive suede jacket.

Shortly after the *Herald* landed on suburban lawns the next morning, the nationwide search ended close to home.

Her name *was* Lisa. The valentine had been signed by her little brother. Her mother read the story and saw her dead daughter's picture. She telephoned the Miami Springs detective who took the missing-persons report on February 16. He was reading the story when she called. "I think that's my daughter," she said, weeping. He agreed.

Lisa had gone out at 6:00 P.M. on Valentine's Day. She never came back. Her father went to Miami Springs police headquarters the next morning to report her missing. They suggested he wait twenty-four hours. A report was taken when he returned the following morning. The detective assured the parents her description would be transmitted statewide by teletype. It was not. Somehow it slipped through the cracks.

The girl was found dead in Miami that day.

For five agonizing months, as she lay in the morgue just seven miles from home, her parents called Miami Springs police each day, hoping for news. Their missing girl was a straight-A student, a senior at Miami Springs High School. Her parents never dreamed she might try drugs. They had never met the man who had registered at the motel with their daughter. They and others who knew her had even seen the earlier newspaper items, but it never occurred to them that the wholesome high school girl they knew could be the same young woman who died of a drug overdose in a sleazy motel room in the company of a criminal.

The mother and the father, a U.S. customs inspector, confirmed the identification at the morgue. "The father couldn't believe it," a detective said.

I talked to the man, as he struggled to hold back his tears. "She had no problems at school and none here at home either," he said. "What can I do? I feel like kicking a hole in the wall."

So did some *Herald* editors. They were furious. The morgue photo of Miss Nobody had greeted readers from the local page of the newspaper, at breakfast time. I really did not understand the objection. The dead girl, with her perfect hairdo and makeup, did not look like someone dead five months. A sheet tucked neatly at her chin, she looked like she was asleep. The problem was, however, that the editors *knew* she was dead.

It had worked; her family got her back. Even tough Libby Everson shed tears of relief, but the editors insisted that the story would have been as effective without the photo. The assistant city editor who put it in the paper, at my urging, caught the heat. He passed it along.

No more pictures of dead people in this newspaper, ever, they decreed, unanimously. Their solemn edict stands unbroken, despite my frequent subtle, and sometimes not-so-subtle, efforts. Some of the morgue pictures I have acquired since were not unpleasant looking at all, and I'm sure, if published, might have identified some other lost people.

Perhaps even the dapper little gray-haired man. A thousand theories crowd my mind when I think of him. He might even have been an escaped Nazi war criminal. Whoever he was, he was clever, very clever at covering his tracks. Why?

A worldwide search by now-retired Miami Homicide Detective Henry Weaver led the detective down bewildering blind alleys to blank walls. It became a personal contest between the investigator and the man with whom he matched wits. The detective did all that was humanly possible, yet the little man who covered his tracks so well remains a mystery fifteen years after his death.

The case nags at Weaver and at me. "It's baffling," the detective says. "It's like he came to Miami to die. He took a lot of pains to make sure he was never identified."

The distinguished-looking gentleman with a gray mustache checked into the Biscayne Terrace Hotel, on Biscayne Boulevard. He appeared to be between sixty and seventy and registered as "J. Williams, 222 Delaware Pl., Jacksonville, Fla. Self-employed salesman." The name is apparently fictitious; the address is a vacant lot.

His three-month stay, in room 708, remained uneventful until the late afternoon of December 29, when an employee went to the roof to lower the flag. The little man, well-dressed as always, in a yellow shirt, brown trousers, and a tasteful tie, was lying on a rooftop sundeck staring skyward. There was a neat hole in his temple, just above his right ear.

His hands were outstretched, his ankles crossed, almost casually. His half-glasses, in a thin gold metal frame, had been knocked askew by the impact of the bullet. It was undoubtedly suicide: A .25-caliber pistol lay at his feet. The body was still warm.

The mystery began back in room 708. The labels had been carefully cut from all of his clothing; the initials had been scraped off his fine leather attaché case. His billfold, which was new, contained five ten-dollar bills, nothing else. He had paid cash for everything. He had made no telephone calls, had no visitors. Police could find only one person who recalled ever speaking to the man, a Spanish-speaking maid. He tipped her fifty cents a day. She thought he spoke with a British accent.

He had been in excellent health, with no scars or tattoos. He had all his own teeth, and his fingerprints were not on record with the FBI or Canadian police. The leather belt he wore was stamped MADE IN FRANCE, but he had removed the manufacturer's name. The Swiss manufacturer of the dead man's Omega watch said that it was delivered to a New York City wholesaler on November 13,

1953. The wholesale firm disposes of records after ten years, so there is no way of learning who received the watch from them. But there was a jeweler's mark inside the cover, inscribed when the watch was repaired. The American Watchmakers Institute researched its files and included the information in its bimonthly newsletter to watchmakers nationwide. The man's eyeglass prescription was published in a national optometry journal with a plea for help. Neither effort brought a clue.

The dead man was five feet three inches tall and 145 pounds. His salt-and-pepper hair was receding. His size-36 undershorts were blue, and in his orthopedic shoes, size 8½ triple-E, he wore Dr. Scholl's arch supports. They could have come from any store in the country that sells Dr. Scholl's.

Among his scant personal effects were a number of books—heavy-reading philosophy and psychology—and two blank sheets of writing paper that bore faint impressions. He evidently wrote a last letter to someone. Crime-lab technicians used every scientific method at their command but could raise no identifiable words from the impressions.

The best clue was the gun. Trace the gun, Detective Weaver thought, and I can track down the name of the man who used it. He and Libby Everson enlisted the aid of Interpol. The response from the international police agency was startling.

The gun had been reported lost or stolen from the Browning factory in Brussels, Belgium, where it had been manufactured in 1917, during World War I. There had been no record of it since, until it killed the dapper little man on a Miami rooftop, half a world and half a century later.

The man's fingerprints and description were circulated through all 113 countries served by Interpol, including England, Australia, and New Zealand. There was no response.

Some suicides are intended to punish with guilt the people left behind. His obviously was not. He wanted to die in secret. Whatever his motive, the quiet little man's final deed was an unmitigated success. He won his posthumous battle of wits. In death he triumphed.

Few missing persons seem to vanish totally and forever, without explanation. Those who do often seem to be the most unlikely candidates for such mysteries.

"It's like a flying saucer swooped down and scooped up her and her car." That is how Miami Missing Persons Detective Saundra Weilbacher described the disappearance of writer-retiree Jean McBride Blocher.

Sandy Weilbacher, a freckled red-haired detective, worked for years on the case. Her intense, long-term investigation found "nothing, just poufff!"

Jean Blocher is an unlikely central character for something so bizarre. Nothing frightening or out of the ordinary ever took place in her well-ordered life, until the day she and her pink sports car vanished.

She left an unfinished page of work still in her typewriter and her cigarettes on the coffee table nearby. In the bedroom, her shoes were polished to a sheen and her lingerie carefully laid out for a sorority luncheon the following day.

Jean Blocher, age sixty-six, obviously stepped out for just a moment.

The moment has stretched into eighteen years.

A retired Social Security employee and the widow of an army officer, she wrote travel articles for magazines and stayed active in church and civic work. Lively and buoyant, she did not lack a sense of humor. Her beloved ten-year-old Kharmann Ghia sports car had recently been repainted, and the color, intended to be fire-engine red, had somehow emerged a hot flamingo pink. Unperturbed, she happily drove what was probably the only flamingo-pink Kharmann Ghia in South Florida.

Her niece telephoned on that October evening to discuss their weekend plans for dinner and golf. No answer. At eight o'clock the next morning, still no answer.

Sara Sekso lived just five minutes away. She drove toward her aunt's apartment near the bay, scanning the neighborhood for the distinctive pink car. She didn't see it. Her aunt's neighbors said it had not been parked in its usual space the night before. Alarmed, she called police. Thus began the weeks, months, and the years of frustration.

Jean Blocher kept little cash at home. She must have needed a few extra dollars for the luncheon the next day and dashed out to cash a check. It was the last check she ever wrote. For a meager ten dollars, it was cashed at a nearby supermarket. It had to have been before dusk—no lights were left on in her apartment. There were no other withdrawals from her bank accounts. Her credit cards vanished with her and were not used again.

Perhaps the well-dressed widow caught the eye of a thief in the store as she cashed the check, even though the paltry amount was not likely to attract a mugger. But even if she was victimized, robbed, or murdered, whatever became of her body and her car? Why didn't the thief ever use her checks or credit cards?

Puzzled police dragged Biscayne Bay and found no clues. Fearing she had blacked out at the wheel and driven off the road into a canal, the niece and her husband hired a diver to probe the murky waterway along the avenue that was Jean Blocher's usual route to their home. The diver found the usual debris, but no small pink car.

The couple continued the search for years. No body resembling Jean Blocher's was ever found. Despite a nationwide alert, the pink car was never sighted. State records reveal it was never reregistered. After eight years the niece's husband died of cancer. His widow told me that she still thought daily of her aunt. "Every time the phone rings, I think maybe she had amnesia and is calling to tell me where I can find her."

After nine years, she told me, "My heart still stops every time I see a Kharmann Ghia."

There are deep lakes, rock pits, and miles of waterways criss-crossing Dade County. Police frequently plumb rusting cars from their depths. Many are dumped by owners who report them stolen and collect insurance; some are stolen and stripped; others are sunken coffins, with accident victims still behind the wheel or homicide victims stuffed in the trunk. Most have not been submerged long, a few for as long as two years.

High-flying police on air patrol constantly monitor the waterways spotting sunken cars. When I am there, or if I hear that they have located a car, I hold my breath to see if it is a Kharmann Ghia.

Detective Sandy Weilbacher retired three years ago and left Miami. A few months ago I called the niece again, just to stay in touch should there ever be news. The number had been disconnected; her name is no longer listed in the Miami telephone directory.

Am I the only person still trying to find Jean Blocher?

People vanish and are not found, corpses surface but are never identified. Where did they come from? Where did they go?

I think of the punchline to an old joke: It's the one about the man who arrives home early and finds his wife in the bedroom, half-dressed. He opens the closet door and is stunned to find a naked man inside. "What are you doing in there?" he cries.

The naked man shrugs: "Everybody gotta be someplace."

It is not funny, but at least one of the dead did play a final practical joke on the world he left behind. I don't believe he expected anyone else to get it; it was a private joke. The punchline still escapes me, but I know I came as close as anyone. And the stranger's final act enabled me to encounter another of the dark princes from my child-hood fantasies.

Hot and sweaty, out at a murder scene all afternoon, I had three other stories to write, was on deadline, and hadn't eaten since dawn. Crazed and impatient, I talked briefly to a young Miami homicide detective about a shooting he was investigating. He, too, was harried and overworked. We were both in a hurry. I just happened to ask what else was going on.

He mentioned a suicide he was handling. A young man on crutches, moving slowly and painfully, had checked into a Miami hotel. His infirmity was so obvious that hotel staff and other guests would rush to help him, opening doors and pulling out chairs. He did not stay long. The following day he managed to crawl over a high balcony railing and plunge headlong to his death.

It seemed a sad and simple case. The man probably ended his life because of his pain. It was still unclear whether his physical condition was due to injury or some progressively crippling disease. The autopsy had not yet been done. The detective was having a problem locating next of kin. The address the man had given at the hotel was fictitious.

What was his name? I asked absently, not terribly interested. The detective consulted his notebook, flipping pages to find it. "George Metesky," he said.

"Are you sure?" I said, suddenly interested. He spelled it out. It couldn't be, I thought. "How old did you say he was?"

The dead man was in his late twenties or early thirties. The real George Metesky must be seventy by now, I thought. Who would name a son after the notorious Mad

Bomber? He had been the scourge of New York. The Mad Bomber and Willie "the Actor" Sutton were contemporaries, sharing front-page space during my childhood years of avid newspaper reading.

This young Latin detective had never heard of the Mad Bomber. I told him about George Metesky. We stared at each other, sharing that sinking feeling. What had seemed a simple suicide might be more complicated. Neither of us had time for this. Now I wanted all the details. I'm certain he was already sorry he had ever mentioned it.

I knew all about George Metesky. A bachelor with no children, he had lived a quiet and circumspect existence with his two spinster sisters, while building bombs in their garage. He waged war on Con Edison. A disgruntled former employee, he felt wronged, blaming the power company for his tuberculosis. He terrorized New York for some time, planting bombs all over the city and writing crazy hate letters against Con Ed. The bombs never killed anyone and eventually, after much excitement and lots of headlines, he was caught and committed to a mental hospital. I recalled reading in recent years that, after half a lifetime, he had been released and had returned once more to dwell with his sisters, hopefully to pursue a new hobby.

Who was this dead man with his name?

At the morgue, the mystery deepened. The doctor who performed the postmortem found no need for the crutches. There was nothing wrong with the man physically, until after he jumped, of course. Why did he struggle about on crutches pretending to be a cripple?

The Mad Bomber might know the answer. I called him in Connecticut. The number was in the phone book. He sounded perfectly sane, a delightful old fellow, kindly and lucid. He had no nephew and no relative named George Metesky. He had never even heard of another George Metesky. Neither did he recognize the young man by physical description.

I recalled that during the national political conventions in the 1970s, along with the Zippies and the Yippies, there was a small group of protesters who called themselves the George Meteskys, the Mad Bombers. But the Mad Bomber himself told me he had never heard from them, and I had no luck in tracking them down. He, too, was curious and asked me to let him know if I ever learned who the dead man was. I promised I would, but I never talked to the Mad Bomber again. I had nothing to report. Despite the story I wrote and the inquiries I made, I still don't know the identity of the young man who pretended to be a cripple or why he chose to die using the name of a notorious madman, captured and locked away in a mental ward before he was even born.

Mike Gonzalez always tells me that logic is useless in trying to figure out such cases because there is none. The people who do these things are not thinking logically.

But I still can't help trying to fathom the mysteries. At night, I sometimes sit by the water and think about all the lost people. The detectives who work on those cases eventually give up. Or, like Sandy Weilbacher and Henry Weaver, they retire or transfer and leave it behind them.

They do the best they can in the time they've got—and then they let it go.

The county employees tag the dead, finish the paper-work, and deliver them, unmourned, to unmarked graves. They let it go.

It is the sane and practical way to handle it, to give it your best shot and let it go.

Why can't I?

TEN

Justice

We all want it, but we rarely find it.

Our system is not one of justice, but of law. Justice is the goal, but it is always elusive, blind, and never certain. People who are in pain and despair are sometimes driven to seek justice in their own ways. Others, who are dedicated and talented, pursue it high-mindedly through the system. They play by all the rules. Sometimes nothing anyone can do is enough.

Many prosecutors pay more attention to their conviction records than to the quest for justice. They take no risks and shun cases that are not neatly served up with a confession, eyewitnesses, and a smoking gun.

Carol King Guralnick was different, different from anything Miami has ever seen. We met when she was Carol King, an intern in the state attorney's office, and I was covering criminal court. We both dated Criminal

Court Judge Paul Baker, an elegant and witty jurist who was between marriages at the time.

Rich, beautiful, and flamboyant, Carol was a former beauty queen and model. She had once clerked for that master of courtroom theatrics, Melvin Belli. She had absorbed everything. At age twenty-three, she became an assistant state attorney, a prosecutor, with her own tiny and drab institutional-style office. The walls were a blah color and the desks were steel-gray. The first thing she did was redecorate.

It did not cost the taxpayers a dime. She had the walls painted powder-blue, a cool backdrop for crushed-velvet drapes of Wedgwood blue, with flocked, white sheer curtains. The carpeting was plush and pale-blue. Her desk was Louis Quatorze; the chair behind it was high-backed and velvet.

She came from a wealthy family. Her lawyer husband, Ronald Guralnick, was also well-to-do. So, she explained, why not?

She was also the star of her own radio talk show. Billed as Lady Law, she took a hard line on crime.

Carol King Guralnick never walked into a courtroom, she made an entrance—and pity the person in her way. Vividly striking, stunningly dressed in designer clothes, with lush long dark hair and flashing dark eyes, she projected enough confidence to stun a whole roomful of lawyers speechless. She always drove an expensive, telephone-equipped sports car. The vanity tag said LADY LAW, and she parked that car any-damn-place-she-wanted-to. She paid the parking tickets without complaint—it was cheaper to her than wasting time looking for a parking space.

Some people, mostly insecure men, disliked her. Her ambition was obvious. Partial to high-publicity cases, she wanted to be a judge. She even envisioned herself on the U.S. Supreme Court someday. "When I'm prepared," she once said, "it will come to me if it's meant to be. I really believe in destiny."

I had to admire her ambition. This woman could be shopping in Paris, partying with the jet set, or having her toenails painted. She did not have to be in that Justice Building zoo every day, prosecuting rapists, robbers, and killers. But she was. Whatever her motives, she was there because she wanted to be. She was not afraid to work— and she cared. She provided warmth and strength to frightened victims and witnesses, who often sobbed in her arms, shedding tears all over her designer suits.

I had not seen Carol for months when I stumbled upon the haunting case of the little boy named Sam. His fifth serious accident finally ended his short life when he was three years and five months old.

Before he drowned in seven inches of bathwater, this beautiful, husky, healthy youngster had:

- swallowed bleach,
- overdosed on pills,
- escaped from his room when it mysteriously burst into flames so intense that they shattered windows, and

• turned blue and stopped breathing, his air cut off
  by a plastic laundry bag found over his head.

On that occasion a police helicopter touched down in
the street in front of his home to rush him to a hospital.
He had been treated in intensive care so often that the
nurses knew him by name.

He drowned in January. I heard about it in June and
began to look into it. At the time of each accident, Sam
was home alone with his twenty-seven-year-old mother.
Twice married, she was divorced from the boy's father, a
Coral Gables police sergeant. In fact, she had been dating
one of the firemen who rushed to the rescue the day
Sam's room caught fire.

The day of his final accident, the mother said she put
her son in the tub for his bath and went to hang laundry.
Ten minutes later, she said, she found him facedown in
the water. The death appeared suspicious, but no prosecutor would touch such a case. There were no witnesses.
What jury would ever believe that any mother could
harm such a beautiful child?

His father had sought custody, particularly after Sam's
earlier escapes from death, but the judge had ruled that a
little boy belongs with his mother.

Six years earlier, in Broward County, while separated
from her first husband, the same woman's first child died.
Also a little boy, he too had drowned while taking a bath.
She had found him submerged after a ten-minute absence to take care of some laundry, according to the old

police reports. The ambulance driver who answered the call was a man she had been dating and planned to marry.

I went to the Coral Gables police station to see Sam's dad. We met alone in a small interrogation room, across a scarred wooden table. Still distraught over his son's death, he blamed his former wife's carelessness for the fatal incident and the boy's earlier injuries. I was puzzled. Wasn't he suspicious in light of the fact that Sam was his ex-wife's second child to drown while being bathed?

He stared at me, speechless, then put his head down on the table and began to sob. He didn't know.

He had met the woman six months after her first child died—of a heart defect, she told him. During their courtship, he even took her to place fresh flowers on the baby's grave.

The mother had also told the detective investigating Sam's death that a heart problem had killed her firstborn. She declined to submit to a polygraph test. She also refused to talk to me, except to say that she could not really explain why she would not take a lie test.

Dr. Ronald Wright, Dade chief deputy medical examiner at the time, concluded that a healthy child Sam's age and size, three feet three inches tall, could not accidentally drown in seven to nine inches of water. It was physically impossible. I wrote the story. There was immediate reaction.

Carol King Guralnick called, demanding to know why no one was prosecuting the case. I told her nobody would take it.

A day or two later, Sam's pudgy, blond mother, now

married to a Coast Guard officer, was arrested on murder charges. A prosecutor had agreed to take the case.

It was, of course, Carol King Guralnick. And I, of course, planned to cover the trial. His father had color photos of Sam swimming—splashing happily in his pool—even diving. Carol had them blown up to life-size, so the jury could see that the boy was healthy and athletic, with no fear of the water.

But there would never be a trial. Neither Sam, nor his mother, ever had their day in court. Even Carol King Guralnick made mistakes.

In a pretrial ruling, Judge Natalie Baskin refused to allow the jury to hear any testimony about the death of the first child or about Sam's four prior near-fatal accidents. It was all inadmissible and irrelevant, she ruled, because the incidents were "remote" to the case.

Carol believed they were the heart of her case and would show the jury a pattern of conduct by the mother.

A jury had already been selected and sworn, but they had not yet heard opening arguments or a single word of evidence. In order to appeal the judge's ruling, Carol moved for a mistrial.

The mother's lawyer, defense attorney Roy Black, one of Miami's best, did not object. He simply smiled.

The judge granted the mistrial—and it was all over. Black, a more experienced attorney, realized something that Carol did not. The jury had already been sworn in, meaning that the trial had officially begun. To try the mother now before another jury would be placing her in double jeopardy. No one can be tried twice for the same crime.

Sam's mother walked out of court free forever on a legal technicality.

What is justice? In the case of Charles Griffith, the father of another innocent child, it is a puzzle to ponder on long and sleepless nights.

I favor Florida's twenty-five-year mandatory minimum prison term for murder in the first degree. Too many criminals, free too soon, hurt somebody else. Outrage stories are legion. And yet, whenever the law is strictured into rigid black-and-white-with-no-exception, and you feel that, at last, the bad guys will be punished and the good guys protected, a Charles Griffith comes along.

I can't forget his face, and I know in my heart that none of us is safer on the street because young Charles Griffith is locked behind bars with no hope of parole until the year 2010.

His mother was a burlesque queen, his father a porno king who owns adult movie theaters and burlesque houses. They are long divorced. Charles grew up in North Carolina, then came to Miami, where his father gave him a job as projectionist at one of his X-rated movie theaters.

Charles and a pretty girl named Becky married young but separated after five years. Only one constantly lovely thing brightened his life: their little girl, Joy, bright, blond, and beautiful. He describes his daughter's blue eyes as "filled with angel dust, with little flecks of light in them."

Something terrible happened in October 1984, when Joy was two and a half years old. At her grandmother's house, as her mother fixed *café con leche* in the kitchen, Joy scampered into the living room to watch cartoons on TV. She climbed into a brown reclining chair and somehow caught her head between the chair and its collapsible footrest. The weight of her thirty-two pounds lowered the footrest, and it strangled her, cutting off the oxygen to her brain.

Her mother found Joy with her head wedged in the chair, her tiny hands clasping the nubby chocolate-colored upholstery. The child was ashen; she was not breathing. Police and paramedics found no pulse or heartbeat. They restarted her heart with drugs. After forty frantic minutes of cardiopulmonary resuscitation, Joy did breathe once again on her own, but her brain was damaged—irreversibly. She would never again regain consciousness.

Her twenty-four-year-old father slept on a hospital-floor mat and visited Joy hourly in intensive care. He learned to take care of her and how to insert a plastic vacuum tube into her throat to suction mucus from her lungs. He took some comfort: "If God takes her, at least we know one thing: She hasn't lived long enough to be afraid. She never had her heart broken. All she knew was laughter and good times."

He asked people to pray for Joy.

Torturous months dragged by, and Charles Griffith searched through medical books and journals. He read about a drug used on coma victims in Europe and pleaded with Miami doctors to try it. They did; it did not help. He worked painstakingly with Joy, touching honey, then lemon to her tongue. He blinked a flashlight into her eyes, rubbed her cheek with silk and then with a rough terry washcloth, trying to reawaken her senses, to stimulate a response. He was certain she could hear him—and that she could feel pain. He agonized when a hole was drilled in her skull for a brain monitor, when doctors cut open her stomach to insert tubes for feeding, when they cut open her throat for a tracheotomy.

Convinced that certain hospital procedures hurt her, he quarreled with hospital workers and technicians he accused of not being gentle enough. Nurses turned the child every two hours. He angrily objected to those who did not speak to her first. "If they can't say, 'Joy, honey, I am going to turn you now,' then I want to be the one to do it," he insisted. "She can't see. It scares her."

He maintained that when he whispered in his daughter's ear, "Joy, this is daddy, if you hear me, blink twice," she responded. "She would do it and start crying. She lifted her left foot for me. I talk about her dog, Benji, and she blinks real fast. If I ask, 'Do you want daddy to hold you?' she blinks real fast. She knows what's going on. She's suffering," he insisted.

He grew more and more depressed and wept at the sight of playgrounds, toys, or small children. He and Becky grew further apart, until finally each was designated specific visiting hours in order to avoid the other. A civil suit was filed in Joy's name, against the chair's manufacturer and distributor. It charged that in order to gain a slight price advantage in a highly competitive market, the recliners were built and sold without a safety device that would have prevented the accident.

On Joy's third birthday, April 4, 1985, Charles wore clown makeup and brought balloons, presents, and a cake to the hospital. He sang "Happy Birthday," guiding her small, limp wrist, as he and his daughter cut the cake together.

Alone at daybreak in his small South Beach apartment he remembered how Joy would wake him, chirping, "Good morning, daddy." At bedtime he recalled how she always tucked in her toy dog and whispered "nighty-nite." Charles kept the stuffed toy on his bed, tucked in by a tiny blanket. He imagined Joy was there with him. He could even smell the baby-shampoo fragrance of her hair. He saw a psychiatrist for help. All the doctor did, he said, was prescribe Valium.

When Joy had been in her coma for eight months, her father telephoned several Miami radio talk shows. Weeping on the air, he asked for somebody to help him.

But no help came.

In his grief, Charles counseled with the only clergyman he knew—the controversial preacher of the so-called First Church of the Last Chance. The mission of the self-named Reverend John 3:16 is to bring "soup, soap, and hope" to people down on their luck. The colorful street preacher, a onetime B-movie actor, found Jesus in the late 1960s and changed his name to the Biblical verse John 3:16: "For God so loved the world, that he gave his only begotten Son, that whosoever believeth in him should not perish, but have everlasting life."

John 3:16 had endured his own troubles and disappointments. Hoping to minister to the poor, he had opened a South Beach mission in a decaying adult movie house owned by Griffith's father, but the city had swiftly shut it down, citing fire-code violations.

The preacher and the young father sat up all night. Charles cried, asking repeatedly: "Is there a heaven, John? Is there really a heaven? I can't let her suffer. Her life has no meaning." Together they pored over the Bible for a sign.

They found no answers.

The following night Charles Griffith went to the hospital nursery for the last time. It was June 28, 1985.

Instead of balloons and toys, he brought a .32-caliber revolver.

He talked and sang to Joy and held her in his arms for two hours. Then he placed the muzzle of the gun to her tiny chest and pulled the trigger twice. Shocked hospital personnel rushed to help, but she died quickly, shot both times in the heart.

Charles did not try to run away. Police arrested him at Joy's bedside and charged him with first-degree murder.

I talked to the medical examiner and the homicide detectives and searched for Griffith's friends, to try to piece together what had happened. I got lucky; John 3:16 called me. He was upset. We agreed to meet in fifteen minutes in front of the shabby South Beach apartment house where Charles lived. The preacher was waiting when I got there. He wore a black suit, a clerical collar, and a large crucifix. His look was anguished; he was distraught. "Pure love shot those bullets into her, pure love," he told me. "And I am a man of the cloth."

When he had urged Charles to pray for a miracle, the

young father had asked him, "Can God make a new brain?"

"I searched the scriptures, but we couldn't find the answers," John 3:16 told me. "He's been going out of his mind. The way he talked, it was mechanical. It wasn't him."

Neighbors talked freely about the father and his hopeless eight-month vigil. "He loved that child so," a grandmotherly woman said. "The look on his face recently . . . It didn't look like Charles. He looked old. The man is no murderer; he is just out of his mind."

It was a hot and muggy day. Over his clerical collar, the preacher's deeply lined face was damp with tears and perspiration. He said that Charles kept Joy's belongings in a small hope chest. "He would hug her dresses and her toys and just cry all night." On the walls, he said, were photographs of Joy, dozens of them. I wanted to see them, to write about them and what had happened to Charles Griffith and his little girl. But I couldn't find anybody with a key who would agree to open the apartment door.

John 3:16 suggested we could find photos of Joy where her father worked, at the X-rated Gayety Theater on Collins Avenue. We took my car. People on the sidewalk stopped and stared as the preacher and I pushed past the turnstile. We passed the sex toys on sale in the lobby— instead of popcorn. The inside of the theater was black as a swamp, far darker than most movie houses. Perhaps these moviegoers are reluctant to be seen, or need the cover of total darkness for reasons I don't even want to think about.

I couldn't see at all as we fumbled about, groping for the door to the projection booth. Afraid of falling, I wondered how I would ever explain breaking a leg inside the Gayety. John 3:16 held my hand tightly. A technicolor orgy was unfolding up on the big screen. "Don't look! Don't look!" cried the Reverend John 3:16.

I looked.

How do you ignore something like that? The quality and the clarity of color was astonishing. I always pictured porno movies as those gritty old black-and-white films the vice squad used to seize—the ones Emmett used to bring home "for review." This was something else entirely.

"Don't look!" the preacher shouted, tugging at my arm. Mercifully we found the door and stumbled into a staircase that took us to the projectionist's niche.

There, in the steamy raunchiness of the Gayety Theater, was a small shrine Charles had dedicated to his daughter. Taped to the walls of the projection booth were more than a dozen color snapshots: Joy on a pony, Joy cuddled in her father's arms, Joy busy at play with a pail and a shovel. Then there was the blond and angelic sleeping beauty on her third birthday, surrounded by stainless steel and electronic machines in a hospital nursery. Joy, oblivious to balloons and toys, watched over by a row of big-eyed dolls.

Charles also kept a small tape recorder at his post and cassettes labeled *Music for Joy*—songs he made up and recorded to play for his dreaming daughter. The projectionist on duty agreed to let me borrow some photos. I took two. In one, Charles, in a T-shirt, is holding Joy. She is smiling, in a sunsuit, as a playful breeze ruffles her golden hair. The other is the sleeping beauty in her small bed, surrounded by sterile machinery. It had to be exactly as she was when the shots rang out.

That picture told the entire story. It was so powerful. Perhaps that was why *Herald* editors chose not to use it. It was never published.

The first photo appeared on the front page in all editions the next day, a Sunday. My story in the first edition quoted the preacher, the neighbors, the homicide detectives, and the medical examiner. It was not enough, I knew. The real story could come only from Charles Griffith, but he was jailed, stripped naked in a safety cell on a suicide watch. The only person who might be allowed to see him at this point was his clergyman. I sent John 3:16 off to the jail. He delivered my message.

Hours later my telephone rang. "This is Charles Griffith," the caller said. "I killed my little girl."

And he started to cry. That is how we got our first-person jailhouse interview with Charles Griffith, telling us how he killed the one he loved most in the world.

"My baby was trapped in a dead body," he explained.

It was almost like a dream, he said. He did not go to the hospital thinking that he was going to kill his daughter.

"I don't even remember what happened last night," he said. "The respiratory therapist came in. He had to slap her on the chest. When he suctioned her, her eyes would open really wide. She couldn't breathe.

"I was crying. I was rubbing her face and saying, 'It is okay. Daddy's here. It won't hurt anymore. It is finished.' Then I heard two bangs."

He did not remember firing the shots, but he knew what they were. "I threw the gun across the room, and I fell on the floor, crying. I was yelling, 'Please don't let her hurt. Please don't let her hurt.' Three men came running. I thought they were going to do something else to her. She went through so much for such a little kid."

The men were hospital employees. Charles Griffith leaped to his feet, screaming, "Don't touch my daughter! You're not going to hurt her anymore. Don't touch her! Don't you go near my baby!"

A husky security guard rushed up and hugged him. "He was holding me up. My knees buckled," Charles said. "I didn't want to see her hurt anymore. She couldn't eat, she couldn't talk, she couldn't move. I just pray that there is a God, and she is up there, laughing and playing and seeing again. I just hope there is. But how could there be—with all she has been put through."

He believes she suffered.

Dr. Charles Wetli disagreed. "She was in a coma and couldn't feel anything," said the Dade chief deputy medical examiner. "She was not brain dead, but, like Karen Anne Quinlan, she could have gone on for years. It's a horrible end to a family tragedy," the physician said. "It's the last place in the world you expect a violent murder to take place—in a hospital nursery."

"I have no idea what's going to happen to me," Charles told me. "I just know I'm not going to do twenty-five years in prison. If they sentence me to that, I'll find a child molester in jail and do something bad to him—so they'll give me the electric chair.

"I'd rather get the electric chair and be with her."

A jury convicted Griffith of murder in the first degree. He was sentenced to life in prison. He must serve the mandatory twenty-five years before parole.

Justice. Everybody wants it, but we rarely find it.

Update: November 2003

Charles Griffith was released on October 24, 1995, after ten years in prison. He won his freedom when Dade County Circuit Judge Alex Ferrer threw out the young father's first-degree murder conviction on the grounds that Griffith did not receive a fair trial because his defense lawyer was apparently more interested in a million-dollar civil suit against the recliner company.

Griffith immediately agreed to plead guilty instead to a lesser charge of second-degree murder. Judge Ferrer sentenced him to seventeen years in prison and six years probation. With all the prison credits he had accumulated over the years, Griffith was immediately eligible for release.

One of his first stops, he said, would be a visit to his small daughter's grave.

"I plan to talk to Joy for a while," he said. "It's been a long time."

ELEVEN

McDuffie

The phone rang at my desk on Friday, December 21, 1979. Life would never be the same again.

That call set into motion events that ended in shocking headlines worldwide, changing the face of Miami forever. Hearts would break, including mine. Eighteen men and women would die and three hundred and fifty people, some of them children, would be hurt. Six hundred people would be arrested and property destruction would exceed $100 million.

The voice on the phone was familiar. It told me that a black motorcyclist was either dead or about to die, brutalized by white Public Safety Department (PSD) officers after a chase. They beat him with their heavy metal flashlights, called Kel-Lites, then faked a traffic accident to explain his fatal injuries, said my source. That was all.

It sounded insane—insane enough to be true. That's how it often seems to be in Miami; the more unbelievable the story, the more likely it is true. We spend a great deal of our time continually checking out rumors, calls, and whispers.

I asked at the medical examiner's office if there was a black motorcyclist in the morgue, a man fatally injured in a police chase.

No, they said, but one was on the way. He had just died at Jackson Memorial Hospital. His name was Arthur Lee McDuffie. He was thirty-three.

I called PSD internal affairs. They investigate when a civilian is hurt during an encounter with police. The commander was familiar with the case, he said, and nothing was amiss. The man simply had an accident trying to outrun the police.

At 1:51 A.M., according to the police story, a patrol sergeant tried to stop McDuffie for a traffic violation. He ran. More than a dozen patrol cars had joined the chase or were on the way, as the pursuit took them to speeds of one hundred miles an hour, across the city limits into Miami. There, they said, the cyclist's Kawasaki 900 crashed at sixty-five miles an hour. His safety helmet flew off on impact, they said. Arthur McDuffie staggered to his feet and tried to escape, forcing them to subdue and restrain him as he fought, the officers said.

I telephoned Dr. Ronald Wright at the morgue, to alert him before the autopsy that perhaps this was no routine accident. Downtown, at PSD headquarters, I listened to a tape of the eight-minute chase. It ended at 1:59 A.M., near a Miami expressway ramp. "We have him . . ." says the sergeant who launched the pursuit. Slightly more than two minutes later, now breathless, the sergeant asks for an ambulance.

On the accident report, I saw the names of the officers involved. A few sprang off the page. I had last seen those names a year earlier—in a *Herald* series on police brutality.

One of them, Michael Watts, was a study in contrasts. An honored Officer of the Month in 1976 for interrupting the rape of a woman hitchhiker and arresting sex killer Robert Carr, Watts had also been accused more than once of assaulting motorists he stopped for traffic violations. One driver required brain surgery as a result. Another, guilty of having an expired inspection sticker, complained that Watts had dragged her out of her car by her boots, bouncing her head on the pavement. Internal affairs had investigated all the complaints against him.

They sustained none.

One night months earlier I had received a call from a concerned cop who was a friend of Watts's. The cop said a supervisor, aware that Watts had difficulty in dealing with blacks, had deliberately transferred him to the predominantly black Central District. Watts was upset, the officer told me, and predicted that in his new assignment he would either "kill or be killed." The officer dared not be quoted. There was little I could do at the time.

The McDuffie accident report listed the name of the towing company that removed the dead man's wrecked orange-and-black Kawasaki. I went to find it.

When I asked for Arthur McDuffie's motorcycle, an employee at Barbon Towing picked up a clipboard. "Sign here," he said. "We were wondering when somebody was going to pick it up."

No investigation was under way. If there was one, the machine would have been seized as the prime piece of evidence. I told the man I had not come to claim it, but just to take a look. He shrugged and showed it to me.

I am no accident investigator. I have written about hundreds of traffic accidents, but I am no expert. It seemed odd, however, that every piece of glass and plastic on the machine was shattered—the speedometer, all of the gauges, all of the lights.

The scuffed and blood-smeared white motorcycle helmet worn by Arthur McDuffie was at the medical examiner's office. The chin strap was missing, cleanly severed, as if it had been sliced rather than torn. Chief medical examiner Dr. Joseph H. Davis was to leave for an island vacation that Saturday morning, but he postponed his departure after my call to Ronald Wright the night before; he wanted to be present for the autopsy on Arthur McDuffie. I did too, but they would not allow me to watch, so I waited.

The doctors reported their findings afterward, to police officers from Internal Affairs. I sat in on the session. Arthur McDuffie's skull had been shattered like an egg. The fatal fracture, directly between the eyes, was typical of the type of injury suffered when a motorcycle rider hurtles over the handlebars head first, smashing into a solid object, such as a pole or a bridge abutment. There were, the doctors acknowledged, other "blunt-impact" injuries that could have been inflicted by police Kel-Lites.

But, as they pointed out, it is an established fact that already fatally injured people often come up swinging and have to be subdued. There were approximately ten head wounds.

I drove out to the crash scene near a windy expressway entrance ramp and walked around looking. For what, I didn't know. One thing I did not see: There was nothing that the motorcycle—or Arthur McDuffie's head—could have hit.

No pole, no bridge abutment, not even a curb.

I left the place where Arthur McDuffie began to die to see where he had lived. He and his sister had shared a modest northwest section home. The house was crowded with grieving family who welcomed me. They, too, had visited the accident scene. His mother, Eula Mae, had combed the pavement for clues to her son's death. She had found the broken frame from his eyeglasses, the chin strap from his helmet, and part of a police sharpshooter's badge, apparently lost from a uniform during a scuffle.

The family made no accusations. They did not know what happened; they were bewildered. Aside from traffic violations, including a suspended driver's license, Arthur McDuffie had never been in trouble with the law. In fact, he had been a policeman himself, in the military. He had also been named the outstanding member of his Marine platoon and the president of the marching band at Booker T. Washington High School in Miami.

One wall of the well-kept living room was covered with plaques. They all had Arthur McDuffie's name engraved on them: awards for achievement—his insurance company sales team had sold more policies than any other in the firm. When I later described Arthur Mc-Duffie in stories as an insurance executive, it drew fire from some quarters. It was startling how many people, not only police officers, raised that question, inferring that the *Herald* had deliberately overstated or "white-washed" McDuffie's status and accomplishments. Many people would have preferred that Arthur McDuffie be out of work, with a spotty reputation and a long criminal record. He was not.

Arthur McDuffie was being groomed for promotion at Coastal States Life Insurance. He was also a notary public and moonlighted on weekends, driving trucks and oper-ating a car wash with the help of unemployed neighbor-hood youngsters, whom he also trained in house painting. With their help he had painted the Range Fu-neral Home, where his burial was now being arranged.

I borrowed a photo of McDuffie; handsome and well-dressed, he was smiling. The divorced father of three chil-dren, eighteen months to eight years old, Arthur McDuffie had been romancing his ex-wife, his childhood sweetheart. They planned to remarry.

Before I left, I held Eula Mae McDuffie's hand in mine and promised to find out what really happened to her son. As I drove back to the *Herald*, I kicked myself. Why did I say that? Maybe because she was crying. How could I ever keep that promise? Especially after the medical ex-aminers' conclusions that it could all have happened just the way police said. Maybe it did. The worst possible sce-nario was personally difficult to accept. I know better than most that it is risky business, very risky business, to lead police on a high-speed chase. What looks like fun and games in *Smokey and the Bandit* is not. In the movies, police cars take to the air and sail off bridges. They splash into rivers, bays, and ditches; they spin into spectacular chain-reaction crashes. No harm done; everyone walks away.

In real life, a thirty-second pursuit is a long chase. Adrenaline kicks in and takes over. One minute seems endless. Eight minutes is an interminably long high-speed chase. When the cops do catch you, they are mad as hell.

You are likely to get hurt.

But knowing all that and accepting that police officers are all too human, it is shocking to even suspect that cops might kill over a traffic offense and then launch a massive conspiracy to cover up their crime. I did not want it to be true. And it seemed unlikely when you considered the logistics. At least a dozen people would have to know. How high up could such a conspiracy go? It would not be easy to persuade that many cops to agree on anything, much less on how to cover up a killing.

Emery Zerick, that crusty, long-time Miami Beach detective, told me many things over the years. One of them was, "When a cop gets in trouble, the other cops all run like thieves." The fabled brotherhood of the men behind the badge, the men in blue, all for one and one for all, is a myth. I have seen proof of that dozens of times since.

So, if the worst is true, I thought, how can they be hanging in so tight? Wouldn't they all be sweating by now? I left messages at the station for all the officers listed on the accident report. None returned my calls.

I did not learn until months later that the officers knew what I was doing and were monitoring my progress.

Saturday night, I called the home of Charlie Black, an assistant chief in charge of the police division, which includes the detective bureaus.

Charlie Black has a fondness for leather jackets. His eyes are heavy-lidded over pale ice-blue, and he has a presence—he is tough and he looks ba-a-a-d. In my book, he is not. A straight-talking veteran street cop, he has always told me the truth and been up front, even when it was not to his advantage. I asked him about Arthur McDuffie—a total blank. The chief had never heard of Arthur McDuffie—six days after the accident.

Provoked, Chief Black drove directly to the home of his Homicide Captain Marshall Frank, to find out why he had not been informed.

A short time later, my home phone rang. Both the chief and the captain were on the line. Arthur McDuffie was news to the captain, too. He had never heard the name. My dinner burned beyond recognition in the kitchen while they both asked me questions and more questions.

The *Herald* newsroom Christmas party was the following day. I missed it. I worked late, writing the story; when I finished I was in no mood to party. An inexperienced editor worked the desk that night. She sharply questioned my descriptions of the helmet strap, the damage to the motorcycle, and the accident scene. "Who can we attribute this to?" she demanded.

We don't have to, I explained, they are fact. I saw them myself. I was having trouble getting this story in the newspaper. Dr. Wright was able to corroborate some of the details. Those that could not be attributed to any outside authority were cut, and I was told to lead the story by reporting that Internal Affairs was investigating the matter.

The story repeated the police version of the accident, the medical examiners' substantiation that it could indeed have happened that way, the backgrounds of some of the officers, and the bewilderment of the McDuffie family. It quoted the dead man's sister, Dorothy, who described her brother as an intelligent man who would not fight police officers.

I learned much later that two of the cops involved were waiting outside the *Herald* that winter morning for a copy of the final edition. In the dark before dawn, they took it to a secluded spot to study the story. They concluded that they might be safe, that they still might be able to pull it off.

They were wrong. It was not a strong story, but it was enough.

It was published on Monday morning, December 24, Christmas Eve. Later in the day, a Miami police officer went to one of his superiors. He had witnessed the beating. The accident, he said, was a fabrication.

My editors also became more interested in the case that day. Now they wanted photos of McDuffie's Kawasaki. But it was no longer at Barbon Towing. Police had seized it. A homicide investigation had begun. It was the prime piece of evidence in the case. Captain Frank, who had been totally unaware that the motorcycle and its rider existed until I told him, now refused to let our photographers shoot or even see it, despite my protests.

On Christmas Day, some of the officers were relieved of duty with pay, pending the outcome of the investigation.

The next day was Wednesday. Officer Charles Veverka, twenty-nine, went to see Captain Frank. He had something to say. Dark-haired, articulate, and boyishly appealing, Veverka was the officer who wrote the accident report. It was fiction, he confirmed. There had been no accident. He falsified the report. It wasn't his idea, he said. He was only following orders.

Veverka, a second-generation policeman and the son of a lieutenant on the same department, told his story. He had been checking out a routine burglar alarm in a warehouse district when it all began.

It was nearly 2:00 A.M., a quiet night. Miami streets, under the eerie orange glow of sodium-vapor lights, were nearly deserted. Blocks away, other officers and a sergeant were talking to a tearful young woman who said she had been raped, when an orange-and-black Kawasaki rolled into their line of vision. At the corner, the rider "popped a wheelie," a dare-devil antic which lifts the front wheel off the pavement.

The stunt prompted the sergeant to chase the cycle, red lights flashing, siren screaming. Another officer piled into his patrol car to follow. More joined in, including

Veverka, who heard the chase via radio and raced to take part. The boredom of a long and uneventful night was broken. Soon nearly every car in the district, as well as some city officers, had joined the wolf pack.

Desperate to lose them, the cyclist succeeded at one point but was spotted again as he rounded a building. An officer fired several shots. That was enough to stop him. The cyclist decelerated and slowed down. He pulled over near the shadows of an expressway ramp, a ramp that would have led to almost certain escape had he used it. Patrol cars screeched to stops. To the man on the motorcycle, it must have looked as if every cop in the world was arriving.

Officer Veverka reached Arthur McDuffie first. The boyish cop who confessed claimed that the 138-pound cyclist, who had just stopped to surrender, took a swing at him. Another version later was that McDuffie simply said, "You got me, I give up."

Whatever happened, Veverka admittedly threw and landed a punch. Suddenly he and his prisoner were the core of a mob. McDuffie, his wrists handcuffed behind him, was torn from Veverka's grasp.

A police officer described the scene later. "It looked like a cartoon, with arms and legs flying out of a pile of dust. They looked like a bunch of animals fighting for meat. His [McDuffie's] face looked like it was sprayed with a can of red paint."

Veverka claims he tried to pull his prisoner free of the pack, but heavy flashlights, fists, and nightsticks were swinging wildly. Hit on the arm and spattered by Mc-Duffie's blood, he says he stepped back.

The prisoner was helpless on the pavement when a Latin officer swung back over his head with both arms, to smash down a two-handed blow with his big metal flashlight. It connected right between the eyes of Arthur McDuffie. One young cop asked another if he knew how to break legs. Then he demonstrated, rapping the dying man's limbs with his nightstick.

A paramedics' rescue van approached, and somebody warned the others to break it up. City of Miami officers who watched the beating but took no part were told, "You didn't see nothing."

Another PSD sergeant arrived, took in the scene, and quickly began to orchestrate a cover-up. Officers smashed all the glass and plastic on the cycle with nightsticks and flashlights, kicked it over, then drove a police car over it. One cop repeatedly pounded McDuffie's helmet on the pavement. Another spotted McDuffie's wristwatch in the grass, pulled his service revolver, and shattered it with a bullet. Arthur McDuffie's keys and identification were hurled up onto a nearby roof, and Veverka was instructed to write a report on the "accident."

After hospital officials reported that McDuffie was in a hopeless coma, two officers drove to Barbon Towing before dawn. The yard was closed and padlocked. The two cops vaulted a fence and battered the motorcycle with concrete blocks to make the damage appear serious enough to explain a dead rider. In the days ahead, the officers repeatedly cautioned each other to "stick to the story."

Veverka confessed on Wednesday, December 26. That night, medical examiners and state attorney's office investigators visited the scene of the accident for the first time, ten days after it took place. With high-intensity fire department lights, they turned darkness into day, and in that brilliant glare they also discovered what was not there— there was no bridge abutment, no pole, no concrete pillar on which Arthur McDuffie could have smashed his skull.

The death was declared a homicide that night. It was official.

The story, stripped across page one in the morning paper, reported that there had been no "accident," that the police reports were faked.

Carol King Guralnick, Lady Law, now in private practice with her husband, plunged into the case with full fervor—representing the McDuffie family. Active in civil rights causes, the couple already represented a black schoolteacher beaten by PSD narcotics detectives who raided the wrong house. Carol called a press conference for the McDuffies. An investigator from the state attorney's office disrupted it as it began. He flashed a subpoena and, as McDuffie's mother wept, seized the items she had found during her pitiful search at the scene. He also confiscated her son's bloodied clothes, returned to the family by hospital officials.

Carol called for immediate intervention by a federal task force. She asked for "an outside in-depth analysis of the inner workings of the Metro Public Safety Department and the Miami Police Department." The request was directed to President Carter, the FBI, the Justice Department, Florida's senators and congressmen, and Senator Edward Kennedy, head of the Senate Judiciary Committee. "The police," she said, "simply cannot police themselves."

She also announced plans to file a multimillion-dollar wrongful-death action against the county, the department, and the officers involved.

It was an election year and the zealous top assistants to the state attorney rushed to file criminal charges. On Friday, December 28, one week after the initial telephone tip to me, Captain Frank arrested five PSD officers, four of them on manslaughter charges. All four had records of commendations for good work, balanced by histories of brutality complaints and lawsuits. The sergeant who initiated the chase had been pulled off the street for "weak leadership." A commander had warned that if he persisted in his ways, somebody who wore a badge "would go to jail." The fifth suspect, charged with being an accessory and fabricating evidence, was Sergeant Skip Evans, the man who masterminded the "accident." He is also the husband of a fresh-faced and friendly Miami Beach policewoman named Patricia. They had been sweethearts since grade school, and she was pregnant at the time of his arrest. She had been my friend for years.

Arthur McDuffie's funeral was the following day.

Hundreds came to see him off to what his preacher promised would be a better world. The promise did little to console the dead man's loved ones. His mother screamed, and his little girl, tearful in white ruffles, called out, "Daddy!" as a Marine honor guard bore the flag-draped casket into the church.

Mourners filled the Jordan Grove Missionary Baptist Church and overflowed into the street outside. Hundreds filed by the open casket. Arthur McDuffie wore his Marine uniform. The brass buttons shone. His hands were folded peacefully. A dozen men and women fainted during the emotionally charged service.

Carol King Guralnick sat with the family, hugging the dead man's weeping child. The choir sang "I'll Fly Away," as the engines of a local motorcycle club present to escort the hearse thundered outside the church.

"Oh, Lord," the Reverend Joe Lewis prayed, "we need you here in Miami today."

The good reverend's words were as true as any ever spoken.

The Southern Christian Leadership Conference and the Achievers of Greater Miami marched three hundred strong that day. With NAACP members and local black leaders among them, they carried a black casket, symbolic of McDuffie's death. They also carried signs:

WHY?????
WHO'S GOING TO POLICE THE POLICE?
JUSTICE NOW!

The manslaughter charges did not satisfy them. They wanted police officers charged with murder. Mingling among marchers and mourners were agents from the Community Relations unit of the Justice Department.

A month later the manslaughter charges against Officer Alex Marrero, believed to have struck the fatal blow, were upgraded to second-degree murder. Jailers kept him in isolation to protect him from other prisoners. His family and friends charged that Marrero was the victim of discrimination and distributed a hundred thousand fliers appealing for public support.

McDuffie coverage passed out of my hands to reporters on the courthouse beat as the case traveled through the system to its inevitable climax. I still had plenty to write about. The year 1979 had been the most violent in Dade County history. The body count continued to mount. Cocaine cowboys were invading public places, spraying bullets wildly, unconcerned about who else got in the way as they tried to kill their intended victims. More citizens were arming themselves against crime and then using the guns to shoot loved ones. The large Jamaican, Haitian, and Latin influx included people overwhelmed and depressed by culture shock, inflation, the job market, and wage disputes. It made them more susceptible to losing their cool—in other words, trigger happy.

Killings were sparked by traffic arguments, lack of parking spaces, and radios played too loud. Various authorities blamed drugs, guns, the economy, and sunspots. There were 360 dead by the year's end.

Little did anyone suspect that 1979 would soon be looked back on as the good old days.

In 1980 there would be 569 murders in Dade County.

In 1981 there would be 622.

And elated officials called it good news when the annual murder toll dropped back down to 538 in 1982.

Little did we know.

At the stroke of midnight Miamians greeted the new decade in the same way they had ended the old: with a fusillade of gunfire. Somehow it had become traditional for celebrants to empty their weapons into the air at midnight. And more and more people had guns.

Thousands of bullets slammed into houses and cars and blacked out entire neighborhoods as they hit power transformers and streetlights. Some even struck an airplane in flight. Downtown Miami sounded like World War III. In prior years as many as half a dozen people were wounded, some were killed; this time, incredibly, nobody died. A twin-engine Cessna, hit in the tail section by bullets fired from the ground, landed safely, its five passengers unhurt. Miami was lucky.

It didn't last. Shortly after midnight police reported one suicide and five unsuccessful attempts by residents reluctant to face the New Year. Three murders were logged by 3:00 P.M., New Year's Day, 1980. I had plenty to do.

Not long after the McDuffie arrests, I chatted with some PSD detectives. They lamented, as usual, their sagging morale. Worse than it had ever been, they said. They blamed it all on the unhappy events of the past year, the ill-considered wrong house raid on the schoolteacher's home, the cocaine scandal among homicide detectives, and the McDuffie case.

I did my best to cheer them up. "At least no policeman was charged with rape last year," I said brightly.

"What about the highway patrolman who attacked the little girl?" a detective said glumly.

"Highway patrolman? What highway patrolman?"

"The one who molested the little girl in his patrol car."

He could recall few details, except that it had occurred several months earlier and that PSD detectives had arrested the trooper. How could we miss that story? How did it slip so quietly and neatly through the system with no media attention?

PSD rape squad detectives were deliberately vague and displeased at my interest. The case was closed, they said. They did not want to discuss it. It all happened months and months ago.

When I insisted on hand-searching their arrest logs for the entire year, they divulged the trooper's name—Willie Thomas Jones—but warned me to let well enough alone. Justice had been served.

Curiosity drove me to the Justice Building, where I pored over the case file. The trooper had pled no contest to lewd and lascivious assault on a child. He could have been sentenced to fifteen years in prison; instead, he got probation—on condition that he undergo treatment and pay for the eleven-year-old girl's psychiatric care. An adjudication of guilt was withheld; he would have no criminal record.

The judge had wished the trooper "a lot of luck" in the record and said he might even terminate the probation early.

Little was mentioned about the young girl.

I found her living in Columbia, South Carolina, where her mother was finishing college. The child was no precociously pubescent Lolita-type; she looked more nine than eleven. Her main interest was not parties or boys, but the French horn.

Always shy, she had regressed to babyhood since her encounter with the trooper. She clung to her mother, wet the bed, and suffered nightmares. Withdrawn and depressed, she was still in treatment. They had never received a dime to pay for it, a condition of the trooper's probation.

The little girl's mother had been told that the disgraced trooper had been fired and would never be allowed to wear a badge again.

It was not true. On the day of his arrest, Trooper Jones was permitted to quietly resign from the Highway Patrol. On his arrest forms, detectives listed his occupation as unemployed. Released in his own custody, he never had to post bond.

His personnel file in Tallahassee, the state capital, reflected that Trooper Jones had resigned to enter private business and that his record was excellent. That is what would-be employers—including police departments— would be told upon checking his references.

While the case was pending, he had failed a polygraph test and was evaluated as "borderline psychotic." A psychiatrist said he strongly suspected that other such crimes had taken place. Four doctors agreed that he was a mentally disordered sex offender.

Then the judge wished him luck and put him on probation.

He was doing much better now. In fact he had been pronounced cured after a few free group-rap sessions at Jackson Memorial Hospital.

The little girl's mother said she had been told that the trooper would plead guilty and go to a mental institution. She and her family had been urged by prosecutors and police to keep silent. They said it was for the child's protection.

It did not appear that the little girl was the one who had been protected.

Neither the trooper nor his attorney would talk to me—at all. The little girl's mother, however, was relieved. She had been troubled about the way the case was handled and was suffering from guilt herself, because she had always instructed her child to trust and obey police officers.

The little girl had been stopped by the trooper as she walked home from elementary school. On duty, in uniform, he told her she was suspected of stealing candy and would have to be searched. He ordered her into the backseat of his patrol car and took her to a desolate area for the search.

The little black girl, sexually molested by a white policeman, was never taken to the rape center and was questioned only by white policemen.

The story I wrote infuriated the judge. He called it "yellow journalism" and denounced me in open court. To prove that everything he did was proper and that the trooper was treated just like any other defendant, the judge appointed Dade County's respected former state attorney, Richard Gerstein, to investigate the entire matter.

After a three-month probe, Gerstein delivered his report. It called the case "a tragedy and a miscarriage of justice" and the police response "insensitive, indifferent, and incomplete." He found that two judges had been lobbied for leniency and that the detective and the prosecutor, who was a former police officer, worked to protect the trooper, not the little girl. "Nobody seemed to care about the plight of this victim," Gerstein reported.

We were right.

Now the judge blamed the prosecutor and the detectives, saying they had misrepresented the facts of the case to him. He sent Gerstein's report to the federal grand jury for further investigation.

During that time, Miami's black community suffered another humiliation. An all-white jury convicted Dade County's first black school superintendent, Johnny Jones, for using taxpayers' money to buy 24-karat gold plumbing fixtures for his vacation home. Eventually he would win his appeal because blacks were excluded from the jury.

Racial tensions continued to mount.

A Miami judge granted a change of venue in the McDuffie case, calling it a "time bomb I don't want to go off in my courtroom or this community." The case was transferred to Tampa, on Florida's west coast. Black groups in Tampa protested, predicting that no justice would be found there. Miami blacks organized fish fries and barbecues to raise money so that Arthur McDuffie's family could attend the lengthy trial.

Officer Veverka and another young officer had agreed to testify for the prosecution. The immunity they had been granted was not enough; they still wanted to be cops and were bitter at being fired. Police work was his life's dream, Veverka protested, complaining that he was ordered to write the false reports.

The trial began in Tampa, in April 1980. It took six weeks. I did not attend, although it wasn't as though they didn't want me. In fact, I was busy dodging defense subpoenas.

From the start I had been aware that I could be subpoenaed and knew that I had to protect the identity of my source, the tipster who told me about Arthur McDuffie. In the months prior to the trial, people speculated about who it might have been. Whenever anyone asked if it was an anonymous caller, I simply smiled and said nothing. Some took that as an acknowledgment, which was exactly what I hoped the attorneys would think. If they didn't bother to subpoena me, it would be simpler.

Ed Carhart, the man who had convicted the Miami cops in the case of Wanda Jean, was no longer a prosecutor. Now in private practice, he was defending one of the McDuffie cops and wanted to question me under oath. If a judge ordered me to identify my source, I could go to jail for refusing.

One afternoon an editor warned me to get out of the building because a subpoena server was in the hallways looking for me. I ducked out the back door—and didn't know where to go. I couldn't go home, they'd probably look for me there too. I couldn't drive away, somebody might be watching my car. So, I ankled over to Omni, a vertical mall a block away, browsed in a store, and bought a pair of yellow shorts on sale. It was the first chance I'd had to go shopping in months.

When I got back to the newsroom, executive editor John McMullan wanted to see me. He took the initial notes I had scribbled on the case and locked them in his safe. Anyone who made a legal attempt to seize them would have to arrest him first. A born fighter, I think he almost hoped they would try it. Then he suggested that I get out of town—out of the country, in fact. The *Herald*, he said, would send me to the Bahamas to hide out.

I may be the only *Herald* employee, possibly the only newspaper reporter in history, to refuse management's offer of a trip to the Bahamas. Running away seemed repugnant to me. I didn't do anything wrong; Miami is my home. Who would water my plants, feed the cats, walk my dog? Besides, who knows what stories I would miss. Hell no, I wouldn't go.

McMullan was incredulous.

I stayed cautious and stopped answering my door. Eventually, once the trial was under way, a sleazy process server oozed up to my front porch and caught me at the door. The *Herald* lawyers challenged the subpoena and won. For some legal reason never clear to me, I did not have to go. I think the trial had already progressed too far for me to be called as a witness.

In the interim, *The Miami News* reported the attempt to subpoena me, prompting my source to call and say, "Don't go to jail. If you have to, you can tell them who I am."

Despite the kind offer, I would not have done it anyway. It's a matter of principle and ethics. I am still relieved it never came to that. I would not have liked jail.

Captain Frank and Dr. Wright both testified that they first heard about McDuffie from me. Reporters covering the trial called from Tampa to interview me about the case. It all seemed bizarre.

Something quite revealing happened at about that time. People generally seemed to believe that my source was an anonymous caller, so somebody decided to use that to his own advantage. An impostor began to claim he was my tipster.

Former Officer Charles Veverka, now employed as a night watchman, was still hoping to be a cop again. Trying hard to protect an earnest all-American-boy image, he called me to deliver another confession. He was my anonymous caller, he said. Tortured by his conscience, he had tipped me off so that the entire conspiracy would unravel.

I was unimpressed.

"No, Charlie," I said. "It wasn't you."

He suggested that I didn't remember his voice because it had been so many months ago. And, oh yes, he said, he had tried to disguise it at the time. Good try, but no cigar. It was not Charles Veverka who telephoned the tip about that fatal night. It was a friend, someone I have known for more than sixteen years. It was not even a police officer. It was not even a man; it was a woman.

TV news coverage of the trial focused, of course, on the most colorful, shocking, and damning testimony. The brief time allotted on the nightly news only permits use of high drama. I remember seeing again and again on TV a husky policeman in suit and tie, both hands raised high over his head as though wielding an axe, demonstrating how the brutish hammer-like blows were struck.

Gene Miller, the *Herald*'s best, reported on the trial. His daily stories from Tampa covered both sides thoroughly. They were not all front-page. On TV, every story is front-page, and lots of people, particularly in low-income neighborhoods, get all their news from TV. What they saw may have convinced them that convictions were certain.

The defense attorneys were all high-powered, top-flight. They said that McDuffie fought and resisted and had to be subdued. One officer won a directed verdict of acquittal after six weeks. The fate of the other four was in the hands of an all-male, all-white jury. The Mariel boatlift was under way at the time, and back in Miami, a crush of Cuban refugees, many of them vicious criminals and mental patients, were arriving; across the nation, Mount Saint Helens was rumbling and about to erupt.

It was Saturday. I was at the office and doubted a verdict could be reached before Monday. After all, there were four defendants charged with a total of thirteen crimes ranging from murder to falsifying police reports. There had been half a dozen lawyers and weeks of testimony. The jurors would need time to digest and weigh all they had seen and heard.

I was wrong.

The jury took two hours and forty-four minutes to acquit everybody of everything.

Defendant Michael Watts sobbed. So did Eula Mae McDuffie as she stumbled out of the courtroom in tears and outrage. "God will take care of them," she said.

The news flashed to Miami in minutes. The timing could not have been worse—three o'clock on a hot, sunny Saturday afternoon. I was concerned. I knew the mood on the street.

I called PSD Director Bobby Jones.

"What are we going to do about tonight?" I envisioned trouble—but nothing like the trouble we got. I was afraid somebody might shoot at some cops.

"What do you mean?" he said.

"Don't you think there'll be problems?"

"Our Safe Streets officers are out there," he said reassuringly. "They'll keep things under control."

Rocks and bottles began to fly within two hours. Some of our photographers rolled out onto the street in their radio-equipped cars. I was checking reports of a shooting, a deranged Mariel refugee shot down by a cop outside a Miami mental health clinic, when I heard garbled shouts. They came from a two-way radio across the room, on the photo desk.

It was Battle Vaughn and two other photographers, Bill Frakes and Michael DuCille. It sounded like they were in trouble, yelling for help. I stood up, straining to hear. The man at the photo desk was chatting on the telephone. Looking annoyed at the racket from the radio, he absently reached over and turned down the volume.

I ran to the desk, reached over his shoulder and turned it up full blast, as the man on the telephone blinked in surprise. The photographers were pinned down, being shot at, their windshield smashed. They were under attack by a mob in Liberty City at the edge of Miami city limits, where jurisdiction is a toss-up between county and city. I made emergency calls to both—and to the fire department rescue squad.

With Battle at the wheel, they escaped without serious injuries but were shaken and cut by flying glass. The *Herald* car had lost its windows and sustained major body damage, torn by bullets and battered by concrete blocks and rocks. It was still early. Traffic could have been diverted, those streets should have been blocked off, but it was the weekend—nobody stepped forward, nobody took command, nobody gave the order.

And as dusk approached, innocent people began to drive down those streets.

Most had not heard the verdict. Some had never even heard of Arthur McDuffie.

Three young people, two men from Pottstown, Pennsylvania, and a woman, on their way home from a day at the beach, drove unknowingly into the area where our photographers had been attacked. A mob was waiting. A brick smashed the windshield, hit the driver, and the car careened out of control. It struck a seventy-three-year-old black man and an eleven-year-old black girl who was playing in front of her house. It pinned her against the building. Her head was injured, her lungs punctured, and her left leg torn off.

The three young whites were dragged from the car and battered with whatever the crowd could lay hands on. The men were shot, stabbed, and run over repeatedly. One died, his brother was maimed, and permanently brain-damaged. The young woman with them escaped death, rescued by a stranger. A black man shoved her into a taxicab that took her to a hospital.

A short time later, Benny Higdon, a twenty-one-year-old father of three, drove his aging Dodge Dart into the same neighborhood.

With him was his pregnant wife's fifteen-year-old brother and the boy's best friend, also fifteen. Homeward bound after a day of fishing, they were dragged from their car. All three were battered to death. The mob used rocks, boards, fists, feet, and a newspaper rack. As the three lay dying in the street, the mob forced an ambulance to turn back. Two Miami police sergeants finally careened down the block in a speeding paddy wagon. Braving a hail of rocks and bottles, they loaded the three victims into the wagon and fled to a hospital. It was too late.

Higdon worked at a local bakery. He had just moved his family out of the small mountain town in Alabama where he had worked as a coal miner. They had come to Miami seeking a better life.

Those savage deaths were just the beginning.

A middle-aged hotel maid on her way home from work was burned to death in her car because she was white. A car driven by an elderly butcher was pounded by rocks. He swerved and slammed into a wall. A crowd turned the car over, set it afire, and jabbed at the man with sticks when he tried to crawl out. He burned to death.

During the mob madness, one police officer found a grotesquely mutilated corpse in the street. He loaded it into his squad car for safekeeping until he could take it to the morgue later.

Policeman Frank Rossi, en route to work, jumped from his car and ran to help a young white couple being dragged from their van by a mob near an expressway ramp. The young couple escaped, but Rossi was badly hurt. In the hospital emergency room, lying on an examining table, he asked a nurse for a telephone and dialed my number at the *Herald*. He wanted to describe what was happening, what was going on out there. His life was saved, he said, because he was not wearing his brown uniform shirt. His attackers did not know he was a cop.

Two black men walked into a fast-food chicken outlet at closing time. A Latin couple was mopping the floors and cleaning up. "This is for McDuffie," the two men said and shot them both.

There were reports that mobs were taking over public buildings, so *Miami Herald* security, unarmed and sparsely manned, took action. Fearing rioters might try to invade the *Herald* building, security personnel locked all but the employees' entrance.

That entrance leads up a narrow hallway, on an incline, to an elevator. I have been told that the chief of security sent out to a supermarket for several cases of Wesson oil; the plan was—if the rioters came—to pour the oil down the hall until it was too slippery for a mob to make it uphill to the elevator. We were lucky. No mob came to the *Herald* that night, only a cop.

Security said a policeman wanted to see me at the employees' entrance. It was Marshall Frank, the homicide captain who had investigated the McDuffie case. I took the back elevator down to meet him. PSD police headquarters was under siege, and he feared for the safety of his men.

The shift commander had called him to report that rioters were breaking into the building. Reports were sketchy. He had raced from his North Dade home intending to join his detectives. As he turned off the I-95 expressway near headquarters, a black man ran up the exit ramp excitedly waving his arms and shouting a warning, "Get back! Get back!"

"It's all right, I'm police," the captain said and swung off the exit anyway. He saw his mistake at once. People were running everywhere in the dark. An overturned car was burning.

A powerful voice, another policeman, bellowed "Turn back! Now! Now!" from an overpass above. He turned, struck by the urgency of the shouts, and saw what appeared to be a sniper leveling a gun at him. He wheeled the car around and got out. As he did, he saw miragelike in the distance what appeared to be a platoon of Miami police in riot gear advancing, marching in military formation.

Frantic to know the fate of his men and the scope of what was happening in the city where he has lived all his life, the veteran cop knew of only one place to find out: *The Miami Herald.*

"How bad is it?" he said, his face grim.

"Bad."

Violence and bloodshed were sweeping south through the city, into Coconut Grove and South Miami. Fires were being set. Looting had begun. Some bodies, burned in their cars, would not be recovered until the next day. Cops under fire were making heroic forays into the riot area, snatching the dead and injured off the street. Many of the heroes were Vietnam combat veterans.

Nothing taught in a police academy could prepare a man or woman for the streets of Miami that night.

Cut off from headquarters and his department, Marshall Frank had instinctively turned to the *Herald*. I felt somehow moved by that, even though I knew he simply wanted to assess the situation by monitoring our radios. In the past, we had been adversaries, on opposite sides; in crisis, we had everything in common. We cared—we had both taken part in the events that led to this. We did the best we could.

I was scared; everything was out of control. It was all coming down around us. We boarded the slow and creaky elevator to the newsroom and simultaneously stepped into each other's arms, hugging tight through the rest of the ride.

At our police desk, the radio traffic was chaotic.

What was to have been a solemn candlelight vigil turned into an ugly mob that took over the Metro Justice Building and surrounded the Public Safety Department headquarters. The thinly spread weekend staff was trapped. Taken by surprise, all the cops inside could do was barricade themselves behind furniture. Their hand-guns would be a last resort when the building was over-whelmed. Nobody knew where to find the key to the locked cabinets where the tear gas and riot gear were stored. Nobody was prepared.

One man, Michael Cosgrove, a baby-faced City of Miami Police major and a Vietnam War hero, took com-mand and saved the county's ass that night. It was Cos-grove's army that Marshall Frank had seen advancing.

He rallied seventy vastly outnumbered city cops and led them to the rescue. In riot gear, they marched down the street, cleared thousands of demonstrators, retook the Justice Building and saved PSD headquarters, along with the county cops trapped inside. He and his men went on to rescue people who would have died that night without them.

More than 270 injured were treated at Jackson Memo-rial Hospital. Casualties would rise to 350 over the next three days. Surgeons and support staff were called in from home. The emergency room and the trauma team had been prepared for a routine Miami Saturday night, but not for this.

At the height of the chaos and confusion in the emer-gency room, a nurse broke down and shouted, "You can thank Edna Buchanan for this!"

I was not there, another reporter heard it and told me.

I don't feel guilty about anything that happened. I am not to blame. It wasn't me who got caught up in an adrenaline-crazed chase. I didn't kill Arthur McDuffie or lie to cover it up. I was only the bad-news messenger, the reporter who found out and wrote the story. I still think about it. If it happened again, what could I do differently? I still don't know.

I do know that Miami was a time bomb. Out on those sweltering streets, in the softness of the night, if you were close to the city, you could hear it ticking. Even if Arthur McDuffie had remained an unknown traffic statistic, something or someone else would have struck the match that lit the fuse.

My conscience is clear, but that does not mean there was no pain. One of the McDuffie jurors, asked later if he felt McDuffie's death should have been left a traffic accident, replied, "The people killed in the riot would probably think so."

The next day, Sunday, was bright and beautiful. I drove the 1.2 mile stretch of causeway west to the *Herald* from my island home. To the east, toward the sea, the fronds of stately royal palms were etched against the brilliant blue of a cloudless sky. To the west, over Miami, the sky was black—Miami was burning. The pall of dense smoke was visible for fifteen miles. It hung like a shroud over the city I love. I had to stop at the side of the road to fight the tears.

If you are a woman in this business, you must never let them see you cry.

Dozens of fires erupted at intersections. Fire fighters were forced back by gunfire. Businesses and stores burned unchecked. "It's absolutely unreal," said Miami Fire Inspector George Bilberry. "They're burning down the whole goddamn north end of town."

Late Sunday, fifteen major blazes still raged out of control. Snipers fired rifles at rescue helicopters. The looting and burning went on for three days. Public schools were closed, and a 8:00 P.M.–6:00 A.M. curfew was established. The National Guard was brought in, eleven hundred strong, to establish order on Miami's turbulent streets. They were quickly joined by twenty-five hundred more guardsmen. It was life in a war zone. Police issued frequent advisories to motorists on safe routes to travel and the streets to avoid to stay alive. Cops went for days and nights without going home, without hot meals, without sleep. It took its toll.

I was in the newsroom Sunday when word came of another death: a Miami police lieutenant. His patrol car slammed up against a tree. He was slumped over the steering wheel. At first they thought a sniper killed him, but medics found no bullet wound. He had died, without warning, of a massive heart attack.

It was Ed McDermott.

The sad and quiet Irish cop—tall, husky, with a stomach as flat as a board—forty-eight years old. Dead.

You must never let them see you cry.

After the National Guard moved in, the U.S. attorney announced immediate action in the McDuffie case. A federal grand jury was impaneled to investigate possible violations of Arthur McDuffie's civil rights.

President Carter visited Miami, and blacks threw bottles at his limousine. Teddy Kennedy, then a presidential contender, asked for a full report on the case. Fidel Castro seized the opportunity to accuse the United States of promoting human rights abroad but not practicing them at home. Attorney General Benjamin Civiletti announced plans to intensify a probe into police brutality in Miami.

Within weeks, the federal grand jury indicted former Trooper Willie Thomas Jones for violating the rights of the little girl in his patrol car. Jones was arrested, then released pending trial. But there was no trial. He fled—leaving behind his wife and three small children. He would remain a federal fugitive for years.

In July, after two months of investigation and testimony, the federal grand jury handed down its first and only civil rights indictment in the McDuffie case.

The defendant: Charles Veverka.

That was a surprise. Many people were indignant; one of the toughest jobs in proving police misconduct is persuading cops to testify against each other. Veverka was the first to tell the truth and did testify against the others. Now the government had gone after the state's key witness. What message would this send to police departments across the country?

Others, however, believed that the indictment was deserved, that Veverka only told the truth to save himself as he saw the conspiracy beginning to fall apart. He was the cop who reached Arthur McDuffie first that night; had he handled his prisoner professionally, the man might have survived. Instead, Veverka hit him, perhaps setting off the spark for the attack that followed.

His trial was moved to Atlanta, then to San Antonio,

Texas. Rumors were that perhaps if he was convicted, other indictments might follow, but they did not. Veverka was acquitted.

Nobody was ever convicted of anything for the death of Arthur McDuffie. But a lot of people paid.

Aftermath

The death toll was eighteen, including Lieutenant Edward McDermott, counted as a riot casualty. The property damage in Miami was estimated at $100 million. The damage to the city's reputation was incalculable.

One of the acquitted McDuffie cops, Michael Watts, later tried to kill himself—with a motorcycle. He rolled it into his apartment and let it run, filling the room with deadly exhaust fumes. The attempt failed when his motorcycle ran out of gas and his ex-wife arrived and found him unconscious.

The Dade County Public Safety Department took away the heavy metal Kel-Lites and gave their officers harmless plastic flashlights. The PSD then put the wrong-house narcotics raid, McDuffie, the riot, and the cocaine scandal all behind it, changing its name to the Metro-Dade Police Department.

Chief Charlie Black, who launched an immediate homicide probe upon hearing of McDuffie's death, was later demoted to captain. The reason given was that acting director Bobby Jones, who had accepted the permanent job, had to build his own management team. And Marshall Frank, the homicide captain with a photographic memory for murder cases, was transferred to a desk job in the civil process bureau. The stated reason: career development.

The baby-faced war hero, Michael Cosgrove, who saved the county the night the riots began, was promoted to assistant chief. But in 1984 he was demoted to captain, ostracized, and forced out of the department after an unblemished seventeen-year career. Politics, Miami style: He was perceived as being loyal to his chief, who had been abruptly fired in a 2:00 A.M. phone call from the city manager.

Cosgrove, the hero, had the last laugh: The city manager's turn came, and he got fired. Beleaguered city politicians, faced with a police department in trouble, pleaded with Cosgrove to return as chief.

He said no.

A fugitive for four years and eight months, former Trooper Willie Thomas Jones quietly surrendered in Miami, saying he was "tired of running." In April of 1985 he pled guilty and was sentenced to a year in federal prison. He wept at the sentencing.

So did the victim's mother, now a social worker. She has forgiven him, she said, for molesting her daughter, now a painfully shy high school senior who has yet to go out on her first date.

The county settled with the McDuffie family for $1 million.

Their lawyer, the woman who said she believed in destiny, never did become a judge.

Carol King Guralnick, the beautiful, brilliant, and

rich Lady Law, was at the wheel of her sunshine yellow Ferrari when it broke down on a Miami street. Exasperated, she left the stalled sports car with the LADY LAW tag. She walked toward a gas station across the street for help and stepped into the path of a van. She was thirty-four.

The young widow of riot victim Benny Higdon had her baby, a little girl he never saw. Left at age twenty-one with four children to raise alone, she sued the county and the city for negligence in her husband's death. She lost. The case was thrown out, and she got nothing.

And Charles Veverka's dream of becoming a cop again came true. He got a job with North Bay Village, a small force with twenty-five officers. He did fine, for a time. He even took part in having another Village cop arrested on cocaine charges. But then Veverka got in trouble again. He was accused of kicking a handcuffed prisoner, a black man, in the groin during an elevator ride at police headquarters. Aboard the same elevator was a witness to what occurred, a county crime-lab technician with a long and spotless record. A religious and idealistic man, he was torn between lying to investigators and handing up a fellow police officer. After a meeting with prosecutors, who threatened to charge him and ruin his career if he did not tell the truth, he went home, put a gun to his head, and shot himself to death.

Without a witness, the charges of kicking the black man were dropped, but Veverka resigned from his police job under pressure.

Michael Watts, completely recovered from his suicide

attempt, also pinned on a badge again, as a cop with the North Lauderdale police department.

A record, a single, was released: "The Ballad of Arthur McDuffie."

It was never a hit.

Anybody who doesn't know what soap
tastes like never washed a dog.
Franklin P. Jones, humorist

SIDEBAR

Rocky Rowf

I was a pushover.

I met Rocky on a sizzling Fourth of July weekend. I never intended to take him home with me. He was sprawled under a park bench on South Beach trying to stay cool. I was there to exercise, to bend and stretch in the shade of the sea grape trees, and to look at the blue-green summer sea. Two elderly men, friendly regulars in the park, were sitting on the bench.

"Is that your dog?" I asked.

They said no. He was so quiet they had barely noticed him. He was panting in the heat, and I grew alarmed as I patted him. His tongue was purple—eggplant purple. I was certain that it meant the animal was dangerously de-hydrated. I filled a paper cup several times from a faucet used by bathers to rinse sand off their feet and he drank politely. But his tongue stayed purple.

That is its normal color, something I did not learn

until later. It may mean he is part chow chow, though he does not look it. He looks like the kind of mutt that everybody has owned at some time in their life: black with buff-colored paws, medium sized, and affable. His ears are floppy, his grin silly. He wore a battered, old leather collar with no tag. After he drank, he watched me exercise, then followed me as I walked along the seawall. This little romance will end now, I thought, as I returned to my car.

When I opened the door, he pushed right past me, scrambling into the front seat. Obviously accustomed to traveling by car, he was determined to have his way. When ordered out, he slunk into the backseat and settled stubbornly on the floor, on the far side, out of arm's reach. What the heck, I thought, I'll keep him until I find his owner. As we pulled away from the curb, however, I reconsidered: I can't take this dog home, what about all those cats?

I stopped at the main lifeguard station, and the dog clambered out after me, trotting right alongside. The guard said he had seen the dog roaming the beach alone for the past three days. He would call Animal Control, he said, and held the dog, so I could get away. "Bye, puppy," I said, and headed for my car. My mistake was in looking back. The dog was whimpering and struggling to follow, his eyes fixed on me, pleading.

"You sure this isn't your dog?" The lifeguard looked suspicious.

I insisted I had never seen that animal before in my life. The lifeguard let go, and the dog bounded to me, wagging his tail.

On the way home we stopped at the supermarket for dog food. It was too hot to leave him in the car, so I left him just outside the store and told him to wait. He'll probably be gone, finding a new friend, by the time I get the dog food through the checkout counter, I thought. But as I turned the next aisle, there he was, trotting past the produce, wriggling with delight when he spotted me. Somebody had opened the door.

"Is that your dog?" the store manager wanted to know. I denied it.

"Are you sure?" he said, staring pointedly at the dog food and the Milk-Bone box in my cart.

He ejected the dog, who was waiting when I came out. I looked around the parking lot vaguely, wondering where I had left my car. He knew. All I had to do was follow as he trotted briskly ahead, found the car, and sat down next to it waiting for me. When we got home, he scampered up the front steps without hesitation and waited as I unlocked the door. It was as though he had lived there all his life. Misty and Flossie were snoozing on the highly polished hardwood floor in the living room when this strange dog walked nonchalantly into their home. Both shot straight up in the air, then fled so fast that for several seconds they ran in place on the slick surface. They skidded into my bedroom and dove out the window. Luckily it was open. The screen landed in the middle of the lawn.

After the initial shock, they sized him up at once. He must have lived with other animals, because he dotes on them, especially smaller ones, and is particularly deferential to cats. He was so obsequious in fact, rolling on his back in abject surrender whenever they entered the room, that they quickly became disgusted at his fawning. Within two days the cats were stealing his food and stepping disdainfully over him as he napped.

For two weeks we walked up and down that stretch of South Beach seawall looking for his owner. Lots of people had seen the friendly dog, but always alone. A middle-aged Puerto Rican busboy with no teeth grinned and greeted him as Blackie. I thought we had found the owner, but he said he had fed the dog a hamburger and some water at about one o'clock the same morning I found him performing his hungry-and-thirsty act.

After two weeks I gave up, took him to the vet, got him a license, and he joined the household.

He chose his own name. I ran through dozens of appropriate possibilities. None appealed to him. He would not even open his eyes at most. But when I said Rocky, he looked up, wagged his tail, and grinned. So Rocky it is— Rocky Rowf.

His past remains a mystery. Housebroken and well-behaved, he did not seem to understand even the most simple commands. Perhaps, I decided, his owner spoke a language other than English. We went to an obedience school, taught by a cop in charge of the Coral Gables police K-9 unit. The only mutt, Rocky was the smartest in the class. However, he did refuse to be a watchdog. In an attempt to agitate him, they thrust him between a Doberman pinscher and a German shepherd. The big dogs were ferocious, leaping in frenzies, snarling, and barking.

Rocky Rowf sat between them, grinning and drooling. A very laid-back dog, he hates trouble, rolling his eyes and whining when the cats quarrel among themselves. If the chips were down and we were attacked by strangers, he would do the sensible thing—run for his life.

The day after his first visit to the vet, I got home from the *Herald* after nine o'clock at night. When I opened the door and called, he did not come bounding in from the yard as usual. I stepped out into the dark and could barely make him out, curled up next to the banana tree. I called to him again and again. He did not move. My heart sank. Frightened, I approached the still form, reached out, and touched the fur, ruffled by a summer breeze. It felt cool.

He was dead.

Poor stray dog, doing fine until I took him home; now he was dead. How did it happen? My mind raced. The vet had said he was in good health thirty-six hours earlier. It had to be poison, or maybe he had been shot. It was too dark to see anything in the yard. I dialed the vet's emergency number. He's dead, I cried accusingly, probably an allergic reaction to the shots you gave him.

"What makes you think he's dead," asked Dr. Hal Nass.

"I know a dead dog when I see one!" I screamed.

He told me to bring the body to his office. He would get dressed and meet me there; together we would find out what happened.

The dog weighed forty-seven pounds. The backyard was dark, and I didn't even own a flashlight. The only neighbor I knew was across the street, in a big house on the bay. When I had moved in months earlier he introduced himself and invited me to call on him if I ever needed help.

His wife answered. They had gone to bed early. I said I needed her husband's assistance. I whimpered to him that somebody or something had killed my dog and asked if he had seen any strangers prowling the neighborhood. I told him I had to get the dead dog out of my shadowy and unlit backyard and into my car. Poor Rocky Rowf's last ride would be to the vet for an autopsy.

A sympathetic man and a good neighbor, Larry Helfer climbed out of bed, got dressed, and brought a flashlight. "I think it was poison," I said, greeting him in tears. "The doctor said he was fine yesterday."

I offered him a blanket to wrap the body in. "Where is it?" he said grimly. Out there, I said, pointing. He pushed open the back door, stared into the darkness, then slowly turned and looked at me, his face strange. I stepped past him to look. Sitting in the back door, gazing up at us was Rocky. He was grinning.

Never taking his eyes off me, Larry Helfer began to back slowly toward the front door. He obviously believed that, using the pretext of a dead dog, I had lured him out of his bed and across the street, for some unknown purpose.

"I could have sworn he was dead. He didn't answer when I called him," I babbled. "He was just lying there."

It was his turn to babble. "My, eh, wife, is worried. I better go tell her everything's all right," he said and made a run for it.

I caught the vet, just as he was leaving his home. "Never mind," I said.

Larry Helfer and his wife avoided me for several years after that. When we did meet by chance, they always asked politely after the health of my dog.

Nowadays, I point an index finger at Rocky Rowf and say, "Bang, you're dead!" He falls on the floor, then rolls over on his back. It's one of the best tricks in his repertoire.

It wasn't difficult to teach him at all. He already knew how.

PART
III

TWELVE

Miami Then and Now

The only constant in Florida is change. South Florida has forged ahead faster in the past twenty-five years than in the prior two thousand.

Indians once journeyed around the Gulf of Mexico, down the peninsula, through the mangroves, and across The Everglades. The Tequestas settled at the mouth of a clear and virgin river and named it Miami—River of the Great Lake.

The Indians vanished long ago, but the river is still alive with pleasure boaters, foreign freighters, boatloads of illegal Haitian immigrants, cargos of smuggled narcotics, and murder victims bobbing to the surface.

When I arrived, Miami was basically still a southern city rarefied by sun-streaked touches of subtropical exotica. The buildings and the flavor were from my favorite time—there are no one-hundred-year-old tenements in Miami—and I loved it. I felt warm and comforted, a patient convalescing from some terrible mishap. I was recovering from the first twenty years of my life: painful childhood, awkward adolescence, all behind me—a gritty, black-and-white newsreel, Paterson, New Jersey. The lights were up, everything was clear, the curtain had lifted. Show time: Me and Miami, we were in Technicolor, wide-screen CinemaScope, and 3-D.

It has not been easy, but it has never been dull.

People ask how I endure this pressure cooker of a job, year after year. The answers are simple: First, it sure beats a coat factory in Paterson, New Jersey. Second, when stress mounts, and the deadlines, dead bodies, and other people's pain are too much to bear—when life *and* Miami are out of control—I retreat to the sea for solace, a war-weary patient seeking the cure. I always find it there, despite all the years and all the changes. The tide goes out, then returns, bringing new life and hope.

Now and then, of course, I am forced to interrupt my soul-searching and therapy to blast my Acme Thunderer authentic police whistle at some swarthy type who insists on displaying his sex organs in front of the tourists.

And the sand is no longer silken. It is gritty now from dredging. And the surf is rougher. It's not as gentle as it was when I first saw Miami.

But, then, nothing is.

On a stroll down Flagler Street in the downtown Miami of twenty-five years ago, you saw fair-skinned middle-aged matrons clad in flowered dresses and sun hats. Some carried umbrellas or parasols to protect their pale, powdered complexions from the sun's scorching rays. They lunched at Burdines' tearoom, where they nibbled salads and, especially if accompanied by a child, indulged in the famous Snow Princess dessert. The doll-face of the Snow Princess smiled coolly from atop a mountain of vanilla ice cream and coconut.

At the start, I admit, I found some Miami Beach senior citizens less than charming. They walk slowly and drive slowly until their cars, too big and powerful for them in the first place, run away with them. Then, mistaking the gas pedal for the brake, they careen out of control, crashing at breakneck speeds into ten or twelve autos, as if playing bumper cars.

As pedestrians, they step defiantly off the curb, one stiff arm raised like a traffic cop, and march right out into moving traffic with often disastrous results. Retired for years, with no place to go and the rest of their lives to get there, they push past you at the lunch counter and sneak ahead of you at the bakery. Forget the supermarket; it is the chariot race in *Ben Hur*.

But my feelings about them changed quickly that first year. Their spirit and resilience overwhelmed me, or maybe just wore me down. The last of a great immigrant generation, they are tough. They overcame hardships, persecution, sweatshops, and a depression. They survived it all. There will be no more like them once they are gone. Their children and grandchildren—"me" generations hooked on instant gratification—are wimps by comparison.

Many of the elderly live and die alone in Miami Beach,

far from the sons and daughters they raised and sent through college. Etta, at age 103, munched on coconut macaroons with her own teeth as we sat in her tiny South Beach kitchen. She described with perfect clarity events that took place when she was a teenager—nearly ninety years ago. I itched to visit her regularly, to record the recollections of this treasure trove of a woman who can remember it all. But there was no time, and she was not easy to catch up with. She was rarely home, and had no telephone.

What brought me there was a missing-persons report Etta had filed with police. The usual parent-child conflict: Her youngest son ran away from home when she refused to buy him a car.

He was seventy-two and he had *always* been a problem.

We found him later, still sulking, up north where they used to live. She promised to buy the car, and he came back. But that is only half the story. As I left Etta's apartment, the landlady shared a secret. The 103-year-old woman's other, more successful son, a Palm Beach dentist who rarely came to visit, had deposited money with her. It was for his mother's burial, so that when the time came, he would not have to face the inconvenience of driving to Miami from Palm Beach, all of sixty-five miles.

Other oldsters are luckier. It's common to see old couples holding hands and cuddling up at dances. Femmes fatales in orthopedic shoes and print dresses, wearing plastic sun shields on their noses, are stalked by dapper little old gentlemen in plaid jackets and bowties.

Sex after seventy is a fact: something to look forward to. For a time I lived next door to a Miami Beach retirement hotel.

"It's hell," the harried desk clerk once told me, "trying to keep them out of each other's rooms."

Hooray.

Passions run high; love triangles are common. One jilted lover, age eighty-one, a man with an unblemished past, was arrested for first-degree arson, a crime punishable by life in prison. He hurled a Molotov cocktail, a gasoline-filled bottle, through his sweetheart's kitchen window. A widow, age sixty-eight, she had rejected him for a younger man in his seventies. A kitchen rug was scorched, but she stomped out the blaze before it could do real damage. She knew the guilty party at once, she told me. He had left a tell-tale clue.

The fire bomb had been fashioned in a prune juice bottle—his brand.

A judge sentenced the defendant to Boston—to the custody of his son who lived there.

That passion for life makes old people's attitudes toward death all the more surprising. As I began to cover police stories, I noticed that the elderly often treat death with a distinct air of nonchalance. Perhaps if you live long enough, death becomes merely a part of life, like eating, sleeping, or going to the bathroom. Or maybe it's that people who fear something imminent tend simply to ignore it, to whistle loudly in the dark and pretend it isn't there.

I noticed it first on the day that something dreadful

occurred in the ornate lobby of a posh oceanfront hotel. A balky elevator descended without warning, crushing to death the repairman who was trying to fix it. His lower extremities were pinned beneath it. His head and shoulders protruded, resting on the lobby floor. He was still wearing his spectacles. Employees behind the busy front desk could not see from their position what had happened.

Eventually, a distinguished elderly man with a cane approached them. "Are you aware," he calmly inquired, "that a man is stuck in your elevator?"

"Oh, I'll take care of it," said a quick young clerk. "That elevator's been giving us trouble all day." He snatched up the elevator keys and stepped jauntily out from behind the desk. When he saw, to his utter horror, that somebody *really* was stuck in the elevator, he promptly lost his lunch. The clerk was gulping deep breaths, his complexion green, his head between his knees when I got there.

It was the height of the winter tourist season. The lobby was full of well-dressed retirees. None screamed, got hysterical, or galloped in circles. The police did not even have to rope off the area to hold back the crowd. The crowd was not interested. The only reaction was from a few people who walked by, shook their heads, and murmured, "Tsk, tsk."

Young people, however, are drawn morbidly to death. They even carry babies and lead small children by the hand to come quick and see this awful something, anything that has happened. But the elderly won't go out of their way to see a dead body. They won't go out of their way to avoid one, either.

Elderly bathers will slip surreptitiously under yellow police lines protecting a body found in an alley and drag their beach chairs down that alleyway, carefully skirting the corpse, of course, simply because it is the most direct route to their destination. Why detour for death?

As police stood glumly on a wind-swept beach one morning, examining a corpse that had rolled in with the tide, I watched the distant approach of a grizzled, solitary jogger—an elderly man who, like clockwork, methodically jogs the same stretch each day.

Closer and closer he came, never looking up, never deviating from his regular path. He was nearly upon us when I realized that he was not going to.

"Sergeant . . ." I began, but too late. The elderly jogger broke through the small knot of investigators, amid startled shouts from detectives and the medical examiner, and hurdled the corpse in a single step, without breaking his stride.

He continued on, never looking back.

Some rare and enlightened Miami Beach public servants understand; they make allowances for this special segment of the population. An agitated elderly woman arrived at Miami Beach police headquarters one morning as I skimmed the crime reports. She was weeping and holding her head as if in pain. "I lost it, I lost it," she sniffled to Richard Caracaus, a middle-aged sergeant manning the front desk.

For a moment he did not recognize her. "The magic box!" she cried. "The magic box. It's gone!" In the process of moving, she said, it had disappeared from her closet.

"Now they're doing it again," she moaned. She rocked back and forth, both hands to her head.

"You sure you lost it?" the sergeant said.

She had searched everywhere.

"I can get you another one," he promised. She clutched at his hands gratefully. He told her to come back at three o'clock, and she shuffled out, looking better already.

"What magic box?" I demanded, and he explained. Miami Beach has more than its allotment of residents who share the delusion of being bombarded by electrical impulses or X-rays that cause them severe headaches and hallucinations, illnesses, and bad dreams.

Many will fixate on an individual or a building they suspect of being the source of their torment. They call police, lodge complaints, and even file lawsuits against innocent people who have no earthly idea what is going on. Sometimes it becomes more serious. I covered the case of a man who complained for months that electrical waves beamed from a service station across the street were making his "heart flutter." He used a gun to put a stop to it. He emptied it at the station and shot two strangers, a customer, and an employee.

The woman at police headquarters had a similar complaint, and Sergeant Caracaus, who repairs antique clocks as a hobby, had built her a magic box to block the harmful rays. For eight months, until she lost it, it worked perfectly. A magic box is simpler to build than a clock. Caracaus uses a few of his kids' marbles, an old cigar box and a roll of black masking tape. Anyone can do it. Drop the marbles inside; wrap the entire box with tape. It works.

He is no Dirty Harry, but Richard Caracaus is a hell of a cop.

A fondness for seniors may be contagious. It tends to clutter your desk. Many share the common fear that when they are gone, their heirs will trash-pile their most precious mementos. A frail woman of eighty, facing serious surgery, lugged a cardboard carton into the *Sun* office. It contained the personal valuables she did not want her children up north to throw away; her handwritten, unpublished poetry, some pressed flowers, and a decades-old plaque from her garden club. Despite my strong protests, she placed the carton on my desk and walked out. I never saw her again.

An impeccably dressed gentleman with snow-white hair and a neatly trimmed mustache presented me with the story of his life, twelve precisely handwritten pages. He included a photo of himself and his "lovely wife," of fifty years, now deceased. He was ailing and wanted somebody who cared to keep it, so they would not be forgotten. I still have it, more than seventeen years later.

Another nagging worry is money. No matter how much they have, they fear that it will not last them the rest of their lives. Who can predict how long he or she will live? And what about inflation? So, many of them, who should be living comfortably, cut corners.

Until theft-proof dispensers were installed in Miami Beach public restrooms, it was nearly always impossible to find bathroom tissue or paper towels when you needed them. I used to curse the city fathers, but it was not their fault—attendants filled the dispensers every morning.

Soon after, old ladies with shopping bags arrived and emptied them.

This did not occur to me until the fatal heart attack of one of them on the street. Detective Emery Zerick, possessed of a genuine warmth and patience in dealing with the elderly, emptied the dead woman's shopping bag. It was full of rolls of institutional toilet paper and stacks of paper towels. A bankbook in her purse reflected a seventy-thousand-dollar balance—but she was stocking up on paper goods from the bathrooms at City Hall, the library, and police headquarters.

Not all the mysteries among the city's elderly are so simply solved. Some are never resolved, like the case of the missing mattress. In his decline, an ailing resident of a South Beach retirement hotel fretted constantly about his money. He had not trusted banks since the depression. Finally he tottered across the street to his bank and withdrew every last cent—eighty thousand dollars—in one-hundred-dollar bills. He sewed it into his mattress, then flipped it over to hide the stitches. He confided the hiding place to a trusted friend and died soon after, of natural causes. His son came quickly from Israel and discovered the bad news at the bank. His father's confidant revealed to him the hiding place. The son and his attorney went at once to the retirement hotel. On the old man's bed: a brand-new mattress.

The son, his lawyer, and the hotel owner fought a free-for-all in the lobby. The owner told police that he had replaced all the mattresses on the tenth floor. Why only the tenth floor, Detective Emery Zerick wanted to know. Because they were in especially shabby condition, the owner explained.

He said he sold them for one dollar each to Dave the Boss, a colorful local junk dealer. Dave the Boss said he had sold some for two dollars each in a poor Liberty City neighborhood, sent a few of the worst to the dump, and still had the rest, mixed up with lots of other old mattresses acquired from various hotels and motels. For months, even on his days off, Zerick, a bald bulldog of a detective, went to the dump and pawed through seedy mattresses. He even had bank officers stack eighty thousand dollars in one-hundred-dollar bills so he would know the exact size of the lump he was seeking. Long after the dead man's son and his lawyer gave the quest up as hopeless, Emery continued his treasure hunt. He must have torn open every discarded mattress in Miami. No luck.

Somewhere out there in Liberty City, somebody dead broke and down on his luck may be sleeping on a fortune. But I doubt it.

I love the sunny streets and the old hotels of South Beach; they remind me of my favorite era: the 1930s and 1940s, years when journalism was more fun, music was sweeter, and movie dialogue better written. Posters for *Casablanca* and *The Maltese Falcon* decorate my study, constant reminders that things are not so simple or romantic anymore, maybe because the times were simpler and more romantic and the good guys always won. Nothing is black and white anymore. I often long for those times when fiction was popular because truth was not stranger. This longing for simpler days, before my time, most often fills my soul on steamy streets, trying not to be robbed, rocked, or bottled as I attempt to find out exactly what the *heck* the not-so-good citizens of Miami are doing to each other now.

Where is Humphrey Bogart when we need him?

In the late 1960s, the Latin influence was just a faint and rhythmic pulsebeat. Cuba was close. People had traveled there from Miami for years to gamble, and to have abortions. The first Cuban exodus of the early 1960s brought penniless refugees; doctors, lawyers and other professionals who labored in Miami as busboys, taxi drivers, and dishwashers.

Members of that first Cuban wave did not stay long at their menial jobs. They rose again to the tops of their professions, becoming the hard-working backbone of Miami's Cuban community. That positive experience set us up for the cruel joke of the Mariel boatlift twenty years later, when Castro flushed his toilets into an unwitting Miami.

Along with eager immigrants, he sent his deranged and retarded, his mentally ill and his convicts—the most ruthless criminals this country has ever seen.

What a coup for Castro. Imagine the advantage if we could simply empty our death rows, our maximum security prisons, our institutions for deranged sex offenders and the criminally insane, and ship them all out—to a place that would welcome them with open arms and set them loose on its streets with unsuspecting citizens. Of course the leaders of no other nation would allow such a thing to happen to them. But that is precisely what happened to us.

The shock sent us reeling. Police work was no longer even somewhat predictable. Many of the refugees were disoriented and confused. They would attempt to rush victims of violence, accident, or illness to a hospital themselves instead of waiting for medics and an ambulance. Unfamiliar with the city, they usually had no idea how to find the hospital.

Panicky friends drove dying patients aimlessly at high speeds, while bewildered police, summoned to an accident or a shooting, raced about at equally high speeds in search of the injured. Sometimes the careening refugees crashed, creating more casualties. One carload of frantic Mariel refugees seeking help for a gravely wounded friend roared wrong way down a one-way street and rammed a police car speeding to the scene of the shooting.

The drivers would seek a hospital until it was too late. Then they would thoughtfully deposit the corpse on the sidewalk outside a police station or some other official-looking public building, causing great consternation among the citizenry who stumbled upon it.

Many other refugee quirks caused concern, such as their penchant for firing gunshots to summon the police. Doing so does win police attention, but makes them inclined to draw their own guns to shoot back. Jittery police tried to convey the message that anyone seeking their help would do better to wave and shout or dial 911.

Officers were issued manuals to consult when needed,

containing emergency commands in Spanish, such as "Stop or I'll shoot," and "Drop the gun," with helpful keys to pronunciation.

At the same time, refugees from Haiti arrived by the boatload. Docile and shy, they presented a total contrast. Yet terrible things happen to them. If such evils as bad karma or ancient curses do exist, they must shadow the lives of the vulnerable and gentle Haitians. Their boats capsize at sea or merciless smugglers steal their money and hurl them overboard. Their bodies wash up on tourist beaches or are never seen again. If they do arrive in Miami, they are locked in a detention center. Those who are not are so eager for work that they will pretend they can do things they cannot do or understand. They get hurt. They get killed.

One day at the morgue, I asked in dismay what on earth had happened to a new arrival who could not help but catch my eye. His job at a Hialeah textile factory had been to keep the knitting machines running no matter what. Working alone, overnight, he had to make sure that no threads caught, that nothing snarled the works. The next morning they found him tangled in the machinery—knitted to death.

Unfortunate Haitians suffer new disasters daily. The power company cuts off their electricity, or perhaps they never accumulate the money to have it turned on. So they burn candles that somehow set themselves and their babies on fire. They want to learn to drive, and somehow in the process they run over their loved ones. They try so hard and pay so dearly. At first the Haitians did not contribute at all to Miami's crime rate—except as victims. Then some of them became Americanized.

Still, they are gentle for the most part. As the oppressive Duvalier regime drew to a close, they sailed their old cars through the streets of Miami's Little Haiti, trailing blue-and-red banners, blowing their horns, shouting, and dancing in the streets. Grim police set up a command post and stood by in riot gear.

As I picked my way across a Little Haiti street in a light rain, the "rioters," leaning on their horns and waving their banners, slammed on their brakes, stopped their cars, and respectfully permitted me to pass. They resumed their "rioting" only when I had stepped safely onto the far curb.

The only policeman shot was wounded by his own gun when he dropped it.

If you must attend a riot, be sure it is one conducted by Haitians.

At a multiple murder scene, I visited the house next door looking for a witness. The occupants, a Haitian family, politely invited me inside. Their home, with just a few modest sticks of furniture, was immaculate. Pictures cut out of old magazines decorated the walls. A huge pot of chicken necks simmered on the stove. The children were well-scrubbed, neatly dressed, and bashful—just like the adults. The father's eyes were red-rimmed from lack of sleep. He scrubbed a Miami Beach hospital by day and cleaned downtown office buildings at night. That family remains more clearly etched in my memory for some reason than the individuals I wrote about that day, the less-memorable people involved in the senseless drug shoot-out next door.

The sad eyes and the shy smiles are everywhere: In the supermarket where I shop, two Haitian men in work clothes lingered at the meat counter, checking, double-checking, and comparing prices, earnestly discussing at length which family-size package of chicken necks was the best buy.

When faced with wretched excess, groaning boards of extravagant fare for the overweight and overindulged among us—you know who you are—I cannot help but think of those careful, sad-eyed shoppers.

They sure know how to spoil a good time.

When I first saw it, Miami Beach was a resort city still in its early years of semi-innocence. Sure there were bizarre crimes, but only from time to time. Miami was the end of the world, the last stop for sun-seeking drifters and people on the run from trouble. And, of course, they brought it with them, all of their blues, excess baggage, and private demons. They always have. They still do.

The Beach had its strip joints, B-girls, and jewel thieves, but, in retrospect, those were the good old days. The problems then were child's play compared to the complexities of today when it is just a short drive from one world to another.

Consider the small municipality of Sweetwater, west of downtown Miami: The town was founded by Russian circus midgets. Now it is becoming heavily settled by Nicaraguan refugees fleeing Communism.

In some neighborhoods native-born Floridians in cowboy hats and boots drive pickup trucks with gun racks in the cab and hound dogs in the back. A few miles away, at a big shopping center, the signs are in Spanish and no English is spoken. Dozens of neighborhoods are changing, none of them into the same thing.

Once a sleepy resort that shut down during the off season, Miami now copes year-round with concentrations of everything corrupt, bizarre, or dangerous from everywhere in the world. It is a city where police on occasion stop drivers for speeding and kill them when the motorists level submachine guns at them. Medics treating auto-accident victims sometimes discover that the injured parties are armed and wearing bullet-proof vests. One man told rescuers that he was wearing body armor because he was on his way to pick avocados.

More is going on than meets the eye.

When five narcs got machine-gunned at a posh ocean-front hotel recently in a drug bust gone awry, the only people who screamed, ran, or scrambled for cover were the cops. Everybody else stayed cool, thinking it was just *Miami Vice* shooting another episode.

Yet one of Miami's problems is an often highly exaggerated reputation for crime and violence. Solid citizens who stay alert are usually safe. There are no tail-gunners on bread trucks. Life in Miami is simply life in the big city, a very attractive and strategically placed big city. Sometimes it is bad, but nowhere near as bad as some people seem to think.

A wealthy man from Tennessee made the mistake of

believing everything he heard about Miami. He stepped off a plane and offered the first person he met at the airport ten thousand dollars to murder his wife. They had been married thirty years. He wanted her strangled. The man he tried to hire, a cab driver, scarcely stopped to consider the offer before calling police.

Even people close to home make the same miscalculation. In neighboring Broward County, a street gang called the Enforcers murdered a colleague and decided to take the corpse to Miami and drop it off where no one would notice. It would be "just another body."

Miami cops accumulate enough dead bodies of their own. They deeply resent people who dump out-of-town corpses inside their city limits. Mike Gonzalez and Louise Vasquez, probably the world's most savvy homicide detectives—they have more practice than anybody else—rounded up the gang in no time.

The crimes of summer, full of passion and newsworthy detail, always seem wilder and more spectacular. August is often the most murderous month. Perhaps it is the season that leads to violence.

Never let anyone tell you that Miami has no seasons. Each wears a distinctive shade of green. Summer green is the fiercest and most brilliant. Trees and flowers bloom lushly here, but only at their appointed time. A fifth season, June through November, spawns hurricanes. You do not know panic until you are a Miami Beach homeowner with no idea where the shutters are stored, much less how to put them up, staring in the face of a tropical storm that is bearing down like a runaway freight train picking up speed.

We Floridians have our own signs and signals of the seasons, courtesy of mother nature. New Jersey has its lilacs and Washington its cherry blossoms; we have water-spouts, sinkholes, Medfly spray spewed at us by crop dusters, and the springtime fires. During a dry spring, lightning sparks Everglades wildfires. Crisp grasslands are ignited, and hundreds, sometimes thousands, of acres are charred. Rain will slow the wildfires to a crawl, but they continue to burn, creeping along and scorching the earth. Sometimes they rage out of control and leap across high-ways, as though daring park personnel and forestry ser-vice fire fighters to try to beat them back.

The fires are not always touched off by lightning. Weedy roadsides become so tinder-dry that a hot muffler will set them ablaze. A highway patrolman pulled a speeder off the road, then smelled something burning as he wrote the motorist a ticket. It was his patrol car. A grass fire had erupted beneath it and quickly enveloped the entire car. He could do nothing but watch it burn to a blackened shell.

Fire is part of the natural cycle of The Everglades. Its gray-brown haze hangs like a shroud over South Florida. Eyes smart as far away as Miami Beach, until the shifting winds bring ocean breezes that scatter the smoke and af-ternoon rains that wash away the sting.

In the sultry, steamy summer months, Sahara dust rides the wind to South Florida in an annual migration. Stormy weather along the African coast scoops up the red sand, passing it off to air currents that stream west. Huge sandstorms, monster clouds of red dust, five hundred or even a thousand miles wide, swirl across the Atlantic, whipped by the desert winds of Africa. Motorists in metropolitan Miami wake up and find their cars coated by a thin red film of dust. Brief summer showers leave cars spotted by mud, and the sky turns milky, with a whitish haze. More common in recent years because of African droughts, it is one of the phenomena of summer.

Out there on a hot night on a breaking story, trying to piece things together, I see the moon, as it hangs fat and low, a sinister silver dollar tarnished by Sahara dust in the eastern sky.

In Miami today, Burdines' tearoom and the Snow Princess are merely memories. But within a short walking distance, anyone can find free-base and drug houses, where the proprietors eagerly dish up miniature mountains of white powder: Miami snow.

The newsroom, too, has changed; its sounds are strangely subdued. I miss the simultaneous clatter of typewriters, all but gone since the arrival of video-display terminals. Even the telephones have been muffled. They bleat softly instead of jangling, dropping the noise level to a humdrum monotone, broken only by frequent shouts of jubilation from investigative reporters as they corner a crook. We reap rich harvests from the dozens of governmental bodies at work in Dade County.

A stroll down Flagler Street is a journey to some exotic foreign capital. Miami *is* Casablanca. The sidewalks seethe with intrigue: undercurrents of international politics, spy versus spy, drug-running, gunrunning, traffic in illegal aliens, and plots of every stripe. The city is exploding with growth, much of it financed by foreign investors and drug money. A new skyline is rising and reaching for the stars. You can hear the beat. You can see it in the faces of every color and description.

I was definitely born in the wrong place on the planet and maybe twenty or thirty years too late; but if not the time, at least the city is right.

It certainly is a fine place to be a reporter.

THIRTEEN

Getting the Story

To entrust to an editor a story over which you have labored and to which your name and reputation are attached can be like sending your daughter off for an
evening with Ted Bundy.

Over the past twenty years I have worked with some
editors who did nothing to my stories but make them
better. For the most part, editors mean well. But I always
warn aspiring reporters to observe three basic rules:

1. Never trust an editor.
2. Never trust an editor.
3. Never trust an editor.

They can be cavalier with your copy. They can embarrass you, lose you your sources, strip the best stuff out of
your story, insert mistakes and misspellings, top it off
with a misleading headline, and get you in trouble. For

example, some editors—and even some reporters—do not know the difference between burglary and robbery. They consider the words interchangeable. They are not. It's the difference between finding a vacant space where your TV set stood and meeting in person a masked man with a gun. That difference can mean as much as twenty years to the perpetrator and far more in trauma to the victim.

Editors and I sometimes disagree on minor points. I hate to continually insert attributions when something is obvious or when it is perfectly clear who is speaking. Yet some editors love to sprinkle them into copy like confetti.

Take a bullet-riddled body lying in plain view in the middle of a shopping center. I saw it and so did thirty people who heard the shots, saw the victim fall, and watched the killer run, smoking gun in hand. I say that we can simply report, "He was shot." We don't have to attribute that information to authorities by writing, "He was shot, police said."

In addition to editors, print reporters often have difficulty with police spokesmen assigned to "handle" the press. For one thing, cops talk funny and write funny. Their press releases are terrible, full of unintelligible police jargon. It is like translating a foreign language. They say things like "The subject left the dwelling and proceeded in a westerly direction in a light color late model vehicle." It makes me want to scream.

Subject does not tell you if the culprit is man, woman, boy, or girl. *Dwelling* gives no clue to whether it is a house, an apartment, or a trailer. Does *vehicle* mean car, van, or pickup truck? Can't they just say, "The man with the gun left the house and drove west in a new light-blue Ford Thunderbird." No, that's too simple.

Cops constantly issue statements saying that a subject "produced a firearm." You produce a Broadway show, not a Saturday night special. And, of course, *firearm* does not give a hint as to whether it was a revolver, shotgun, Uzi submachine gun, or a bazooka. If they would only say, "The robber pulled a sawed-off shotgun from under his jacket" or "drew a handgun from his waistband."

There is also a space on police reports to record what the perpetrator said. I saw one recently that quoted the robber as saying, "I demand your United States currency." If he really talked like that, he should not have been difficult to locate.

I think I know where the cops pick it up; from our law-makers. We don't have "rape" in Florida anymore; it is now called "involuntary sexual battery." Rape is rape and that is what I want to call it, unless, of course, it is some other kind of sex crime, and then I try to tell it like it was.

For the clearest, most succinct account of what really happened, reporters need to find the actual detective, patrolman, or fireman involved. The most accurate information and the best quotes always come from the man or woman who saved a life, ducked a bullet, or tackled a fugitive. I don't want to talk to a police public-information officer who was at his desk drinking coffee when it happened, would not know a good quote if he heard it, or recognize a good story if it stuck to his shoe.

What a reporter needs is detail, detail, detail.

If a man is shot for playing the same song on the juke-box too many times, I've got to name that tune. Questions unimportant to police often add the color and detail that make a story human. What movie did they see? What color was their car? What did they have in their pockets? What were they doing at the precise moment the bomb exploded or the tornado touched down?

Miami Homicide Lieutenant Mike Gonzalez, who has spent some thirty years solving murders, tells me that he now asks those questions and suggests to rookies that they do the same. The answers may not be relevant to an investigation, but he tells them, "Edna Buchanan will ask you, and you'll feel stupid if you don't know."

A question I always ask is: What was everybody wearing? It has little to do with style. It has everything to do with the time I *failed* to ask. A man was shot and dumped into the street by a killer in a pickup truck. The case seemed somewhat routine—if one can ever call murder routine. But later, I learned that at the time the victim was shot he was wearing a black taffeta cocktail dress and red high heels. I tracked down the detectives and asked, "Why didn't you tell me?"

"You didn't ask," they chorused. Now I always ask.

I also want to know what was in their pockets. The contents of a corpse's pockets sometimes tells the whole story. I covered a case where killers, determined that their victim never be identified, hacked off his hands and his head to eliminate fingerprints and dental work. Their hard work went to waste because they missed a slip of paper tucked deep in the pocket of the dead man's blue jeans.

It was a receipt bearing his name and address.

A hit-and-run driver killed a seventy-five-year-old veteran as he rolled south in a wheelchair on U.S. 1 at one o'clock in the morning. The wheelchair was everywhere. It looked like it exploded. What was in the dead man's pockets? Any clue to why he was out there? Of no importance to the troopers investigating the accident, it was important to me, to the victim, and to a lot of people: The dead man had two nickels and a dime, a Key West ID, hospital discharge papers, and printed forms from various county social agencies rejecting his appeals for help in returning to Key West.

A social agency in Key West had put this amputee on a Greyhound to the Miami VA hospital. The hospital rolled him back out onto the street. Nobody made any provision to get him back home. He made the rounds of government offices and county agencies saying he wanted to go home. Finally exasperated by all the bureaucratic red tape, the feisty vet tried to make it back to Key West alone.

He covered about seven miles when a college kid in a Corvette killed him. He had 149 to go.

If the TV was on when the shooting started, I want to know what everybody was watching. It could be ironic, it could be relevant, it could also help piece together a timetable for when it all happened and who, therefore, the guilty party might be. An entire life-and-death chain of events can be reconstructed by what everyone concerned was watching on television at the time.

In the case of Gus Kloszewski, accused of beating his

chubby bride to death with a hammer and battering his mother-in-law into a hopeless coma, a parade of witnesses swore they "knew" what time it was, not by any clock, but by the show on their TV screen. An alibi witness insisted she arrived during *Mork and Mindy* and left fifteen minutes before the end of *Soap*. Other witnesses said they got home just after the start of *MASH*. The mother of the accused heard Gus in his room during the eleven o'clock nightly news. His father heard a door slam during the news, then went to bed after Johnny Carson's monologue. Police pored over a *TV Guide*, and an expert witness for the defense was a TV executive who explained how his industry keeps time. The jury acquitted. Had he been guilty, they reasoned, the defendant could never have been home in time to catch the news at eleven.

TV mesmerizes all of us. One young man looked me in the eye and earnestly insisted that he was so engrossed in a rerun of *Gilligan's Island* that he did not hear the quintuple murder—eight people machine-gunned, three survivors—in the apartment next door.

Sometimes details simply add an ironic twist to an otherwise-routine story. A teenage girl who was fed up pulled a pearl-handled revolver from her purse and gunned down a college student who had made a lewd remark to her on the street. He fell, bleeding, in front of a movie theater. Witnesses dragged the wounded man to safety in the lobby. On the marquee: *Cease Fire*.

A young woman decapitated by her boyfriend was wearing a T-shirt with the message STICKS AND STONES MAY BREAK MY BONES, BUT WHIPS AND CHAINS EXCITE ME.

Print reporters need to know who called the police or the fire department. Who got there first? We need color, background, ages, details, and how to reach victims and survivors. We need to talk to witnesses. Police try to shield them, but some people don't need or want to be protected. The decision should be theirs.

I want to talk to them if I can. It is important to be sensitive and kind, but most of all, it is important to get there first. Otherwise, other reporters will have already driven everyone to distraction, and the victims or survivors may no longer wish to talk at all.

I want to know what happened and what they want to say about it. Some will not talk. But for every one who refuses, several are eager to get something off their chests. It can be a catharsis; sharing can help them through a difficult period. Some survivors, like police widows I have interviewed, want the world to know what has been lost. And if there is anything at all suspicious about a death or disaster, going public often helps loved ones learn what really did happen.

So when somebody hangs up the telephone or slams a door, I give them sixty seconds to think it over, then redial or knock again. It is not easy; nobody likes rejection. If it is by telephone, I say, "We were cut off." Often they immediately regret hanging up, or someone else tells them, "You should have talked to that reporter . . ." If they hang up again, I do not dial a third time. But at least half the time somebody wants to talk on the second call. I always give people the chance to reconsider.

*   *   *

Charles Curzio was sixty-three and operated a small neighborhood TV repair shop. On New Year's Eve he stayed later than he had planned so that some of his customers could pick up their sets in time to watch the King Orange Jamboree Parade. His kindness cost him his life. A robber took it. He beat Curzio to death with a rifle butt for what little money he had.

I called the dead man's home. One of his sons answered, loudly cursed at me in a hysterical rage, and slammed down the telephone. He was in pain. What a way to spend New Year's Eve. A lump in my throat, I redialed. The other son answered. He spoke freely and warmly about his father and made several quotable comments on capital punishment, a controversy in the news at the time.

It made the difference between a two-paragraph brief and a story stripped across the top of the local page about the wanton slaying of a good and decent man.

"I don't see anybody out protesting that my father is dead," the son of Charles Curzio said. "Not one person in the street. Yet my father got no trial, no stay of execution, no Supreme Court hearing. Nothing—just some maniac who smashed his brains in with a rifle butt—That's all he got."

That said it all.

My natural curiosity helps. When bad things happen I always want to know why; being a reporter gives me a legitimate reason to ask. If a car crashes, or somebody is shot at a traffic light, I want to know what quirk of man or fate put them there. Where was he or she going? Was he speeding on a rain-slick street because his boss threatened to fire him for being late? Have there been other accidents at that intersection? Has there been a traffic study at that corner?

Cops and other people I deal with may become irate when I ask so many questions, but some, I hope, respect my persistence. Cops sometimes tell stories about our encounters.

A detective repeated one to a group I attended recently. Until he did, I had totally forgotten the incident. A woman had been shot in broad daylight, inside a Cuban restaurant. The victim had contacted the *Herald* just a day earlier, saying that someone was trying to kill her. She was right.

I greeted a homicide detective at the curb. He could tell me nothing, he said, pointing out that he had just arrived. I persisted, but he kept insisting that he knew nothing. Still asking questions, I followed him and a companion, the man telling the story, until blocked by the yellow rope. They ducked under the police line, stepped into the restaurant, and as they did, the telephone rang. It was for the homicide detective. He took the phone and his friend heard him repeat, "Edna, I *told* you, we just got here, and I don't know anything yet."

There was a pay phone on the sidewalk outside.

I know it sounds foolish, but often people uncomfortable at being seen talking to a reporter will speak more freely over the telephone. It never hurts to remind them that you are out there, waiting. If they know that you never give up, never go away, sometimes they will tell you what you need to know—out of sheer self-defense.

Quick and accurate coverage of sensitive or controversial cases is urgent in a community often volatile and divided. The Donald Harp case is a good example:

Two boyhood buddies, one home on leave from the service, got drunk, hot-rodded around town, and wound up in a little fender-bender with a taxicab. Damage was minor, but they had been drinking, so they ran. The cab driver radioed for police. After a chase, the young men's Camaro skidded off the road to a stop. It was 4:30 A.M. A cop pulled the driver from the car. The passenger, Donald Harp, was so drunk he was nearly unconscious. A cop yanked his arm up and out the window to cuff him. As he did so, Harp's other arm went down. Another cop saw the sudden movement, assumed, supposedly, that it meant the passenger was reaching for a weapon and shot him dead.

There was no weapon. This was a white cop and a black victim in a community where two major riots were sparked by white cops killing black men with what appeared to many as insufficient cause.

I talked to the cops, canvassed the neighborhood, and went back to the office to write a story for the early edition. The *Herald* had some rookie reporters at the scene and one called in excited. He had found a witness, a young black woman who happened to be looking out her window and saw the whole thing. She said police pulled the passenger from the car, dragged him to the middle of the street, surrounded him, and then she heard the shot.

That sounded like murder. But I had seen the car. The passenger seat was bloodsoaked, not the street. And she just happened to be looking out the window? At 4:30 A.M.?

I asked the reporter more about his witness. She had told him she was twenty-two and lived with her mother who was at work. He described their home. I had been there that morning and talked with a sixteen-year-old girl and her mother. Neither one had seen a thing. The mother had heard brakes screeching and the shot. The girl had slept soundly through it all. I asked the reporter to double-check the age of his eyewitness. She now wavered and said she was seventeen. He said she had also been telling her story to TV reporters. Despite the time factor and the competition, who would air it at 6:00 P.M., I left her inflammatory account out of our first-edition story and called the lead homicide investigator.

I asked if they had taken this young woman's statement. Why should we, he said. She didn't see a thing. I told him what she said she saw. He sent detectives out to find her. She gave an official statement, and she told the truth: She hadn't seen a thing. But she wanted to be on TV with a popular local newsman. She was.

Cops distribute a six-line press release and expect everybody to go away happy. It is never enough for print reporters. We need so much more, more color, more detail. Most TV reporters are content if they have the brief press release and sixty seconds of dynamite film—leaping flames and firemen running. Radio people need only seconds.

Print reporters work harder. When we leave the scene our job has just begun. Once we have the story, we still have to write it.

FOURTEEN

Home at Last

The police beat is about people and what makes them tick, what turns them into heroes or homicidal maniacs, what brings out the best in them, what drives them berserk. It has it all: greed, sex, violence, comedy, and tragedy. You learn more about people than you would on any other newspaper job. The police reporter has a finger on the pulse of the community and is the first to know. Many of the biggest front-page stories in the nation originate on the police beat. It has always been that way.

I have never understood reporters who consider covering the cops the least desirable beat, the one to escape as quickly as possible if they are unfortunate enough to be assigned it, the job to avoid if they can, as they forge onward and upward in their journalistic careers.

Watergate grew out of a police-blotter burglary and made police reporting a bit more respectable. To a lesser degree, so did something that happened on Thursday,

April 17, 1986, fifteen years, six months, and two days after I was hired at the *Herald*. At 3:00 P.M., a news bulletin appeared on video terminal screens in the newsroom.

NEW YORK (UPI)——EDNA BUCHANAN OF THE MIAMI HERALD THURSDAY WON THE 1986 PULITZER PRIZE FOR GENERAL NEWS REPORTING.

What meant the most to me that afternoon was the genuine happiness on the part of those around me. I am not the most popular person in the newsroom; I don't go to parties or the local bar where all the reporters hang out. I go home. Yet the excitement shone in their faces, their eyes. They all owned a piece of this. It proved that all things are possible, that a reporter out in the trenches, fighting the good fight every day, can win the biggest prize in journalism. I choked, wanting to cry, but held it back. Fighting tears is second nature now.

Never let them see you cry.

It made me think back to the beginning, when I never even thought to ask about salary, when I just wanted a job.

It was impossible to sleep that night. I think I was afraid that if I did, I might wake up and find it was just a dream. At 7:15 A.M., a black stretch limo from the *CBS Morning News* arrived to take me to a studio for an appearance with fellow winners Jimmy Breslin and Jules Feiffer. The uniformed chauffeur was a woman named Shirley. She owns a poodle and a cat, and she keeps a .38-caliber revolver next to her bed. She told me that she had had the opportunity to use it recently, but did not. She had a choice: let the burglar escape or shoot and run the risk that he would bleed all over her new champagne-colored carpeting. She opted to save the carpet.

Made sense to me.

I am very lucky to be able to do what I love. You must care about this job in order to do it. I've reported more than five thousand violent deaths and covered kidnappings, mass murders, plane crashes, riots, and other catastrophes. Writing about the new sewer-bond issue or upcoming referendum is less stressful, the hours are better, and the surroundings more pleasant, but the rewards are not the same.

It is never easy. You give up a great deal when you work the police beat: decent hours, regular meals, stable relationships, and weekends off. Few major crimes or disasters occur between nine and five, Monday through Friday. The beat becomes more a way of life than just a job.

When I decided to buy a house, I called the bank to ask about mortgage rates. The loan officer cried out, "We know each other, don't you remember me?"

Puzzled, I could not place his name at all.

"You were a guest in my home," he said, sounding crestfallen that I did not recall. "Remember? When my neighbors were murdered . . ."

And as I attempted to fathom the sizes and complexities of window shades for my new abode, the woman taking the order wanted only to talk about her murdered sister. She showed me pictures. Her sister's sweetheart, who was the killer, had tried to stuff the body in a duffel bag.

And shortly after another reporter and I teamed up on an investigative piece close to our hearts—sexist dry-cleaning establishments that charge higher prices to launder women's shirts than men's—there seemed to be some question about my check at the supermarket. A suspicious employee regarded me with narrowed eyes and took it to the office as I trailed along. I heard her whisper a warning to the manager, "It's Edna Buchanan. She claims she's here to buy groceries."

The days are hectic and the nights solitary—but I would have it no other way. Some people ask if I regret not having a family. Not at all. Some women are cut out to be mommies. Some are superwomen with the stamina to do it all. I am not one of them. My elementary school math teacher was right: I would have been a lousy housewife. Instead I am lucky enough to work and interact with talented and stimulating people on a job where no day is ever the same as any other. And I get to touch thousands of people in some way.

There are drawbacks that lend a poignancy to many encounters. Reporters are like cops in yet another way: We suddenly appear in someone's life at a crucial, often emotional point, suddenly their best friend, confessor, defender, confidant, and shoulder-to-cry-on. We share the same foxhole for a short time, then we are gone with our story, slam-bam-thank-you-ma'am. It is often difficult for both of us. Sometimes I feel very close to the people I interview. They share their intimate secrets and pain, they tell me things they never told anyone—mostly because other people were too polite to ask.

Often, particularly with the elderly or with the very young and bereft, we become such pals that as I leave, they ask, "When are you coming back?" The answer, of course, is probably never. Tomorrow I will be thrust into some new close encounter with somebody else I may never see again.

The problem is, I truly like many of these people and want to reach out to them. I would be their friend if the circumstances were different and we had met some other way. But it is unprofessional to become involved with anyone you write about. And the daily whirlwind of news leaves little time for anything, much less the nurturing of new friends.

Communicating, however, being read by strangers, is a joy, and so is living here. I am still hooked, still in love with Miami. We have both changed a great deal over the years. We grew up, and in doing so we survived the good times and the bad. Life comes in cycles, and Miami and I are on a high right now. The city is being rediscovered as a place to film movies and commercials. A lot of the cops who quit after the riots are coming home. A lot of the people who left have realized that there is no place like Miami and wish they were here.

The doomsayers who point at the cocaine crack houses as the ultimate downfall of us all pointed at the heroin shooting galleries with the same alarm nearly twenty years ago. They are right; it is terrible. It was terrible then, too.

We survived. We will survive.

I still return to where it all began, where the sea is turquoise and glowing, as though lit from within, where the sky is a perfect blue, with pink clouds stacking on the horizon. The house I live in is full of light and reflections off the water. There are red, pink, and purple flowers, and banana, avocado, mango, and palm trees in my yard. The wind chimes sing in the night. It could not be further from a coat factory in Paterson, New Jersey. It is thirteen hundred miles and a million light-years away.

And I am still hooked on stories. I still want to know the end.

On a bad day, exhausted by constant battles with the outside world on the streets and the inside world of editors who suffer from itchy cursor fingers, a good story will still banish the blues, the headache, that tired, run-down feeling. Slumped and weary, yearning to go home, hungry, feverish, weak from the flu, desperate to escape, my mind an overloaded computer about to crash, I can feel the adrenaline pump and the brain cells kick back into life if somebody dangles something resembling a good story. The blood begins to tingle, the curiosity begins to pique. It is a lifelong addiction.

The best day is the one when I can write a lead that will cause a reader at his breakfast table next morning to spit up his coffee, clutch at his heart, and shout, "My God! Martha, did you read this?"

That's my kind of day.

Update: 2004

Only change is certain. Dr. Joe Davis, Miami Police Sergeant Mike Gonzalez, and Detective Louise Vasquez are all retired now.

Former Miami Beach Detective Sherwood Griscom, the cop with fast reflexes, deadly aim, and a legendary sixth sense, has retired with his wife, Fran, to Gulf Breeze, Florida.

Gulf Breeze is best known for its UFO sightings, among the most in the nation.

Nothing would surprise me.

Emery Zerick, the bald, cigar-smoking detective who had seen it all—and more—pulled over on the expressway while driving alone to the airport and slumped dead over the steering wheel. His heart, they said.

Metro-Dade Rape Squad Sergeant Christine Echroll, the strong and beautiful Viking Princess, never found her prince. She died young instead, after a fierce battle with cancer.

And me, I am still hooked on stories.

Once a news junkie, always a news junkie. I write occasionally for The Miami Herald *but never returned to the paper full time after taking a long-ago one-year leave to write a novel. Instead, it was another year, another book, then another and another.*

Cold Case Squad *is my fourteenth book, and I am at work on the next one.*

I still live in a house full of light and reflections off the water. I still love stories and want to know the end. Most of all, I love Miami.

Life is good.

SIMON & SCHUSTER
PROUDLY PRESENTS

COLD CASE SQUAD
EDNA BUCHANAN

Now available in hardcover
from Simon & Schuster

Turn the page for a preview of
Cold Case Squad. . . .

CHAPTER ONE

Like all things good and bad in the world, it began with a woman.

She was a blonde, with a complaint about her ex-husband. She saw him everywhere she went. Turn around and there he was. She knew he was trying to send her a message, she said.

Problem was, the man was dead, gone from this earth for twelve long years.

Some guys just don't know when to let go.

My name is Craig Burch, a sergeant on the Miami Police Department's Cold Case Squad. My assignment is relatively new. I worked homicide for eighteen years, mostly on the midnight shift. I fought like hell to land this job. Why not? It's every big city homicide cop's wet dream. This squad is armed with a detective's most powerful weapon: time. The luxury of enough time to investigate old, unsolved cases without interruption. I wanted that. I wanted the change. I wanted to see the faces of murderers who suddenly realize their pasts and I have caught up with them. The job has other perks as well. No daily dealing with fresh corpses or, worse yet, corpses less than fresh. No more stepping cautiously through messy crime scenes in dark woods, warehouses, or alleyways, trying to avoid stepping in blood, brains, or worse. No more trying to forget the pain-filled screams of inconsolable survivors whose unearthly cries will scar your soul and echo in your dreams asleep or awake. No more watching autopsies that suddenly and unexpectedly replay in your mind's eye at inopportune moments. And no more throwing my back out when lifting dead weight. *Real* dead weight.

This job also reduces my chances of being rocked, bottled, and/or shot at by the unruly Miamians who cluster bright-eyed and belligerent at every nasty crime scene in neighborhoods where trouble is a way of life and violence is contagious.

I quit confronting new deaths. Instead I breathe new life into old, cold cases and track killers whose trails vanished long ago like footprints on a sea-washed beach.

Loved the concept. Still do. And I yearned for what came with it—mostly regular, daylight hours, giving me the chance to spend more time with my family before the kids are grown and gone. Made sense to me. It was long overdue. I looked forward to it. Connie couldn't have been happier—in the beginning. What's not to like? Weekends off together for the first time? The man in the mirror suntanned instead of wearing a prison pallor from sleeping days and working nights?

Now I know why people say: Be careful what you wish for—you might get it. At the moment, I live alone. Last time I called home, one of the kids hung up on me. Every job in my line of business has a downside.

This one has ghosts.

My detectives are hand-picked self-starters. They don't hear the screams, see the blood, or feel the moral outrage cops experience at fresh murder scenes. Instead, they dissect dusty files and stacks of typewritten reports as cold and unemotional as a killer's heart.

Our standard operating procedure is to reread the case files of old, unsolved murders, pass them around, and brainstorm on which have the most potential. We also field tips on old homicides from our own cops, other agencies, confidential informants, prison inmates, and the friends and families of victims.

She was one of the latter: a walk-in. Our team had just voted on whether to pursue the high-profile triple homicide of a man, his pregnant wife, and their toddler. Murdered nearly twenty-five years ago, they were presumed casualties of the time—collateral damage in the drug wars of the eighties. But one of my guys suspects another motive, something more personal. Two of my detectives, Sam Stone and Pete Nazario, were still arguing about it when the secretary steered a stranger their way.

Her hair was feathery, tousled in an expensive, wavy style intended to look natural, the kind that costs more to look as though it was never touched by professionals.

Stone sprang to his feet when the secretary brought her past my desk, directly across from theirs. He grew up in Miami's bleakest, blackest, toughest neighborhood. Sharp, edgy, young, and focused, he has a passion for high technology and is as aggressive as hell. Sometimes he's a runaway freight train and you have to hold him back.

Well-dressed in blue that matched her eyes, she was your typical soccer mom with a little mileage on her.

Nazario offered her a chair. He came to Miami alone as a small child, one of the thousands of Pedro Pan kids airlifted out of Cuba and taken in by the Catholic church when Castro refused to allow the parents to leave the island. Nazario never saw his parents again and grew up a stranger in a strange land, shuttled to shelters and foster homes all over the country by the archdiocese. Maybe because he lived with strangers who didn't speak his native language or maybe he was born with it, but Nazario is blessed with an uncanny talent—it's invaluable to a detective, even though it's not admissible in court or probable cause for a warrant: He knows, without fail, when somebody is lying to him. Stone and Nazario are among the best, and I don't say that just because they work for me.

The woman in blue chewed her lower lip, her face pinched with apprehension. She looked to be in her late thirties but it's tough to tell the age of most women. Her name was April Terrell, she said. A plastic tag identifying her as a visitor to the building was clipped to her short, crisp jacket. Her summery dress flared at the hip and quit just above a nice pair of knees. She held a little purse demurely in her lap while apologizing for showing up unannounced. I listened, trying not to look up and be obvious.

"It's about my husband," she said, then corrected herself. "My ex-husband."

They married in college, she said. She quit and worked as a legal secretary to put him through pharmaceutical school. "I thought I knew him. The divorce caught me off guard. Our children were three and five. That was almost fourteen years ago."

She gave the guys a sad-eyed, self-deprecating smile. "He found someone else, younger, his second year in business. He remarried right away and started a new family."

The guys itched to hear the point. I know I did.

"It's funny." Her lower lip quivered, indicating the opposite. "All of a sudden, after all this time, he's there. I see him everywhere I go."

Nazario frowned. "He's stalking you?"

"Our domestic violence unit has a felony stalking squad." Stone reached for the phone on his desk. "You need to talk to one of them. We're homicide. Cold cases. I'll call downstairs and find you someone."

"Wait." She spoke briskly. "Obviously I haven't made myself clear. I know who you are. You investigate old deaths. That's why I'm here. Charles was killed twelve years ago."

I look up. Nazario and Stone exchange glances.

"Oh," Stone said accommodatingly. "And you say you've seen him lately?"

"Yes." Her voice held steady.

"On what sort of occasions?" Stone steepled his long fingers in front of him, his liquid eyes wandering to a window, past the grimy streaks to a patch of innocent blue sky above the neighborhood where he was born.

She raised her voice and her right hand slightly, as though to recapture his attention. "You know what I mean. Like at the bank yesterday . . . I saw another customer, his back was to me. He looked so much like Charles that for a moment I forgot he was dead and almost called out his name. The man turned around later and, of course, he didn't look like Charles at all." She shrugged. "You know how it is. You catch a glimpse of someone familiar but it turns out not to be them. It's happening to me more and more. He's in my dreams almost every night now."

"When did this start?" Nazario asked, his face solemn.

"Last year. I keep asking myself why, after all this time? Why?" She leaned forward, speaking clearly, voice persuasive. "The only explanation is that Charles is trying to tell me something."

Her shoulders squared, head high in a regal pose, reacting to something in their eyes. She shot me a quick glance, suddenly aware that I was listening, too.

"I'm not crazy," she said quickly. "Please don't think that. It's just that it's made me realize that I never felt right about what happened to him. I think I always suspected, but I had two little children to raise alone, a boy and a girl."

"Did you seek grief counseling at the time?" Nazario asked softly.

The blond waves bounced as she tossed her head. "Who had time for that?" She opened her hands in a helpless gesture, pale palms exposed. "I had to take care of business and get on with life because of the children. How could I allow myself the time to obsess, to cave in to anger, bitterness—or grief? You've heard people say, 'If I only had the time, I'd have a nervous breakdown'? Our children worshiped their dad. The divorce was tough enough on them, on all of us. He and his new wife had a baby. Their dad's death was the final crushing blow. They'd never see him again, call him on the telephone, or spend another weekend or vacation together. Now that they're older and asking questions, I realize there are no answers. The whole thing didn't make sense . . ."

"Sometimes," Nazario gently interjected, "when you suppress a traumatic incident and don't deal with it, it comes back to trouble you later, when you least expect it."

She shook her head forlornly, staring down at her naked fingers for a moment. She wore no rings.

"Can you at least look into it?" she said, raising those blue eyes.

"Into what?" Stone's brow furrowed.

Lieutenant K. C. Riley, our boss, suddenly appeared, slamming an office door, lean and mean, a folder in hand, expression impatient.

"He burned to death," April Terrell's voice rose, quavering slightly. "In a flash fire. It was horrible. They had to have a closed casket. There wasn't enough . . ."

Talk about timing.

K. C. Riley reacted as though slapped.

This can't be good, I thought.

"My ex-husband, the father of my children," April told the lieutenant without introductions. "His death was no accident. I'm sure he was murdered."

"When did this happen?" Riley's pale lips were tight, arms crossed.

"Twelve years ago: May 26, 1992. It happened on a Saturday." Charles had confided the last time he'd dropped off their children that he and their new stepmother of just a year were not getting along. The brief marriage, a bumpy ride, was already off track. Natasha, wife number two, spent extravagantly. And there was, of course, a big life insurance policy.

She had since lost track of the widow, she said.

"That sort of accident was totally out of character for Charles. He was skilled and competent, precise and careful about everything he did."

Riley lapped it up, never missed a beat. "Thanks for coming in Ms. . . . ?"

"Terrell, April Terrell."

"I'm K. C. Riley."

The two women shook hands.

"It's certainly worth looking into," Riley said. "My detectives will get right on it. Right, Sergeant?"

Three jaws dropped as one: mine, Stone's, and Nazario's.

Charles Terrell was no candidate for us and Riley knew that. We don't investigate accidents. We solve murders. Old cold ones. We had enough ghosts on our hands.

But timing, tragedy, and a chance encounter conspired

against us. Had the lieutenant stayed red-eyed and brooding behind closed doors as usual lately, it would have been different. We knew why she did it. No doubt about it. Haunted by a ghost of her own, K. C. Riley was taking it out on us.